S0-CBK-798

KEY CONCEPTS IN
EASTERN PHILOSOPHY

KEY CONCEPTS IN EASTERN PHILOSOPHY

Oliver Leaman

London and New York

First published by Routledge
11 New Fetter Lane, London EC4P 4EE

simultaneously published in the USA and Canada
by Routledge
29 West 35th Street, New York, NY 10001

Routledge is an imprint of the Taylor & Francis Group

© Oliver Leaman

First Indian Reprint 2004

Typeset in Bembo by The Florence Group,
Stoodleigh, Devon

Printed at Chennai Micro Print Pvt. Ltd. Export Division 100% EOU
No. 34, Nelson Manickam Road, Aminijikarai, Chennai 600 029, India

All rights reserved. No part of this book may be reprinted or
reproduced or utilized in any form or by any electronic, mechanical,
or other means, now known or hereafter invented, including
photocopying and recording, or in any information storage or retrieval
system, without permission in writing from the publishers.

ISBN 0-415-17363-9 (pbk)

For Sale in South Asia only

In fond memory of Norman Calder

CONTENTS

INTRODUCTION

There are many problems in knowing how to discuss the key
concepts of Eastern philosophy. The first is in deciding what
Eastern philosophy actually is, that is, what counts as the East.
There are no problems in including East Asian thought, especially that of India, China and Japan, and the related civilizations
in that part of the world. I have included Islamic and Zoroastrian
philosophy since so much of it took place within Persia and
then went further East, but it should be pointed out that some
of its main thinkers were very much part of what is generally
called the Western world, even living as far West as what is
today Spain. On the other hand, many important East Asian
thinkers have also spent at least some time in the West, and it
seemed to me appropriate to include Islamic philosophy within
the description of Eastern. I was influenced in this by the
discussion within Islamic philosophy itself as to how Eastern or
otherwise it was.

The second problem is in differentiating between philosophy
and religion. It is often held that there are several basic distinctions between Eastern and Western philosophy. Eastern philosophy is sometimes taken to be more holistic, and has sought as
its end some form of enlightenment, while Western philosophy
is more concerned with truth, logic, reason and individualism.
This is not the place to debate the differences, if any, between
these two forms of thought, since such a debate would be far
beyond the scope of this book, and certainly of this introduction.

I do not think that these generalizations about Eastern and Western philosophy really lead us anywhere, although I realize that with that statement I have just produced a generalization of my own.

One of the things that strike many of those who are predominantly trained within the Western tradition when they approach Eastern philosophy is both how similar it is, and how different. It is true that more of the problems that arise within the Eastern traditions are clothed within the language of a particular religion than is the case any more in the West, but this clothing often appears to be quite superficial. The logic of the controversies which lies beneath the appearance is much the same as in the West, or even exactly the same. It would be rash to insist that the arguments are always the same, of course, since every significant thinker puts his or her own style of expression on the problems they consider. Many of the arguments produced in Eastern philosophy are very different from anything that exists in the West, and often there appears to be an entirely different way of looking at the notion of being and change. In any case, saying anything sensible about vast collections of philosophical traditions stretching over thousands of years and even more square miles is even less likely to be sensible. I have attempted to express the ideas of these philosophical traditions in clear and accessible language, and with no direct reference to Western philosophy. If there is comparative philosophy in this book, it is between the different Eastern philosophical traditions, which are often genuinely linked both historically and culturally. Yet it has to be acknowledged that there is much in Eastern philosophy that will strike those unfamiliar with this tradition as very different from what might be called Western philosophy, in the sense that it has at its basis a culture and view of the world that frequently appears to be very distinct from those prevailing elsewhere. There is no assumption in this book that Eastern and Western philosophy follow a similar approach. It would be highly misleading to adopt such a strategy, since there are huge differences in some of the working practices and techniques of many of the traditions within the East and the West, if we can use these terms usefully.

The premise on which I am working here is that Eastern philosophy is philosophy, and not something special and esoteric which we need special non-philosophical tools to operate. On the other hand, there is no doubt that Eastern philosophy is closely connected with the religions of the East, and it is impossible to understand that philosophy unless one also understands something of the religions. I have tried to explain enough about the relevant religion or culture to make the context of the philosophy comprehensible. For this reason I have included some material that is far more relevant to religion than to philosophy. It is always difficult to know if one has gone into enough depth, and if one has spent too much time on the religion and not enough on the philosophy. This is a book on philosophy, and not on religion, and a book on religion would include far more discussion of the key religious concepts than I have done. I have tried to write in such a way as to presuppose no knowledge of Eastern religions, nor philosophy itself, and I have tried to explain to the reader how particular theoretical problems arose within a specific cultural context. I should not wish to argue that Eastern religions have acted as parameters within which the philosophy operated, since often the thinkers themselves have stretched the religion within which they are working to such an extent that it is not reasonable to see that religion as constraining the philosophical thought. If it was the case that Eastern philosophers were always faithful to a literal understanding of their religions in their philosophical output then they would be poor philosophers. It is because they felt the need to follow the argument wherever it went that their philosophy is worth the name of philosophy and is not part of the history of ideas or theology.

Clearly readers will benefit from following the cross-references and reading about the network of concepts that relate to a particular topic. One might try to force readers to do this by not saying anything about a term that is explained elsewhere in the book. While I hope readers will explore the whole gamut of concepts in this book, I have tried to make the content of each section work fairly independently of everything else. As a result, there is some repetition, since a term that I suspect readers may not know will often, but not always, be explained briefly whenever it comes up, and readers will not always be obliged to go to the section dealing with that term alone. I chose this approach as a result of talking to a variety of people about how they like entries to be written. The general view was that if one was reading something in which a new philosophical concept figured what one wanted was a quick answer to the question as to what it means. Later on one could browse through the volume to deepen one's grasp both of that term and of the terms to which it is linked. In the interests of brevity, though, I have not always explained each technical term in each section, and it will be easy for readers to go to the appropriate section if they find any terms with which they are not familiar. Every foreign term is provided either with its own entry or with a definition of its meaning together with a reference to an entry that has discussion of it. Where there is no definition of its meaning, it should be assumed that it means exactly the term that is referred to as being the relevant entry. So, for example, the term *bheda* is represented as '*bheda*, difference, *see* Dvaita', where a discussion of this Sanskrit term may be found within a context in which it plays a part in a theory.

There is a particular problem in writing this sort of book about *philosophical* terms, and that lies in the essentially argumentative nature of philosophy. Every time I write something making a claim about a particular philosophical position, a voice in my head says 'But this is only one view, and there are others who take a different view.' In an article or a book on a particular topic or thinker one has the space to look at a whole range of interpretations, and one can then argue in favour of what one takes to be the correct interpretation. I am constantly aware here that I have not had the opportunity to do that, and readers should be warned that the content here is entirely dependent on my view. I have tried to present what I take to be the most generally accepted view, since in a book of this kind it is not appropriate to do anything else. On the other hand, there is no doubt that I have presented my own line of interpretation on a whole range of issues, and readers will no doubt appreciate that this is just one person's understanding of the issue. If they follow up the references to relevant books, they will find a wide variety of both supporting and critical arguments on all these concepts.

Another aspect of presenting such a book on philosophical concepts is that I have tried to display something of the ways in which the concepts are used in arguments, which is after all the main activity of philosophy. Rather than say that A believed p and B suggested that not-p I have tried to point out where different thinkers challenged each other and what the main points of their arguments were. Of course, it is not easy to do this within a short space, but I hope it has been possible to convey something of the flavour of the arguments that constitute Eastern philosophy. Had I shortened each section I could have included many more concepts, but I felt that it is better to discuss a rather more limited set of concepts and have some opportunity to explain what arguments relate to those concepts. After all, we are talking about philosophical concepts, and they find their life within arguments, so it is difficult to explain their meaning unless something of their argumentative structure is explained.

It is necessary to say something about the choice of the particular concepts themselves. The list was arrived at as a result of asking a number of people which concepts they felt ought to be included, and also many years of teaching experience on my part. One decision that had to be taken was whether to limit the list of concepts to those occurring within Eastern philosophy itself, so that the key concepts would only be terms in Eastern languages. The problem with this approach is that readers would not be clear on how different terms in various cultures are linked to similar philosophical concepts. What I have tended to do, then, is have entries on some key concepts in Eastern languages, together with fairly long sections on general concepts, themselves incorporating a variety of such Eastern linguistic terms. This has the advantage of showing the links between particular discussions in Eastern philosophy and the general concept that those discussions illustrate. It has the disadvantage of implying that those discussions actually relate to a specific Western concept, which is often the case in only a tangential sense. Yet this is a constant problem of translating and linking concepts from one culture to another, and is inescapable when dealing in one language with concepts that originate and have their life within an entirely distinct language and culture. As a result there are often quite short sections devoted to key Eastern concepts in the entry headed by the name of the concept, yet much fuller treatments of those terms within wider sections dealing with a more general concept.

Those with whom I work tend to find particular concepts within the Eastern tradition puzzling, and I have sought to respond to these here. But there are some important concepts that I have totally ignored, and some that I have included which some readers will think are not so important. I tried to avoid being mechanistic in dealing with each concept, so that while there are often accounts of the treatment of the concept within a variety of cultural traditions, it is never the case that every Eastern tradition is mentioned. This is not because that concept is not discussed within that tradition, but choices have to be made about which discussions are most important and interesting. Finally, the reader should be aware that the equivalents in Eastern languages of the concepts discussed here are rarely exact, and no claim is being made that the Chinese, Japanese, Indian, Islamic, etc. interpretations of a particular concept are all precisely the same concept. The English renderings of the concepts are always full of difficulty and only indicative. Readers should also be alerted to the fact that I have had to be concise, and each of the concepts in this book has books devoted to it, often whole libraries of books. I am presenting here no more than a very thin slice of an enormous philosophical tradition. I hope that the slice is sufficiently rich to give the reader a genuine taste of the area as a whole, but if not I would urge the reader to try other introductory works in the area. Eastern philosophy is a fascinating subject, indeed, collection of subjects, and its study is a rewarding activity both intellectually and personally.

Having made all these excuses, I have to admit that no one apart from me is to be blamed for either the selection of concepts or their treatment.

NOTES ON TEXT

Transliteration

I have not followed the standard rules about transliteration in all the relevant Asian languages since these are only really appropriate for specialists in the area, and are unnecessary in an essentially introductory text such as this. I am assuming that readers will not wish to know precisely how the terms are to be translated back into their original languages. I have tried to present terms in ways that make them pronounceable as accurately as possible by English-speakers. I have omitted all macrons and diacritics. The standard form of Chinese is given in pinyin (e.g. Mao Ze Dong or Mao Zedong), although Wade-Giles (e.g. Mao Tse Tung) is also used occasionally in the case of well-known terms, since readers will often find the latter system used in standard works, particularly older ones. Indian terms are generally given in both Sanskrit and Pali forms. Those names that are generally known in latinized form (e.g. Confucius) are presented in that form, although the pinyin form is given as well at least once. For Tibetan I have used a form of transliteration that helps the reader know how the term is pronounced. Readers who move on to more specialized works in the area would be advised to study the transliteration guides for those works and they should be easily able to work out what the fully transliterated terms correspond to in this book.

Cross-referencing

Most foreign words are italicized in the text, and if they have their own entry they are also represented in bold on first mention in the entry. Most terms that have their own entry are represented in bold when they first occur in a different entry. This is not always the case; some terms are so ubiquitous (e.g. Buddhist philosophy, God) that they are not represented in bold, and some foreign terms are common enough in English (e.g. yoga, zen) not to require constant italicization. Readers are expected to work out that if they are informed that a term is used in Tibetan philosophy then there will be relevant information on the context of that term within the entry on Tibetan philosophy, for example. The index also, of course, provides information on where concepts are to be found throughout the text, apart from their own entry, should they have one. At the end of each entry there are suggestions of other relevant entries which are not directly mentioned in the above entry, and appropriate readings are recommended. For the sake of simplicity references are to the volume in which the information may be found, and some of these references are very general. In such cases the reader will need to look for the specific term or name in question in that volume. The names of authors are not always the surnames but the names that tend to be regarded as the surname within the English-speaking world. Terms in bold are not always precisely the term represented in the entry, since sometimes terms are highlighted in bold when they are some form of an entry (e.g. **meditator** for the entry term **meditation**). At the start of the book a list of concepts is given. Where the concept stands alone, this indicates that it has its own entry. Where a concept does not have its own entry, there is a reference in the list to the entries in which it can be located.

KEY THINKERS AND DATES

This is a list of the thinkers who are mentioned in this book, with relevant dates. These dates do not, as a result, figure in the list of key concepts themselves.

Al-Ash`ari d.935

Averroes, *see* ibn Rushd

Avicenna, *see* ibn Sina

Badarayana fifth century BCE

Bhartrihari *c.*fifth century

Candrakirti *c.*seventh century

Chen Duxiu 1879–1942

Cheng Hao 1032–85

Cheng Yi 1033–1108

Chinul 1158–1210

Confucius 551–479 BCE

Dhalla 1875–1956

Dharmakirti *c.*seventh century

Dignaga *c.*480–*c.*540

Dogen 1200–53

Dong Zhongshu *c.*195–*c.*115 BCE

Eisai 1141–1215

Al-Farabi *c.*870–950

Fazang 643–712

Gandhi 1869–1948

Al-Ghazali 1058–1111

Gongsun Long *c.*320–*c.*250 BCE

Han Fei *c.*280–*c.*233 BCE

Huishi *c.*370–*c.*310 BCE

Honen 1133–1212

Hu Shi 1891–1962

Ibn Matta 870–940

Ibn Rushd 1126–1198

Ibn Sina 980–1037

Ibn Taymiyya 1263–1328

Iqbal, Muhammad 1876–1938

Jin Yuelin 1895–1988

Jizang 540–623

Al-Jubba'i d.915

Kanada c.fifth century
Al-Kindi c.812–c.873
Kukai 774–835

Laozi c.sixth century BCE

Madhva 1238–1317
Mao Tse Tung, see Mao
  Zedong
Mao Zedong c.1895–1976
Mengzi (Mencius) 372–289
  BCE
Miskawayh 936–1030
Motada Eifu 1818–91
Mozi 468–376 BCE
Mulla Sadra 1571–1641
Myoe 1173–1232

Nagarjuna c.second/third
  century
Nichiren 1222–82
Nishida Kitaro 1870–1945
Nishitani 1900–90

Patanjali c.200 BCE/400 CE
  to c.150 BCE/450 CE

Radhakrishnan 1888–1975
Ramanuja c.1017–c.1100
Al-Razi, Abu Bakr d.925 or
  932

Saicho 767–822
Shankara 788–822
Shinran 1173–1262
Shosan Suzuki 1579–1655
Al-Sirafi 893–979
Shotoku 574–622
Sri Aurobindo 1870–1950
Al-Suhrawardi c.1170–1208
Sun Yatsen 1866–1925
Suzuki, D. T. 1870–1966

T'oegye 1501–1570
Tsongkhapa 1357–1419

Vacaspati b.842

Wanbi 226–49
Wang Shuren 1472–1528
Wonhyo 617–686

Yan Fu 1854–1921
Yi T'oegye, see T'oegye
Yi Yulgok, see Yulgok
Yulgok 1536–84

Xunzi c.325–238 BCE

Zeami 1363–1443
Zhang Dongsun 1886–1962
Zhangzai 1020–77
Zhou Dunyi 1017–1073
Zhiyi 538–97
Zhuangzi c.369–c.286 BCE
Zhu xi 1130–1200

KEY CONCEPTS

A

Abhidhamma *see* Abhidharma Buddhism
Abhidharma Buddhism
action
active intellect
adhyasa see avidya
Advaita
aesthetics
afterlife and rebirth
ahimsa
Ahriman, see Ahura Mazda
Ahura Mazda
ajiva see cosmology
Ajivikas *see* asceticism, fatalism
alayavijnana see consciousness, *tathagatagarbha*, Yogachara
ambiguity
Amida *see* enlightenment, *nembutsu*, Pure Land
Analects see Confucianism
analysis
anatman see anatta
anatta
Angra Mainyu *see* death, evil
anicca
animals

anumana see inference
al-`aql see law
al-`aql al-fa``l see active intellect
arahat
arhat see arahat
ariya saca see Four Noble Truths
artha
arya satya see Four Noble Truths
asceticism
Ash`ariyya and Mu`tazila
atman
atomism
atta see atman
avatara
avidya
avija see avidya
awareness *see* knowledge

B

badha
bardo
being
benevolence *see* love
Bhagavad Gita
bhakti
bhakti yoga see yoga
bkeda see Dvaita
bi-la kayfa see Ash`ariyya
bodhi
bodhichitta
bodhidruma see bodhi
bodhisatta see bodhisattva
bodhisattva
Book of Changes
brahman
Brahmanas see brahman
Brahmasutras see brahman

Buddha
buddha nature
buddhata
buddhi see yoga
bushido see death

C

caste
causation
chan see zen
Chandogya Upanishad see causation
change *see* causation
cheng see Book of Changes, enlightenment, human nature
Chinese philosophy
chitta see mind
Chittamatra *see* Yogachara
communism
compassion *see karuna*
conditioned arising *see* dependent origination
Confucianism
consciousness
cosmology
creation

D

dahr see time
Daoism
Dao de jing
Dao zue see Neoconfucianism
darshana
de
death
democracy
dependent origination
desire *see* love
destiny *see karma*

guna see Dvaita, *prakriti*
guru

H

hadith
harmony
hatha yoga
heaven *see* human nature, *tian*
himsa see asceticism
Hinayana
hoben see skilful means
hongaku see Tendai
hua yan see Chinese philosophy, Korean philosophy
human nature
humanism
hwadu see Korean philosophy

I

i see humanism
I Ching see Book of Changes
ignorance
ijma` see law
Ikhwan al-Safa´
illuminationist philosophy
`ilm al-huduri see* illuminationist philosophy
imagination
imam see fundamentalism
immortality see afterlife
indeterminacy of meaning *see* ambiguity
Indian philosophy
inference
isha see God
ishraq see illuminationist philosophy
ishvara see God, *jiva*
Islamic philosophy

J

jada see brahman
jahaliyya see fundamentalism
Jain philosophy
Japanese philosophy
jian see love
jianai see love, Mohism
jihad see violence
jina see Jain philosophy
jing see human nature
jiu see time
jiva
jivanmukti
jivatman see jiva
jnana see knowledge
jnana yoga
ju see education
jue see education
justice

K

kalam see Islamic philosophy
kalpana see imagination
kamma see karma
karma
karma yoga
karuna
khilafa see fundamentalism
knowledge
koan
kongan see koan, Korean philosophy
Korean philosophy
kyong see human nature

L

language
law
Legalism
li
Li xue see Neoconfucianism
liberation
lila
logic
Lokayata *see* consciousness, materialism
Lotus Sutra see Chinese and Japanese philosophy, faith, harmony,
  skilful means
love

M

Madhyamaka/Madhyamika
mahamudra see Tibetan philosophy
Mahayana
manas see mind
mappo see time
materialism
maya
meditation
Mimamsa
mind
ming jiao see Neodaoism, rectification of names
Mohism
moksha
momentariness
mu see emptiness
Mu`tazila *see* Ash`ariyya and Mu`tazila

N

nafs see mind
nahda see enlightenment

Naiyayikas *see* Nyaya-Vaisheshika
nana see jnana yoga, knowledge
nembutsu
Neoconfucianism
Neodaoism
nibbana
Nichiren Buddhism *see* faith
nirguna brahman see lila
nirvana see nibbana
niyati see fatalism
noesis see knowledge, *prajna*
non-violence *see ahimsa*
nothingness *see* emptiness
nous poetikos see active intellect
Nyaya-Vaisheshika
nyorizo see tathagatagarbha

O

Ohrmazd *see* evil
orientalism

P

panna see prajna
paradox *see koan,* logic
perception *see* inference, knowledge, *prajna*
personality
prajna
prajnaparamita
prakriti
prama see knowledge
pramana see knowledge
pratityasamutpada see fatalism
pudgala see personality
Pure Land
purusha
Purva Mimamsa *see* Mimamsa

Q

qi

R

rajas see Dvaita, *prakriti*, yoga
rectification of names
ren
ru lai zang see tathagatagarbha

S

saguna brahman see lila
samadhi see meditation, *prajna*
samatha see meditation
samsara
samsari see Jain philosophy
Sankhya
sarupya see knowledge
Sarvastivada
sattva see Dvaita, *prakriti*, yoga
shari`a see law
shaykh see guru, Sufism
sheng see causation
shi see Legalism
Shi`a, Shi`ism
*shi`at allah see* Shi`ism
shila see prajna
Shingon Buddhism
shu see Legalism
shunya see emptiness, Madhyamaka
shunyata see emptiness
Shunyatavada *see* emptiness, Madhyamaka, Mahayana
shura see democracy
skandhas see personality
skilful means
song see human nature
suchness *see tathagata*

suf see Sufism
Sufism
Sunna, **Sunni Islam**
susupti see atman
svadharma see dharma

T

tamas see Dvaita, *prakriti*, yoga
tanha see Four Noble Truths
tantra
Taoism *see* Daoism
Tao Te Ching see Dao De Jing
tasawwur see knowledge, logic
tasdiq see logic
tat tvam asi see Vedanta
tathagata
tathagatagarbha
tathata see tathagatagarbha
tawhid see Sufism
Tendai
Theravada Buddhism
tian
tianli see human nature
tian tai *see* Chinese philosophy, emptiness, Korean philosophy,
  Tendai
tianzi see Mohism
Tibetan philosophy
time
triaratna see ethics
trishna see Four Noble Truths

U

umma see violence
universals
Upanishads
upaya see skilful means

V

Vaisheshika
Veda
Vedanta
vikalpa see imagination
violence
vipissana see Madhyamaka, meditation
Vishishtadvaita
vyapti see logic

W

wei see Daoism
wei wu wei see Daoism
wu see Neodaoism, zen
wu nian see meditation
wu xin see meditation
wu yu see Neoconfucianism

X

xi see Daoism
xuan xue see Neodaoism
xue see enlightenment

Y

yana see skilful means
yi see Daoism, Mohism
Yi jing, see Book of Changes
Yin-Yang school
yoga
Yogachara

Z

zaman see time
zazen
zen
Zhou yi see Book of Changes

Abhidhamma – *see* **Abhidharma Buddhism**

Abhidharma Buddhism   A doctrinal development and body
of literature originating from 400–300 BCE in India
(Abhidhamma in Pali), and meaning a systematic or supple-
mentary arrangement of the *dharma*s, the basic concepts
and teaching of Buddhism. It is regarded as the second of
the three 'baskets' that make up the Tripitika, the body
of Buddhist scriptures. It is particularly interesting for its
treatment of the conditioned constituents of all existence,
including mental as well as physical factors, inner consciousness as well as outer bodily existence. Real beings are *dharma*s,
and everything that we experience as outside of us is just
a series of instantaneous flashes of *dharma*s. Even what is
commonly referred to as the soul is only a mass of momentary episodes, and we are trapped through our ignorance into
acknowledging the reality of what really is not real at all.
The momentary events do really take place, but we only
notice them or are interested in them because of *karma*, our
repertoire of desires and actions. Once we realize this, we
appreciate that what we take to be the self has no more reality
than what it takes to be outside itself, and once we eradicate the self from our thinking (or perhaps better, from
thought) we no longer look on the world as a site for the

1

satisfaction of our desires or a source of our frustrations. The point of studying the lists and types of *dharma*s is to be able to work out as systematically as possible how things really are, and so we may be enabled to transcend the *karma* involved in any kind of purposive activity. As a result we may be able to bring about the cessation of craving based on ignorance.

See also: **atman**
Further reading: Guenther 1976, Pruden 1988–90.

action   The aphorism 'it is easy to know but difficult to act' has played an important role in Chinese philosophy. It suggests that it is far easier to have a theoretical understanding of something than to act upon it. The implication is that one does not really have **knowledge** unless one is able to apply it in practice. When Cheng Hao put the emphasis on the difficulty of acquiring knowledge in using the slogan, he sought to establish a form of subjective idealism, and the necessity to take steps to find out what is the case. Sun Yatsen criticized the slogan, arguing that it suggested a form of inaction and political pacifism. He turned it round, arguing that it is easy to act, but difficult to know. People have often acted without thinking clearly about what they were doing. Mao Zedong in his *On Practice* advocated the synthesis of theory and practice in revolutionary behaviour. This is actually the culmination of many centuries of speculation in Chinese thought, where **materialists** tended to stress action as the basis of morality, as opposed to idealists, who often saw thought as the basis of action. For Mao, social practice was not just the basis of human knowledge but also the criterion of that knowledge's validity. There is a dialectical process according to which practice and knowledge both develop in tandem, and reach ever higher levels of human attainment.

In Indian philosophy the relevant term here is *karma*, which is identified with movement. Action is a property of substance, a dynamic quality that links one substance with another. On the **Nyaya-Vaisheshika** system motion or movement is not an essential aspect of matter. Rather, it comes from outside it. There is often an argument that **enlightenment** is only accessible through certain kinds of action, the performance of duties, prayer and worship.

The Japanese philosopher Dogen discusses action in his account of *dharma*, the way of life appropriate to each individual. He pours scorn on the idea of the separation between practice and the attainment of what the practice is aiming at, between setting out to do something and actually achieving it. Enlightenment is then not dependent on practice, nor is awakening based on action. To have a **buddha nature** is to be a **Buddha**, and one cannot be a Buddha without having a buddha nature. Dogen represents this relationship as dynamic, and criticized the idea that one could just awaken as Buddha. The identity of action and the end of the action is a crucial aspect of zen thought. Of course, action is only successfully linked with the acquisition of the buddha nature if it is carried out perfectly and with the absence of intention, but once it is performed in the correct way, the result is inevitable. Action and the goal of action are just one thing really.

Islamic philosophy took over a controversy that originated in theology and considered whether we are free to carry out our own actions, or whether what we call our actions are just reflections of what God does. Many thinkers influenced by **Ash`arism** argued that only God really acts, so that what we do is only possible in achieving certain ends because God has brought those ends about, and has also allowed us to think that the world is an orderly place in which we have some impact. Al-Ghazali often produced this sort of view, and he suggested that only acceptance of such a thorough-going occasionalism gives appropriate status to God's power as compared with our inability to do things without his assistance. The Peripatetic thinkers like ibn Rushd argued by contrast that unless we can really act we can form no view of the world as an environment in which there are stable and independently existing entities. Moreover, if what makes an action feasible is God bringing it about in every case, this makes the addition of God's agency empty, since we merely

3

redescribe our ordinary actions in every case as presupposing God's activity.

See: **ethics, materialism**
Further reading: Abe 1992, Cheng 1989, Leaman 1985, 1997, Mao 1961, Schram 1989.

active intellect   In Islamic philosophy this is a crucial concept, which is sometimes translated also as the agent intellect. In Arabic *al-`aql al-fa``al* and in Greek *nous poetikos*, this expression comes indirectly from Aristotle. The active intellect is often described as a transcendent immaterial entity equivalent to the sphere of the moon which acts as an intermediary between the divine mind and the human intellect. Once the latter has achieved a state of relative perfection by becoming the acquired intellect, the state of understanding the universal and abstract principles behind reality, it receives from the active intellect an emanation from heaven. The active intellect makes the acquired intellect possible, by transmitting from the transcendental world the power that manages to link it with the sublunary world. The active intellect represents the highest level of thought which we human beings can attain, and it reflects the necessity of something outside of us to move our capacity to think into alignment with transcendental reality.

Further reading: Leaman 1985, 1997.

adhyasa superimposition or the attribution of incorrect features to something that is experienced – *see avidya*

Advaita   A school of **Vedanta** which literally means 'not two' or 'not dual', and whose major thinker was Shankara. The group of texts discussed in most detail is the **Upanishads**, and the varied ways in which that text deals with the links between *brahman* and the individual soul, and the former's links with the universe. The term 'non-dual' is based on the idea that reality is one and not to be differentiated. This reality is *brahman,* divine power, knowledge of which leads to *moksha* or liberation. The crucial notion here is of a hierarchy of levels of viewing reality. The more crude level is that where we rely on the senses and which is only an aspect of a more basic reality, a reality that is more accessible to us through dreams, and most accessible through dreamless sleep and yogic trances. *Brahman* is available to a degree at each level of reality, but really it exists without any attributes at all. The common idea that we are separated from reality is due to human ignorance, *maya* or *avidya*, the illusions that persist as a result of our apparent individuality. One of the ways of cementing us in this ignorance is by trying to escape from it, since such effort means **action**, and action implies the acquisition of karmic traces (*karma*) and merely deepens bondage.

One view offered by Advaita was that *brahman* is both identical and different from the individual soul and the world. In itself it is entirely one, but within that unity resides the ability to comprehend an infinite variety, both the variety of the soul and the rather more limited diversity found within the physical world. This is plausible if one sees creation as not the production of entirely new things, but rather the instantiation of aspects that already exist within the *brahman.* One of the interesting implications of this view is that it suggests a dual strategy to liberation, which is going to be neither entirely through following one's moral and religious obligations, nor through acquiring knowledge, but in some combination of the two. The former strategy helps bring about detachment from the influences of the world, while the latter encourages acknowledgement of the oneness of reality, and so leads to the ending of ignorance. The progress of this attempted solution was brought to an end by Shankara, who argued that all it does is restate the original problem without contributing to its solution. How can one thing encompass both similarity and dissimilarity? These are contradictory concepts and claiming that they both characterize the same subject is to involve oneself in self-contradiction. Shankara agrees that whatever the Upanishads say must be true, but that the references made to the diversity of reality are not an account of what is deeper reality. All diversity is in itself an illusion. On the other hand, it does not follow that the world itself is unreal, since it constitutes a stream of appearances which do depend on a principle of reality. We need to distinguish between two sorts of unreality, one where an object is mistaken for something that it is not, and this is different from the case where we take ordinary experience to be ultimate reality, which it is not when compared with the one principle of reality, *brahman*, itself. The individual self is not illusory in the first sense, since it is *brahman* appearing to us in a particular way, in the only way that would make sense to us given our physical and mental constitution. Seeing *brahman* in this way leads to errors about its real nature, but none the less it gives us a glimpse of that real nature. What we need to do is to work from where we are to gain a deeper idea of where the self genuinely originates. We have to make a distinction between the status of the self and the world, for while the latter may be illusory, the former is not similarly illusory, since if it were, there would be no prospect of the liberation of the self.

The doctrine then is that *brahman* is the one reality which manifests itself in two ways, once as the world and also as the individual self. The former manifestation is an illusory aspect of *brahman*, while the latter is *brahman* itself, albeit under the distorting aspect of the illusory universe. We should not see this link between *brahman* and the world as causal, since causal relations only obtain between empirical phenomena. Physical change means that one thing becomes part of something else, but is not entirely destroyed, nor is the new thing entirely new, since it came about through the causal efficacy of something else, which remains part of the 'new' thing. Although the universe is *maya* and so unreal, it is not incomprehensible. By contrast with the **Sankhya-Yoga** metaphysics, the principle of the material is not real. It is not unreal either, since it is influenced by reality, and there is no point in looking to matter itself as the ground of the physical universe. On the other hand, it obviously has a part to play in such an explanation, but not an ultimate role. The ultimate ground is of course *brahman*, and when we deny the reality of the world all that we are doing is denying its reality apart from its origins in *brahman*. The latter in itself does not change, but without it there would be no possible ·experience of physical change. The position is even more complicated than might immediately appear to be the case in that *brahman* is really neither simple nor diverse, but is entirely without features.

How then could it lead to anything else? After all, in the empirical example of illusion where a rope is taken for a snake, there is some degree of resemblance between the rope and the snake. Shankara gives the example of the way in which we are aware of our own self as the foundation of everything we do, which is neither a precise understanding of the self, nor a completely mysterious relationship to it. *Brahman* is like this, one can be as certain of it as one can of the existence of one's own self. Like the self, it appears to be some sort of thing but it is impossible to say what characteristics it has in itself.

The whole universe is the effect of *maya*, and its parts are derived from the ignorance we employ when thinking about things. Actually, the differences that appear to exist between different selves are entirely the effect of this ignorance. Does that mean that the selves and *brahman* are one and the same? This is not the case, since the selves are very much part of the world of illusion, in so far as they concentrate on that world. From the point of view of ultimate reality, there is no such thing as diversity, but from the point of view of this world, it does indeed exist. The individual self is equivalent to *brahman*, and its apparent distinction from it is based on the illusions on which it concentrates. Correct knowledge results when we appreciate the illusory nature of this sort of experience and the concepts that go with it, and can result in liberation. It is not enough, though, just to have the right attitude towards these illusions, we also need to act from a motivation of complete disinterestedness. Such action helps us to rid our minds of the dualistic illusions with which they are otherwise replete, and the pursuit of duty is a vital part of the path to liberation. The intellectual aspect of following this route is taken up with formal study, reflection and meditation – all processes that emphasize the intellectual and personal aspects of the understanding of the unity of the individual and reality. Both the mind and the body require training, and the Vedanta should be studied with a teacher. The end of the process is reached when all erroneous views are removed and beliefs in the truths of the Vedanta are held in a steady and permanent manner. The final proposition that is grasped is that the meditator is *brahman*, and he contemplates this truth calmly and makes it an essential aspect of his thinking. The eventual end of *moksha* is not knowing *brahman* but becoming *brahman*. Such an individual may continue to carry out ordinary human actions, and we should recall that he will still be subject to a degree of previous *karma*, but the motive from which the actions will be done will be different, entirely spontaneous and unconstrained by desire for personal success or fear of pain. Duty continues to be a requirement, but it is done through a deep belief in the unity of everything. The individual no longer identifies himself with his body, so the false identification of the self with the body, and the separation of the self from *brahman*, disappears and takes bondage with it. Although liberation can thus be achieved, the agent can continue to exist in the world, but after liberation he does not identify with the body nor with the world, and is unattached to the sufferings of phenomenal existence. This lifestyle is called **jivanmukti** and refers to the liberation of someone who is still alive. He lives in complete **harmony** with the world, having no desire of his own to fulfil his own ambitions, with the exception of the intention to relieve the sufferings of others and liberate everyone. Even this intention, though, is pure and unconnected with the desire to satisfy a personal craving. In having this intention the individual merely represents the principle of *brahman* itself and its potential role for universal liberation.

See also: **badha**
Further reading: Deutsch and Van Buitenen 1971, Ramamurty 1996.

aesthetics In **Islamic philosophy** a strong distinction was made between intellectual and sensible notions of beauty. Al-Farabi accepts that the immediate notion of beauty is visual and so more closely related to the sensations, and yet he also claims that it represents an advanced stage along a thing's progress to its final perfection. God, the most perfect thing, is therefore also the most beautiful. His beauty is different from everything else because it is part of his essence; by contrast, the beauty of everything else is linked with physical and accidental features that are not the same as their own essence. God's pleasure in his beauty comes about through self-contemplation, where the knower and the known become the same, and is obviously eternal and continual, by contrast again with lesser forms of beauty which are only temporary and occasional experiences in life. Ibn Sina develops this thesis to argue that there is an innate aesthetic tendency in everyone which can be noble if it is applied to the intelligible and the rational, something that results when there is cooperation between the animal and the rational aspects of the soul.

One of the interesting aspects of Islamic philosophy is its determination to treat all kinds of proposition as having a logical kernel, so that even poetry and rhetoric, which are primarily designed to move us emotionally, are basically the popular presentation of a rational claim. Religion is often seen as the reflection and popularization of philosophy, since it has the same message, albeit wrapped up in a more graceful and beautiful form.

Aesthetic theory based on **Advaita Vedanta** tends to stress the unity of everything, refusing to see art as a separate activity from the contemplation of reality itself. **Zen** theory also insists on the inclusion of art as part of the route to **enlightenment.** Art can help us distance ourselves from the notion of a permanent self and towards a feeling of integration with reality, while at the same time helping us appreciate the **emptiness** of everything. The romantic notion of the artist as a unique creative individual is replaced by the idea that everyone is an artist, capable of appreciating the real nature of the world, of integrating the theoretical, practical and aesthetic aspects

9

of life. The Japanese thinker Zeami developed an account of training for *No* theatre that identified the actor's training with the awakening (*satori*) of the zen practitioner, and which argued that the highest form of theatre is far more than merely a matter of appearance, but is rather the communication of a deeper emotional beauty to the audience.

Further reading: Deutsch 1975, Izutsu and Izutsu 1981, Kemal 1991, Patnaik 1997.

afterlife and rebirth   There existed an important **materialist** tradition in Indian thought which saw human beings as the product of physical elements, which decay on **death** and lead to the dissolution of the human being. **Consciousness** is no different from anything else, and when its parts are dissipated, it is itself dissipated. The doctrine of rebirth is ridiculous since there is a close relationship between a particular type of body and its consciousness, so that the idea of a human soul entering an animal's body is out of the question. Finally, there is no memory of a previous life, and so no reason to believe in it. This argument could be broadened to suggest that memory is an important aspect of self-identity and so without it there is no self-identity. There are some difficulties with these arguments which are frequently brought against the materialists. Conscious states seem to be rather different from physical states, and since we cannot observe the connection between them, how can we be sure that when the body dies, the soul dies also? A more popular view in Indian thought is that we are part of a constant cycle of birth and rebirth, until the final **liberation** through **enlightenment**. The fate of souls after death is determined by their behaviour during their lives, which tends to be reflected in the sort of transmigration that they can undergo.

Buddhist ideas do not go in the direction of an afterlife that represents another life abstracted from the ordinary world. **Karma** and rebirth takes place all the time, and the soul is not a permanent thing that can take up residence in another world, but just a series of existences. What has an afterlife is not the unitary soul – there is no such thing – but the character of what was the original or latest person. This continues until the ambitions and aversions of the individual are overcome and there is an end of their application to the world (i.e. so leading to *nirvana*). It is up to the individual to rid herself of *karma*, since the latter leads to confusion about what is the source of existence and so leads to suffering. It is up to the individual to achieve *nirvana*, perhaps with the aid of a teacher, and it is for the individual to practise a morally beneficial life. What is crucial to a grasp of the Buddhist notion of rebirth is the significance of **causality**. Everything that happens has a cause, so if something is without a cause, it must be permanent and changeless. So if our consciousness was not caused by a prior consciousness, it would be permanent, yet we know from our experience that it is not. In opposition to the argument that we do not remember previous lives, it was often suggested that people do remember such lives, or parts of them. If such recall is not universal, then this can be blamed on the traumatic effects of death and then rebirth.

Some kinds of rebirth envisaged by Buddhism are rather unpleasant, in particular those that involve long periods in hell, or as ghosts and animals of various kinds. Other kinds are preferable, since they are human rebirths, or even in heaven where one's companions are gods, albeit non-eternal deities. There is a hierarchy in operation here, at the bottom of which lie beings who are close to the realm of the senses and desires, while the higher up one goes the more refined and pure are the thoughts of the individual. These higher states are often identified with different stages of the meditation process.

A serious problem to do with rebirth arises from the Buddhist suspicion of the notion of the **self** as a permanent substance. If the self is not real, then how far can we say that the same person is reborn, or even that the same person escapes the cycle of birth and rebirth? The solution seems to be that rebirth does not require a permanent self, but a permanent or continuing idea of the self, which lies at the base of the significance that we apply to the notion of ourselves. This attitude emerges again and again in new minds and leads us to treat seriously the phenomenon of desire and the experiences that we have. These aspects of ignorance reinforce the notion that is perhaps even more crucially an aspect of ignorance, that is, that we have a real and continuing self that is far more important than any other selves in existence.

A central problem with the notion of the afterlife in Islamic philosophy is the fact that the soul is generally regarded as the form of the body, so that when the body dies the form is no longer applicable, and would be expected to disappear immediately. Some, like ibn Sina, escaped this problem by adhering to a view of the soul as non-material, so that only the non-rational part of the soul decays on death, the possibility of a spiritual afterlife remaining for the rational soul. He argues that the rational soul is indestructible since it is simple and so cannot be broken up into its parts. Others, like al-Farabi, argue that the only eternal aspect of the soul is its ability to come into contact with eternal ideas, so that only those souls with such contact manage to remain in existence after the death of the bodies. Ibn Rushd pushed this notion rather further, arguing that only one intellect is permanent, and everyone can participate in it, if they perfect their intellects. So there is no individual survival of death for him, merely an eternal blending of the individual soul into the principle of the abstract ideas themselves. The problems that the philosophers had with understanding the notion of an individual afterlife was attacked by al-Ghazali, who argued for a philosophical justification of the literal Qur'anic notion of a physical afterlife. On the other hand, he later followed the Sufi understanding of such an afterlife as being largely descriptive of an advanced spiritual state, not a direct enjoyment of physical goods.

The discussion of the afterlife in Islamic philosophy had to deal with the difficulty of reconciling the rather physical descriptions of the next world in the Qur'an with the Aristotelian understanding of the soul as the form of the person. If the person is an ensouled body, then when the body perishes there is nothing left to inform, and so the soul might be expected to disappear. In any case, there is a problem with understanding how after the death of the person another person, or the same person in a different guise, could reappear in the next life, given the fact that this would go against the natural process by which matter decays and is not reassembled. This could come about through miracle, of course, but again this runs against the naturalistic interpretation of most Peripatetic philosophy in the Islamic world. Al-Ghazali claimed that anyone who denies the possibility of physical resurrection is guilty of unbelief, but his objections are not only theological. He wonders why there should be any problem in imagining a physical afterlife, and if we can imagine it, this shows it is logically possible, and if it is logically possible, then surely God would have no difficulty bringing it about. Ibn Rushd replies that not everything that can be imagined is logically possible, since it is only possible to think of an individual afterlife if God were to re-create us through miracle, and if miracles took place we should lose our grasp both of the course of nature and of the meanings of the terms we use. He argues for a sort of universal afterlife in the sense that we are immortal in so far as we concentrate on immortal subjects, and as immortal we cannot distinguish between different individuals, since the source of our immortality is our concentration on the impersonal abstract truths. Why then does the Qur'an talk about personal immortality? This is because most people will find it difficult to behave virtuously unless they think that their fate in the next life is going to depend on their behaviour in this life, and since they think that the most important part of themselves is their bodies, advice about how to conduct themselves will need to be presented in physical terms. Philosophers are able to understand that we ought to behave well for its own reward, and that the consequences of our actions continue after our death through their effects on others, but most people will need to have this explained to them in more physical terms. Hence the account of the afterlife in the Qur'an. So ibn Rushd argues that there is no need

13

for God to bring us back to life in the next world after we have died in this world, just the need to explain to us that the results of our actions are more durable than the lives of those who perform those actions.

See: **action, mind,** *samsara*
Further reading: Basham 1971, Eliade 1958, Leaman 1985, 1997, Ling 1981, Ma`sumian 1997, Raju 1985.

ahimsa A term from Hindu, and especially **Jain**, thought meaning 'non-violence' or not harming, also very important in Buddhist thought. It is of particular significance in Jain thought, which sets out to avoid harming any form of life whatsoever. Non-violence is also an important idea in Buddhist thought, and it came to become an ideal of Hindu life, leading to the low status of those who were left with the caste role (*dharma*) of killing or working with dead things. Although in practice this ideal did not lead to the ending of killing or fighting, it contributed to the growth of vegetarianism in Hinduism. Non-violence was turned into an important political principle in the twentieth century by Gandhi, who saw its application to economics as possible through what he called 'bread labour', the participation of everyone in productive work, preferably involving the production of food. This brings out what is the positive side of non-violence for Gandhi, which is charity and **love** for all. It involves three vows, the vows of self-control, fearlessness and universal social equality, including untouchables.

See: *karma*, **violence**
Further reading: Bondurant 1965, Chapple 1993, Chatterjee 1983, 1996, Gandhi 1969.

Ahriman – *see* **evil**

Ahura Mazda A name created by Zoroaster for God, literally meaning 'The Wise Lord'. Zoroaster took the notion of an already existing deity, a 'lord' (*ahura*) and built it up into a unique role as the sole good creator. In Pahlavi this term became *Ohrmazd*, and came to represent the good creator who stood against the **evil** *Ahriman*, both of whom exist eternally. *Ohrmazd* is the source of all the good in the world, including light, life, health and happiness, and his influence leads to **harmony** and order. He is not omnipotent, though, and has no control over the forces of evil.

Further reading: Boyce 1975, 1984, Hinnells 1978.

ajiva, absence of mind or inanimate substance – *see* **cosmology**

Ajivikas – *see* **asceticism, fatalism**

alayavijnana – *see* **consciousness**, *tathagatagarbha*, **Yogachara**

ambiguity   A term has meaning that can either be literal or metaphorical. Some Indian theories suggest that it is God who lays down the meanings of words, although others insist that it is human beings who give meanings to words. These varying arguments of the **Naiyayikas** are rejected by those who believe that the Vedas themselves give meaning to the terms included in them. This has led to a theory of meaning in which it is the sentence and not the word that has primary semantic value, and so the sentence that gives meaning to the word. It will then be the sentence that makes a word ambiguous, since it will have no clear or univocal sense given its use in the sentence.

In Chinese thought many schools of philosophy placed great reliance on the **Rectification of Names**, an idea initially put forward by Confucius which saw ambiguity and indeterminacy of meaning as a great enemy of social stability and clear thought.

In **Islamic philosophy** the notion of ambiguity became important, since many of the verses of the Qur'an appear to

15

be ambiguous, and there was often argument as to how this should be understood. Some thinkers argued that the best way to understand such passages is to take their literal sense and leave it at that, while many philosophers suggested that these verses needed to be understood figuratively, as pointing to a hidden meaning which the apparent difficulty of the text itself shows but does not say. Al-Ghazali claims that religious language ought to be understood as literally true, so that when the **afterlife**, for example, is described in very physical terms, then this is precisely how we must accept it as being. Ibn Rushd, by contrast, used the notion of the ambiguous nature of the language of the text here to argue that the text points out to ordinary believers how important it is for them to do their duty in order to enjoy the next life, while the philosophically sophisticated understand by this that the consequences of their behaviour have a wider extension than just being limited to this life. Religion speaks to different people in different ways, in analytical ways to the more intelligent, and in poetic and rhetorical ways to the simpler members of the community. What we should do with this language, ibn Rushd argues, is not try to simplify it by suggesting that it embodies only one meaning, but we should respect the variety of meanings and interpretations that a particular term and sentence may have.

Further reading: Chatterjee 1965, Confucius 1993, Leaman 1997.

Amida, Buddha-image of Pure Land school – *see* **enlightenment**, *nembutsu*, **Pure Land**

Analects – *see* **Confucianism**

analysis In Buddhist thought analysis is the investigation of the way things' really are, and is linked to the process of **meditation**. The first step in the process is throwing doubt on the notion of the inherent existence of the objects that confront us, and this is established through argument.

Such arguments demonstrate that we are not justified in having confidence in the existence of any such inherent existences, and they generally consist in dialectical attacks on the arguments that present the thesis that there is such a thing as inherent existence. The successful refutation of that thesis leads to the conclusion that . all that exists is really **emptiness**, not in the sense of a substantive reality but as the defining feature of everything, and then emptiness itself can function as the object of thought, in particular meditation. The thinker will consider the contrast between putative inherent existence and how existence appears to us. The difficult aspect of this meditation, from the **Madhyamaka** perspective, will be to remain in the middle in the contrasting of the existence and non-existence of such essences.

See: **logic**
Further reading: Cabezon 1994, Kalupahana 1986, Williams 1989.

anatman, absence of self – *see anatta*

anatta A Pali term used in Buddhist thought and meaning 'not-self' (Sanskrit, *anatman*). This is one of the three marks of all conditioned existence and is central to Buddhist teaching. It was devised to stand in opposition to the notion of *atman*, the idea of a constant and eternal self, a significant notion in Indian philosophy at the time of the Buddha. The Buddhist theory of selflessness is predominantly a rejection of Hindu orthodox philosophy, and has led to a very creative debate between the traditions. Buddhist philosophers regard the Hindu notion of the self as an expression of the reification that binds humanity to a misguided notion of what is real, while Hindu thinkers regard the denial of the self as equivalent to nihilism. The idea of such a self is misleading, according to Buddhism, since it is no more than an idea that we apply to the flow of **consciousness**, and if we closely examine the contents of consciousness we can find no such

17

self in it. For Buddhism this is a crucial point, since it is the illusion that there is a self which leads to an incorrect view of reality and so to suffering (*dukkha*). Once we rid ourselves of this notion, we are on the route to escape from suffering. It is difficult to overemphasize the significance of this notion in Buddhist philosophy.

An interesting question has often been asked about the doctrine of not-self, and that is why the self is not actually denied, while the not-self is described as a vital notion for us to grasp. The reason seems to be the desire to avoid the appearance of Buddhism being nihilist, and also to vindicate the role of the not-self for our salvation. The not-self doctrine can be regarded as an example of **skilful means** to employ a device that human beings want to use to transcend the negative consequences of that device. The idea of the self is a leading instance of attachment, and it is through such attachment that we become linked to suffering and frustration, since we do not realize that what we are attached to is constantly changing and impermanent. The notion of the real self is a useful notion in that it explains what we find so attractive about the idea of a permanent subject of consciousness, and can be used to encapsulate so much of what is in fact illusory but which seems to be solid. The point of identifying things with not-self is to point out how illusory they are, and how we should let go of them in just the same way that we should let go of the self. What we need to do is appreciate how suffering, change and not-self characterize everything in which we ordinarily have confidence, and this exercise sets us on the route to *nirvana*.

The role of the not-self, then, is to provide us with a reason to let go of the phenomena that imply the existence of a self. There is no need to attack the notion of the self directly, since contemplating the nature of the experiences that presuppose that notion brings out not only how empty they are, but also how empty is the notion that they presuppose. The point is to embody one's suspicion of the reality of phenomena in one's practice, and not disprove a particular concept which can then remain unconnected' to our behaviour. One of the interesting features of Buddhist philosophy is the suspicion of philosophy itself, in the sense of the defence of or attack on different theoretical views. There is even an uneasiness about what might be regarded as correct views, since adhering to these is also a form of attachment, and they are held by us due to some prior cause which links that attachment to the impermanent and eventually leads to impermanence and frustration. On the other hand, one can hold the right views in the right way, which involves going beyond the process of holding views entirely because it is identified with a form of direct intuition. From this it follows that adhering to a doctrine of not-self can be just as destructive as believing in the self. What we need to do is change until we can see things as not-self. The question remains, however, is this not itself a view that has been defended and to which we might well become attached, albeit through practice instead of in theory?

One of the characteristics of *nirvana* is that it is the opposite of everything that characterizes the appearance of our world, in the sense that it is permanent and happy. One might expect it also to be the opposite of not-self, but this is not the case. *Nirvana* is the highest form of emptiness, and since it is empty, it cannot include the self. The self is intimately connected to the human personality, and as the forms of attachment implicit in the personality are weakened and eventually replaced, the self certainly does not make a comeback. The notion of the permanent self disappears, and as a result *nirvana* is realized. The characteristics of the self, its permanence and immutability, do survive in *nirvana*, and indeed represent the nature of the ultimate end, but not as parts of a reconstructed real self. The notion of a real self is shown to be illusory in *nirvana* since the latter involves establishing as real and permanent what goes far beyond the narrow and selfish aspects of the ordinary notion of the human self. The latter characteristics cannot survive in *nirvana*, which is precisely its opposite.

Further reading: Collins 1982, Griffiths 1986.

Angra Mainyu, personification of evil in Zoroastrianism – *see* **death**, **evil**

anicca   A Pali term (*anitya* in Sanskrit), meaning impermanent or transient. One of the triad of marks that characterize all existence in this world, along with *dukkha* and *anatta*. This is a central Buddhist concept designed to contrast with the permanent and enduring sense (*atman*) of Hinduism. It is supposed to capture more than the idea that everything in life is transient, and to show that the sorts of things that most people regard as fulfillment are very impermanent. Buddhists frequently do not even contemplate the possibility of a permanent form of fulfillment. A suitable object of **meditation** is the constant change of all the phenomena of experience. This kind of awareness is crucial to Buddhist **cosmology** and brings vividly to mind the impossibility of trusting in the apparent stability of our ideas and impressions.

Further reading: Murti 1960.

animals   There is evidence in some Buddhist texts of a general sympathy with the sufferings of animals. After all, if the **buddha nature** is in everything, then everything must be respected. This leads to a problem, though, in that plants are just as worthy of preservation as animals, so it would seem that Buddhists can eat nothing at all. Many Buddhists are vegetarians, but this often seems to have more to do with their living in countries where vegetarianism is traditionally practised than for any other reason. Had vegetarianism been a Buddhist doctrine, it would have failed to become popular in parts of Asia where meat-eating is popular. On the other hand, there is a general acknowledgement in Buddhism of the interconnection between diverse forms of life, along with the necessity to be **compassionate**, which suggests an attitude of sympathy with animals. Buddhistic monastic rules forbid monks or nuns to eat meat which they suspect has been killed for them, and some forms of Buddhism equate meat eating with killing animals.

Further reading: Chapple 1993.

anumana – *see* **inference**

al-ʿaql, reason – *see* **law**

al-ʿaql al-faʿʿal, active or agent intellect – *see* **active intellect**

arahat A Pali expression (*arhat* in Sanskrit) from Theravada Buddhism and early Buddhism for someone who has attained the goal of **enlightenment** or *nirvana*. The successful individual will have completely understood the **Four Noble Truths** and left behind all types of emotion and error. The mind of the *arahat* is pure, and leads to actions that are entirely the result of **compassion**, wisdom and selflessness. There are important implications of this sort of achievement, in that the *arahat* escapes the bonds of *samsara*, the cycle of rebirth, and so does not return after death to this world. Even if one is not successful in reaching such heights, there are lesser but still important roles available to those who travel along most of the way. (This approach to salvation was vigorously criticized by Mahayana Buddhism for selfishly stressing personal salvation and not dedicating the individual to the relief of suffering in general. They called the form of salvation enjoined by the *arahat* a selfish *nirvana*.) The *arahat* experiences *nirvana* in this life and the highest developed type of saint enters it on death, not returning to any other form of existence. Interesting questions arise over how far the same individual becomes an *arahat*, since if what we call the self is just a reflection of the ways in which different people respond to the phenomenon of desire, then the abandonment of desire experienced by the *arahat* will also lead to the abandonment of individuality. Yet this would mean that the *arahat* would become a literally different person. This is too dramatic a conclusion, though, since all that is really required is for him to transcend the use of the ordinary sense of 'I'. He can use that label, but in a self-critical manner, making no assumptions about any underlying reality to which it applies. Nor does the status of the *arahat* imply a general coldness to everything, but rather extending the compassionate love a mother feels for her child to all sentient beings.

When the **bodhisattva** reaches a high level of enlightenment he has a choice as to whether to become an *arahat* and pursue a personal peace, or to devote his life to others by continuing to develop on the route to Buddhahood. He has abandoned his attachments at the *arahat* stage, and so can bring the *samsara* process to an end. The *arahat* has let go of everything, including the aspects of his personality and the ways in which they seemed to constitute some kind of 'self'

See also: **asceticism**
Further reading: Aronson 1980, Gombrich 1988, 1997, Griffiths 1994.

arhat, someone who has achieved enlightenment – *see* **arahat**

ariya saca – *see* **Four Noble Truths**

artha *Artha* is one of the four goals of life in Hinduism (together with **kamma**, **dharma** and **moksha**). *Artha* refers to the practical world, to the acquisition of wealth and the maintenance of material possessions. It is also used to refer to a disposition to act in a particular way, and is used in philosophy to outline the duties we are taken to have with respect to the material world. Although spiritual goals are clearly of greatest significance, it is often argued that these cannot be realized without first satisfying our material welfare. While it is important to make adequate provision for material welfare, care should be taken to do this honestly and fairly, since otherwise one interferes with one's *dharma* or correct way of life. *Artha* also means 'referent' or the meaning of a word in the sense of its denotation.

Further reading: Potter 1988, Puligandla 1975, Radhakrishnan and Moore 1957.

arya satya – *see* **Four Noble Truths**

asceticism   The Buddha represented his position as a moderate one, between the two extremes of hedonism and asceticism. It is commonly thought that he advocated extreme asceticism, but this is not the case. On the other hand, early Buddhism was very much linked to monasticism, where monks and nuns turn away from their families and society in general. The renunciation of the world and the orientation towards other-worldliness fits in well with the idea that the experience we have of the external world is radically misleading, and that the route to **enlightenment** is through rejecting desires and ambitions. Although Theravada Buddhism often follows such an ascetic path, Mahayana Buddhism does not, and criticized attempting to be solitary and rejecting the material world. The Mahayana argued that the ascetic path is in fact a less worthy route to enlightenment, since it restricts the path to a few special individuals. Japanese thinkers were particularly scathing about asceticism, and both Shotoku and Suzuki Shosan emphasized the desirability of participating in social life. Suzuki himself advocated the ordinary carrying out of one's duties, as opposed to meditation, arguing that this could lead to becoming a buddha if entered into with complete commitment. This is based on the idea that to follow one's particular vocation is to follow one's original self, in other words, the **buddha nature**. Some Japanese Buddhists even argued that there was no need to criticize the basic social distinctions in society, since these are like the distinctions between mountains and valleys, and so there is no need to turn one's back on society and seek to act outside it.

Many Indian philosophical traditions are committed firmly to asceticism. **Jainism** regards the physical body as something to be subdued in order to reduce the influence of individuality. This does not mean that they would advocate suicide, since this is classed as *himsa* or harm, interfering with natural processes. The Buddhist attitude to the body is somewhat less hostile, arguing that what is necessary is for the **mind** (*manas*) to eradicate from itself the concept of individuality (*anatta*). According to the **Sankhya Yoga** theory, it is sometimes necessary to subjugate the individual self to higher duty, and even to die or take others' lives (as is the case with Arjuna in the *Bhagavad Gita*). In any case, since the soul (*atman* or *jiva*) is eternal and infinite, it is hardly affected by the fate of the body.

Zoroastrian philosophy is also not explicitly ascetic, although the honourable poor individual is awarded a high religious rank. There is nothing wrong with wealth, provided that it is acquired fairly and used in appropriate ways. On the other hand, there are varieties of Zoroastrianism that ally it closely with Hinduism, and so make it more sympathetic to various ascetic strategies.

There is a consistent ascetic strain in Islamic philosophy. This is often identified initially with the figure of Socrates, and was taken up by many in the **Sufi** movement. Al-Kindi argued that the proper attitude to sorrow, which is an inevitable part of human life in the world of generation and corruption, is to appreciate that sorrow comes about either from our actions or from those of others. If it comes from our actions, then if we are rational we shall stop acting to bring it about. If from others, we shall prevent them from acting to cause us to suffer, and if we cannot prevent them, there is no point in being upset at what transpires. We may suffer as a result of their actions, but we should bear it without complaint, and in any case any material possessions that we may lose are only temporary possessions of ours. The great Muslim physician Abu Bakr al-Razi followed the logic of this to argue in his work on spiritual medicine that we should allow the rational part of our souls to control the physical and emotional parts, and only then will we be in control of ourselves and our feelings. Seeking a life of pleasure is to enslave oneself, and results in sadness since so many of these pleasures are short-lived. The wise individual does not experience sorrow, since he realizes that nothing in this world is long-lasting, and that whatever cannot be prevented must be endured or ignored.

See also: *ahimsa*
Further reading: Nasr and Leaman 1996, Zaehner 1969, 1975.

Ash`ariyya and Mu`tazila The Mu`tazila became an influential theological movement in the early Islamic world, but came under attack from al-Ash`ari. He criticized what came to be thought of as the extreme rationalism of the Mu`tazila and replaced it with what came to be seen as a more compliant attitude towards revelation. There were principles on which the Mu`tazila and the Ash`ariyya were united, in particular in sharing an **atomistic** analysis of the universe. They were impressed by the fact that a thing can take on different properties across **time** and space, and yet there are some properties they cannot take on, given their original nature. All bodies are made up of identical material substances or atoms which are provided by God with incorporeal accidents. By themselves the atoms are as invisible as mathematical points, but in combination they have a variety of properties which lead us to see them as different bodies. Some of these properties are definitive of the bodies they characterize, while others are changeable. This sort of approach to the nature of being was shared by most of the Mu`tazilites, and was not regarded as controversial by their opponents. The main principles of the Mu`tazila were belief in the unity of God, the prevalence of divine **justice**, the availability of rewards and punishments, and the necessity of the individual to pursue virtue and avoid **evil**. The first principle appears not to be controversial, since it is one of the bases of Islam itself, yet the difficulty comes in knowing how to interpret those scriptural references that imply that God has a body or parts.

The Mu`tazilites argued that God is essentially one, so that he cannot have a body nor any of the characteristics of a body, and the language in the Qur´an that implies otherwise has to be interpreted allegorically. The Ash`arite response was that this sort of language is to be accepted *bi-la kayfa*, without trying to understand how it works, since God is so far apart from us that our concepts cannot be expected to encompass his greatness. The Mu`tazilites argued that there was a time when God did not act, and so the Qur´an, his speech, came about at a certain time and is not eternal. For the Ash`arites, this is impossible, since in that case he could have brought the Qur´an about either himself or through someone else. If he had done it himself, he would be the basis of things coming into being, which is not the case. He is far above that. If it had been brought about by someone else, then it is that person and not God who produced God's speech, which is also impossible. Thus the Qur´an must be **eternal** and uncreated.

Another important area of dissension was over the nature of justice. The Mu`tazilites argued that we are free to decide how to act, and that if we are virtuous God must reward us. The divine **law** that God establishes has to accord with objective principles of justice, so that God defines the good in terms of what is good, not just in his commands. Al-Ash`ari famously raised this issue with his Mu`tazilite teacher al-Jubba´i. The latter claimed that God is obliged to prolong the life of an unbeliever if he knows that he will eventually improve and repent. Al-Ash`ari asked what would be the position of three brothers, one a believer, one an unbeliever and one who perished as a child. Al-Jubba´i is said to have replied that the first would be saved, the second punished and the third neither punished nor rewarded, and to the objection that God should have allowed the last to live in order that he should be rewarded had he become a believer, al-Jubba´i suggests that God allowed him to die as a child since he knew that he would become an unbeliever. Al-Ash`ari then produced what he took to be the decisive objection that God should have brought about the early death of the unbeliever in order to allow him to escape damnation. Al-Ash`ari then uses this to argue that what makes morality worth pursuing is that it is God's command, not anything objective in it, that gives it validity. Within that interpretation it is, of course, open to God to do as he wishes with us, possibly punishing the innocent and rewarding the guilty, if that is his wish. There are no constraints on God at all.

Further reading: Hourani 1985, Leaman 1985, Martin and Woodward 1997.

atman A term (*atta* in Pali) that originally means 'self' but which came to mean 'the true self' or essence of living beings that does not change when they go through the process of death and rebirth. Some versions of **yoga** argue that through their spiritual practices one can come into direct contact with one's real self or *atman*, while other Hindu doctrines suggest that the *atman* possessed by each individual is a reflection of the **brahman** or absolute in the universe. The real immortal self of human beings is identical with *brahman*. Spiritual **liberation** or *moksha* takes place when the *atman* and the *brahman* become united. This is a possibility that was anathema to Buddhist philosophy, which based itself rather on the absence of a real self, **anatman**. Buddhism denies the existence of the *atman*. The notion of the self is closely linked with that of the **personality** and the construction of the parts of the individual, and many arguments arose within Buddhism about its nature, or better, lack of essential nature.

In order for the self to achieve liberation, it has to come to know reality, both its own and that of the ultimate cause of the world. Does the individuality of the self survive after liberation? According to Shankara it does not, but Ramanuja argues that it does. He suggests that the self is what lies behind **consciousness**, which itself is similar to light. Consciousness and what lies behind it are both the same sort of thing, and the self is the basis to the activity of consciousness. Consciousness is the way in which the self expresses itself, it represents the manner in which it acts. But it is important to make a

clear distinction here between them, he claims, by contrast
with the Advaitin who mixes them up. What scope is there
to distinguish between the self and consciousness in this way?
We have experience of a self that is different from its acts of
consciousness, since the latter are always changing while the
former seems to be relatively permanent. He goes on to argue
that not only is the self the basis of consciousness, it is also
the object of consciousness. This is the case because in every
act of knowledge the self is aware through consciousness of
something else, and it is also aware that it is aware; in other
words, it is also aware of itself. This is not a separate act of
consciousness, but rather is part and parcel of the activity
of consciousness itself. The significance of this doctrine
emerges when it is contrasted with Shankara's concept of
dreamless sleep (*susupti*). According to Shankara, in such sleep
the individual self disappears, and all that remains is consciousness, which is to be identified with the absolute self. From
this it follows that the individual self is really an illusion.
There is an eternal self which is presupposed by individual
experiences. The nature of the self is something that we
intuit, it is known through our experience. Shankara disapproved of the **Nyaya** argument that we can know the self
through **inference**. This argument starts with a series of
experiences, and then appeals to the notion of a self to which
they belong. Shankara suggests that we have no reason to
think that those experiences are part of my self as opposed
to someone else unless we already accept the existence of
such a self, which would be circular. Such a self can be
accepted as existing right from the start of experience, although
its real status has to be qualified. Ramanuja agrees that
consciousness persists in dreamless sleep, but does not accept
Shankara's conclusion, since the former argues that a type
of self-awareness continues in the experience of dreamless
sleep. After all, when we wake up we attribute the experience to an individual self, and so have no reason not to think
that such a self persisted during the sleep. In such sleep the
self is aware of itself only as a subject, but he discounts
the significance of the dreamless sleep. This does indeed

provide an example of bliss, the same sort of bliss that arises on liberation, but this is only a pale reflection of the fully fledged bliss of liberation. Dreamless sleep merely provides a temporary relief from *samsara*, while when the self is in contact with *brahman* complete relief is effected. By contrast, Ramanuja argued that our experience is essentially dualist, since we distinguish between the knower and the object of knowledge. Madhva also suggested that the individual differences between people must be based on their different selves, and went further than Ramanuja in arguing that souls cannot be alike.

Atman has two rather contrasting meanings, in that it can mean the ultimate reality of a person and also the superficial aspects of the personality with which we tend to identify ourselves. The more we get to know ourselves as we really are, the further we can see behind the superficial to the essential aspects of ourselves. But these superficial aspects can be important as well. According to **Advaita Vedanta**, only the universal *brahman* is ultimately real, and the ordinary personality and its notion of identity is illusory, yet there is also an elaborate theory of the personality and how it survives during change, in particular transmigration. Although the self may not be ultimately real, it is still real enough as a part of our experience to be analysable in terms of a self that can undergo change and yet remain to a degree the same. Advaitins are particularly interested in the nature of *brahman*, while at the same time they are keenly aware of the conceptual difficulties in describing the nature of something that is absolutely one and without differentiation.

Buddhist philosophy argues that were there to be a real self it would have to possess certain characteristics. These include permanence, immutability, absence of suffering and being unaffected by prior events. A real self would be happy since it would be aware of itself, it would not change and it would not depend on anything else. But the self, in so far as we experience it, is very different from such a description, which suggests that the real self and the human self are entirely distinct. The notion of a persistent self is an illusion

29

from which we ought to free ourselves, and such mental liberation is a stage on the route to liberation.

See: **afterlife**

Further reading: Chakraborty 1996, Carr and Mahalingam 1997, Collins 1982, Radhakrishnan 1966, Smart 1964.

atomism The **materialist** Indian school of Lokayata seemed to believe that atoms are either the smallest perceptible particles of reality, or cannot be seen but constitute the smallest parts which can be seen. The **Vaisheshika** argued that the world must come from atoms since the character of a material cause is reproduced in its effects, so there must be some element of the causes in the effects. However, the evidence seems to go against this, as they pointed out, since intelligent *brahman* produced a material and crass form of existence, our world. There are taken to be four kinds of atom – earth, air, fire and water – and they go to make up ordinary things. They operate in space, which is not itself to be analysed in terms of atoms. Living things are also made up of atoms, and the **mind** itself as a physical entity, the *manas*, is itself atomic. Critics of this view like Shankara point out that there are great problems in explaining how atoms can combine. Their very definition emphasizes their separability, and the atomists stress that what brings about change is a quality of the soul which can only come about through a body, that is, after the combination of atoms has taken place. The notion of atom is also used by Ramanuja to contrast the smallness of the individual self when compared with reality of *brahman*. It is also used to contrast anything material, and so divisible, with what is not material and so can be permanent and not part of something greater. Ramanuja argued that the human self is atomic, and at the same time it is divine. Because it is atomic it is far too small in itself to link up with the body, and it requires something to mediate between it and the body. The soul in itself is **eternal** and capable of attaining bliss, since when it is liberated it is free from desires and divine, but unlike our soul, the soul of God fills the world due to its size.

For the Jains, the smallest imperceptible part of matter is the atom, of which there are four kinds – air, fire, water and earth. The combination of these atoms leads to the ordinary objects with which we are familiar. It may be that this theory comes from a version of Buddhist materialism, which defines the atoms in terms of solidity, fluidity, heat and motion, the basic aspects of physical reality. There are corresponding atoms that make up human beings, and these are the cognitive, emotional, volitional and perceptual. All these atoms change all the time, and they constitute what we call people and material objects. This leads to the difficulty that there is no explanation as to how these apparently arbitrary collections of atoms coalesce in the particular ways in which they do. There is an attempted solution in the suggestion that the organization of atoms in one aggregate leads to a different but linked aggregate, so we get regularity in our ordinary experience. Critics of Buddhism suggest that if there is such regularity, then there can be no transformation of one form into a different form, which there has to be for rebirth to be possible, and if there is not regularity, then our experience could be chaotic and change all the time without explanation. There was in fact a major controversy within Buddhism between a defence of atomism and those who argued that if atoms existed they should be perceptible. This might seem just wrong, since atoms are often supposed to be so small that it is not possible to perceive them. But the opponents of atoms argued that analysing our experience in terms of atoms which really exist is to contravene the central Buddhist argument that nothing really exists.

Most of the early Islamic thinkers were atomists, believing that the universe is kept in existence at each moment by a freely creating God. The point of such a theory is to emphasize the role of God, but the problem with it is that it empties the world of **causal** power. If God keeps creating at each time the different events of the world, the latter have no underlying logic or pattern, only that regularity that God makes us think they have through the grace of his agency. Such a thoroughgoing occasionalism (the idea that all action is really divine action) stands in strong contrast with the view of many philosophers that the world has a logical structure, that events follow causes as conclusions follow premises, and that only in this way can we do justice to the regularity of the lawlike structure of the natural world.

See also: **afterlife**, *atman*, **emptiness**
Further reading: Basham 1971, Kalupahana 1975, Nasr and Leaman 1996, Potter 1988, Radhakrishnan 1966.

atta, self – *see atman*

avatara Given God's concern for human beings, he is prepared to descend (hence this term in Indian philosophy) into our affairs and help us find salvation. One might have thought that God would not wish to lower himself into the world of *samsara* when he could after all remain constantly at the level of perfection and immutability. But fortunately for us he freely decides to set out to restore religious **law**, help his followers and bring to a satisfactory conclusion a particular type of being. Although the way in which this descent takes place may result in the creation of a body, this is a very different sort of body from the rest of the bodies in the realm of *samsara*, since this body is not brought about as a result of *karma* and the prolongation of selfish motives. This prevents God from becoming part and parcel of the world of suffering that he is trying to relieve. The doctrine of *avatara* as incarnation makes it possible for some Hindus to regard Jesus as an *avatara*.

Further reading: Parrinder 1997.

avidya A Sanskrit term meaning 'non-knowledge' or ignorance of the nature of reality. In its Pali form *avija* it is often more limited and relates to ignorance of the **Four Noble Truths**, representing the Buddhist idea that failing to appreciate the true nature of things is the basis of all **evil**, in the sense of being a fetter that binds us to the conditional realm of *samsara* and hence of *dukkha*. Sometimes the finite aspect of the individual self is identified as *avidya*, and is used to contrast with the cosmic **maya** of the **brahman**. *Maya* is the whole, and the *avidya*s are the parts of it, since all the individual selves think that they are important and that their ideas of the nature of reality are reliable. The point is that if the universe can be seen to have been caused by *maya*, then the parts of the whole can be regarded as based on ignorance. It is *avidya* that creates the idea of the distinction between the self and reality itself, and between one self and another self. Since the self incorporates ignorance, it takes this with it during its journey through other lives. In itself the self is equivalent to reality, but since it sees itself as individual it relates more to the mind, the senses, the intellect and the will than to reality, which are all reflections of ignorance.

Some have argued that this notion has been adapted from Buddhism by Shankara, but this seems wrong, since the notion is at least implicit in the **Upanishads**. *Avidya* is sometimes described as being neither real nor completely unreal. It is not real since it does not accurately describe reality, but on the other hand it is not absolutely unreal since it does serve a practical end. This problematic nature is important, since if it were not problematic, it would be entirely real, and so not ignorance. It cannot be an aspect of reality, since reality is simple, and *avidya* is the source of diversity. On the other hand, it cannot be an aspect of the selves, since the selves themselves presuppose *avidya*. Ignorance directs itself towards reality, but it conceals that reality, and so the nature of the experiences we have are similarly opaque versions of the real. These experiences are themselves neither real nor unreal, existent nor non-existent, since they share in the characteristics of *avidya* itself. They are not real, since they stem from ignorance, but they are also not unreal, since they have as their basis reality. Once **liberation** is achieved, these experiences are disregarded and understood as what had previously been confused with reality.

There is an interesting analysis of *avidya* as *adhyasa* or super-imposition. The idea is that it is the appearance of one thing as another thing, where the appearance of a thing, as 'this', is taken to be a genuine indication of that thing, a 'that'. It is this complexity of *avidya*, which is itself the source of the apparent complexity of the world, that makes it such a useful concept in Indian metaphysics. Superimposition or confusion of the not-self as the self is the source of the bondage of the finite self, *jiva*, and this was used by thinkers like Vacaspati and Shankara to argue that it is only through **knowledge**, in particular through the study of the **Vedic** texts, that one can achieve *moksha* and escape from ignorance.

See: **badha**

Further reading: Deutsch 1968, Radhakrishnan 1966.

avija, ignorance – *see* **avidya**

awareness – *see* **knowledge**

B

badha An important concept in Shankara's theory of **brahman**, the one reality which is describable in a number of different ways. *Badha* is sublation or cancellation, and involves correcting a judgement once one has an experience that contradicts it. There are three layers of being which are connected by sublation. Absolute reality or being cannot be sublated by any other experience since it is a complete unity. Nothing can be regarded as a conflicting proposition or experience, since there is nothing really apart from it. Then there is the ordinary world of experience, which appears to be real, but which is sublated with respect to experience of *brahman*. That is, once we get some understanding of the nature of reality we realize that our ordinary world of experience is not real at all, but merely a faint reflection of the real. Finally, there are illusions, which are themselves sublated by coming up against our ordinary experience. The notion of *badha* enables Shankara to present clearly the **Advaita Vedanta** hierarchy of being, and we can appreciate how according to it what is most real is what cannot be contradicted or replaced by something else.

Further reading: Carr and Mahalingam 1997, Deutsch 1968, Ramamurty 1996.

bardo A Buddhist doctrine that emphasizes the significance of the intermediate state between **death** and rebirth. This is

35

discussed in detail in what is often referred to as *The Tibetan Book of the Dead*, on which there are important commentaries by Tibetan thinkers. *Bardo* is a Tibetan term that literally means 'between two' and has a use in explaining how ordinary life tends to be contrasted with dreaming experiences, but both are really part of the illusions caused by **samsara**. There is no point in using logical thought to understand the nature of human existence, what is required is the ability to experience reality through ascetic practice and the guidance of an appropriate **guru**. The Tibetan method of **enlightenment** involved what came to be known as the practice of *mahamudra*, the **yoga** of the great symbol. The first stage is to concentrate on one object, and thus achieve inner peace. Next one abandons conceptual thought and experiences existence as a **buddha nature**, through getting away from the distinctions that are ever-present in our concepts. Then one experiences the unity between *nirvana* and *samsara*, which represents the complete blending of the Buddha and human experience, and prepares the way for the final stage, that of actually achieving buddha status. At the final stage there is no longer any difference between **meditating** and the meditator, since all dualities have been abandoned.

Further reading: Bishop 1993, Cabezon 1994, Gyatso 1992, Karmay 1988.

being In Daoism (Taoism) the nature of the dao (tao) is defined in terms of what it is not, as compared with what it is. This is why it is often identified with *wu* or nothing/non-existence. Using this sort of language is an attempt at transcending the dualism of nothing/being which gets us into the same confusions as existence/non-existence, reality/illusion and subject/object. This point is sometimes expressed in the analogy of **emptiness** existing like the eternal ocean, while being is its waves. The idea is that really there is no difference between the ocean and the waves, they are just two different ways of looking at the same thing. Dao is the origin and principle of being. Dao is both all beings and all possible beings. Some thinkers like Jin Yuelin made the theory more sophisticated by incorporating **Neoconfucian** ideas, so that *li* or principle (form) describes the mode of being of everything possible, while *qi* or spirit is that which brings some of the possible things into actuality.

In Buddhism there was a lively discussion of the nature of the being of the **buddha nature**. Some thinkers identified it with an actual entity within each individual, but this approach was also often criticized. Jizang of the Nirvana School of Daosheng argued that the buddha nature is not a being, but rather a state of mind which has managed to eradicate the self/no-self distinction. It is a disposition to treat the world as though it were empty. This discussion brings out nicely how important it is to think clearly about questions of ontology, since there is often a tendency to confuse the ontological status of the buddha nature, the soul, self and emptiness. It is because he tried to get away from this way of talking that Dogen insisted that the whole of being *is* the buddha nature rather than *has* the buddha nature. Thinking of the buddha nature as either present in the world or as above the world is systematically misleading. Since he identifies the buddha nature with impermanence, it is an easy step to further identification of being, or buddha nature, with **time**. His notion of time is more complicated than that of a passage, though, and he argues that there is an aspect of time during which it does not change, that is, the present. The buddha nature is present time, and it represents the negation of temporality. This idea is interesting especially for its ability to get around the notion of the buddha nature as something that is apart from the world. On the contrary, buddha nature is present all the time. Yet how can we talk about time not changing, especially if the notion of the world's impermanence is so important? Dogen is describing what he sees as the culmination of religious life, in particular *zazen*. Through religion everything in the universe can achieve **enlightenment** and become permanent, yet this takes place in the present, and we can appreciate the unity of being, albeit at the same time observing its differentiation into selves and others.

The Buddha described three aspects of being: the suffering inevitably present in it, its impermanence and the non-abiding self. Being is transitory, a truth from which we are excluded given our fascination with satisfying our desires. These desires presuppose the permanence of being, since it would be hardly sensible to seek to pursue impermanent and changing things. The self has no being, in the sense that there is nothing permanent about it, nor does it do more than represent what in fact are just a passing series of images. Finally, since in reality everything is in flux, being cannot be the source of our happiness, since what is constantly changing cannot be the source of a happiness that is not itself constantly in flux and so incomplete.

In Islamic philosophy the links between being and existence are a particularly controversial issue. Some thinkers such as ibn Sina, al-Farabi and al-Suhrawardi argued that being and existence are not only logically but also ontologically distinct, so that what we can say about a thing is distinct from how or whether that thing actually exists. This leads to a theory of **creation** in accordance with which there are possible beings that only have **existence** if they are brought into existence by a creator, ultimately a creator who exists necessarily since his existence follows from his being or essence. A different line was taken by ibn Rushd and Mulla Sadra who argued that, on the contrary, the aspects of something that exists are an essential part of its meaning, so that one cannot differentiate significantly between the notion of something existing as compared with its being or essence. Then the ways in which things exist are an essential aspect of their meaning, so that in a sense it is existence that comes first and essence follows on from it.

Further reading: Graham 1989, Heine 1993, Hoffman 1987, Leaman 1997, Nasr and Leaman 1996.

benevolence – *see* **love**

Bhagavad Gita   A highly significant verse *upanishad* from the
Mahabharata. In the story Arjuna is contemplating participation in the war and is reluctant to fight. He wishes to regain
the kingdom that was taken from him by his cousins. On
the other hand, the army opposing him is made up of his
relations, teachers and friends. His charioteer Krishna sets out
before him a range of arguments to persuade him to join the
battle, and some of these arguments are particularly important. There is much use of the argument that really no one
kills or is killed anyway, since the self merely changes bodies.
Everyone has an immortal spiritual essence. This passage marks
a change from the idea of perfection through contemplation
to *karma yoga*, the argument that a particular form of **action**
is what is required. Of course, the form of action has to be
carefully selected, and should be without attachment or desire
for reward. It is important to follow one's *dharma*, one's role
in society, but if one is to escape the bounds of *karma* it is
necessary to act out of a pure sense of duty. What is important is the motivation that lies at the base of activity, rather
than the actions themselves. Disinterested action can be
regarded as genuine renunciation, as compared with total inactivity. Towards the end of the poem Krishna manifests himself
as a deity, with the message of *bhakti yoga*, which stresses
action and **love** as the basis of perfection. Much of the text
is taken up with discussion of the nature of the highest deity,
which results in Arjuna's attitude of devotion. Devotion is
placed at the summit of the hierarchy of how people are to
behave, with **knowledge** and action regarded as also important but of a lower order. This epic is highly significant for
its presentation of a way of life that is available to people in
general, and is often seen as a synthesis of the **Upanishads**
as a whole in an attempt at creating an accessible form of
Hinduism.

   It is especially interesting for its introduction of the notion
of God as the self, and indeed as the originator of everything in the universe. It is not enough to do one's duty
selflessly, but one should do it for the sake of God, which is
in a sense a higher form of action even than duty.

Like all major religious texts, the *Bhagavad Gita* has been interpreted in a wide variety of ways. Since it points to a variety of routes to **liberation**, it has been easy for later commentators to point to one route as the main route, and the others as subsidiary. So Shankara, for example, is able to prioritize the route through knowledge, while Ramanuja, by contrast, argues that the devotional route is primary and the others secondary. Some have argued that the fact that Krishna persuades Arjuna of the necessity to engage in **violence** shows the acceptability of violence, but Gandhi took this passage in another sense, as showing that we are not to reject the struggle against **evil** impulses within ourselves. The best way to win that struggle is to forgo the engagement with physical violence against those whom we regard as our enemies.

See: **atman, bhakti yoga, violence**
Further reading: *Bhagavad Gita* 1994, Zaehner 1969.

bhakti Devotion to God, and one of the main routes to salvation in Hinduism. In the *Bhagavad Gita* this notion is much discussed towards the end of the text, and it is identified with loyalty and subservience to the supreme deity. A long period of Indian thought starting in the second millennium CE is called the 'Bhakti period' because it stresses the relationship of the individual with God. This had radical consequences for philosophy, since it means that the route to salvation is through linking everything with God, and accepting God's role in the shape of the world. The implication is that we need no longer seek to renounce the world, since it is divinely inspired, but we should accept it or at least resign ourselves to it. A school called **Dvaita Vedanta** embodied these approaches, arguing that everything is dependent on God and has a fate entirely determined by the decisions of God.

The stress on devotion often leads to concentration upon a particular deity, and was popular among major poets. Its main philosophical exponent was Ramanuja. He argued that *bhakti yoga* can exist at different levels of devotion to God, some where the power of the selfish **personality** is still quite strong as compared with other kinds. The route to salvation is through a combination of **action** and **knowledge**, where the action involves the carrying out of the appropriate rituals and sacrifices, and the following of virtue. The more such a mixture of action and knowledge is developed the more the thinker understands the relationship between ultimate reality and the world, and the purer his knowledge of God becomes. In the end he becomes perfectly integrated, in harmony both with himself and with God. This results in the wearing away of the accumulated *karma* and the acquisition of the state of **yoga** itself. The highest level of *bhakti* is where a complete and overwhelming love of God becomes possible, and God responds to this by displaying his grace to the thinker. The latter comes into contact with God through being able to **imagine** the divine form in a direct and personal kind of way. This is not actually the same as seeing God, but is as close as we can come before being liberated finally. In the *Bhagavad Gita* Krishna discusses the role of the path of devotion (*bhakti yoga*) for the attainment of **liberation**, suggesting that God may release someone completely devoted to him from the cycle of birth and rebirth. Krishna sometimes suggests that this route to liberation is the best, but he also claims that the other routes, those of action and knowledge, are also effective for individuals with different sorts of personality.

See: **samsara**

Further reading: Bhatt 1975, Brockington 1996, Dasgupta 1975, Murti 1960.

bhakti yoga, the path to enlightenment through worship – *see* **yoga**

bheda, difference – *see* **Dvaita**

bi-la kayfa, not knowing how – *see* **Ash`ariyya**

bodhi The Bodhi tree (*bodhidruma* in Sanskrit) is according to tradition the tree under which Buddhas attain **enlightenment** (*bodhi*), and is often taken as a metaphor for the insubstantiality of the body. It is frequently identified with the banana tree, whose stem can be stripped away gradually without revealing anything solid. This notion of stripping away proved to be the source of a complex controversy within Buddhism about the best approach to enlightenment. Some chan (zen) thinkers followed quietist paths, meditating without following any religious practices or studying texts. Other thinkers advocated the practice of gradual **meditation** and the purification of the self of passions that obscure the mind by following a method like peeling an onion (a Chinese metaphor) or a banana tree (more appropriate to India). The trouble is, from the chan point of view, there is nothing at all to peel!

Further reading: Gregory 1987, Griffiths 1994.

bodhichitta It is very important from the perspective of Mahayana Buddhism that actions are carried out with the correct motivation, and this is called *bodhichitta* or the awakened **mind**. This sort of **consciousness** is a result of a deep **compassion** for the suffering of others. This is the prime principle of **action** of the *bodhisattva*, and extends to everything in existence. But, of course, it is not exactly easy to acquire. We start off with being interested in achieving our own selfish ends in this world, and we have to work through **meditation** to achieve **liberation** from this world, from *samsara*, along a route with a number of stages. First of all one meditates on the rarity and value of human rebirth if it is accompanied by the ability to practise the *dharma*. Then the meditator thinks about **death** and the mutability of everything, so that there is a point to concentrating on those aspects of our lives that relate to our spiritual development. This leads to a genuine concern with virtue which will lead to positive future rebirths, and a higher moral and spiritual point of view. Then one thinks about the varieties of rebirth and suffering that are available to creatures, which emphasizes the unsatisfactoriness of rebirth as a whole for the individual. Such a process of meditation, if often repeated, may lead to a genuine renunciation of all rebirth in *samsara* and a desire to develop *bodhichitta*.

There are two sorts of meditation that are very helpful to reaching this state. One is that whereby we visualize people and situations that created strong passions in us, and we are encouraged to develop an attitude of equanimity towards them. In this way we realize that **friends** can become enemies, and vice versa, so really there is no difference between a friend and an enemy. Also, since we have spent an infinite amount of time in *samsara*, at some stage or another we have been cared for by low creatures, which is a thought designed to suggest that there is no distinction between different levels of sentient being and we should reverence anything that might have been our parent or protector in a past life. Hence the need for a general **compassion**, and the motivation to help others as far as one can. The most help that one can provide is through becoming a Buddha oneself, and this is the aim of *bodhichitta*, the attainment of **enlightenment** out of a sincere desire to work for the welfare of sentient beings in general. The process of meditation generates the *bodhichitta*, and that goes on to change us and perfect us.

Another powerful form of meditation in this respect is thinking about the large number of individuals in existence, and the fact that they all crave the same sorts of things, and seek to avoid pain. We should use the previous process of achieving equanimity, but also grasp that there are so many more others than ourself that it is our duty to work for them and benefit them. A meditative process that is supposed to be very effective is imagining the sufferings of others, inhaling their sufferings with one's breath, as it were, and then exhaling happiness, a process which if sufficiently developed is supposed to enable the *bodhisattva* to take on the sufferings of others and so relieve them. There are actually two kinds of *bodhichitta*. One kind leads to the *bodhisattva* wishing to organize his or her life in such a way as to wish to help others in a total sense. The other kind actually gets them to put the desire into action.

See: **afterlife and rebirth**
Further reading: Griffiths 1986, Hoffman 1987, Tominaga 1990.

bodhidruma, the *bodhi* tree – *see* **bodhi**

bodhisatta, someone who sets out to become a Buddha – *see* **bodhisattva**

bodhisattva Someone in Buddhism who has taken the vow to become a perfect **Buddha** and who acts accordingly. The *bodhisattva* renounces entry into *nirvana* until all other beings have become enlightened. This notion is given different interpretations in different forms of Buddhism. In Mahayana Buddhism, for instance, becoming a *bodhisattva* (*bodhisatta* in Pali) is to be distinguished from becoming an **arahat**, which was criticized for being too individualistic and limited in scope. The real *bodhisattva*, according to the Mahayana school, wants everyone to become *bodhisattva*s, and not only himself or herself. Everything lacks its own nature and so is empty. *Nirvana* is also empty, and is attainable through the empty **consciousness** of the meditator. There is a tendency to think of the essence of the world as being **emptiness**, which is the same as the nature of *nirvana*. The conclusion is that we can all reach *nirvana*, we can all reach the ultimate truth, and we all have the **buddha nature**. We all should be *bodhisattva*s, we should all seek to realize our buddha natures. Most of the usual virtues of Buddhism are present in the Mahayana conception of *bodhisattva*, including giving, moral behaviour, patience, energy, **meditation** and wisdom. In some ways this idea manages to reconcile the social and the monastic virtues, although really it seems far more likely that the higher stages are only attainable through an **ascetic** lifestyle. On the other hand, the Mahayana literature does have *bodhisattva*s who are very much involved in the world, and yet who are able to reach this high level of spiritual development. Dogen, for example, states explicitly that **enlightenment** is in principle available to everyone, lay or monk, but it seems clear that the descriptions of the zen techniques are most likely to be applied within ascetic and monastic contexts.

In all Buddhist doctrines the process of becoming perfect is a long and difficult one, taking far more than just one lifetime. The **mind** first has to be enlightened, which means turning from concentration on the self to **compassion** for all. This protracted process is described in different ways, but on one thing all the authorities are clear, and that is that this is a highly complex path with many levels of perfection. The descriptions given of it often emphasize the role of the *bodhisattva* as someone who educates others in the knowledge of the path.

Once the *bodhichitta*, the principle of enlightenment, has been produced in the individual, she is on the route to becoming a Buddha. To make progress involves increasing in wisdom, and the five perfections – morality, patience, effort, giving and meditation. The important point here is that the Mahayana *bodhisattva* cannot ignore the interests of others and proceed to her own enlightenment, she has to use **skilful means** to help others. A whole hierarchy of mental perfection is constructed, and through the knowledge that is acquired along with the training in calm thought, one acquires a deeper understanding of emptiness and of the falsity of dualism and conceptual manipulation. But this is just the start of a long and highly complex route, along which the individual perfects herself and becomes purer and less constrained by the phenomena of *samsara* and ignorance.

Further reading: Griffiths 1994, Guenther 1972, Murti 1960, Williams 1989.

Book of Changes – *I Ching* (*Yi jing*)   A text, sometimes known as the *Zhou yi* (The Changes of Zhou), that deals with the philosophy of change, in terms of **yin** and **yang**, and the five powers theory of nature (metal, wood, fire, water and earth). *The Book of Changes* was originally a book of divination, and has become through additions and commentaries a fundamental work of Chinese cosmological and philosophical speculation. It represents a form of correlative thought that links all phenomena together in a universal dynamic pattern of symbolic correspondences. *Yin* and *yang* are the opposing forces of negative and positive, dark and light, passive and active, which through their interplay bring about and control events. The Five Powers or Elements are dynamic forces that make up the structure of the world and direct the pattern of all life. Different combinations of the latter, expressing their generative and destructive forces, provide an account of the structure of **being** and **cosmology**. These concepts are represented schematically through eight trigrams and their combination in sixty-four hexagrams. This constitutes a symbolic representation of the order of the world and can be used to predict the future and explain the past. There is an orientation away from heaven and towards the earth, which explains the detailed accounts of natural events in the text. It can also easily be extended to provide a philosophy of history, which comes out as a kind of political **humanism** and organic naturalism. It is interesting how a book that deals with the occult structure of the world can have such important use in Chinese metaphysics and ethics.

There certainly seems to be a close connection with the orientation of Daoism, and the *Book of Changes* has even been detected in the thought of Mao Zedong, especially in his reflections that change is the only constant phenomenon in the universe. A range of Chinese philosophy has its origins in both Daoism and the *Book of Changes*, and can then have as its basic concepts a constant process of change and alteration, production and reproduction. In the Han period the *Book* became one of the Confucian classics. A modern thinker like Yan Fu could even argue that the Darwinian theory of evolution was quite similar to Daoist views, and to the *Book of Changes*. After all, according to the latter the universe is a natural process of evolution and development in which being comes from non-being and undifferentiated being is changed into different kinds of things.

Much of what is important in the *Book* is actually found in the appendices which have been added by those who wished to extend the meaning of the text itself. While we find extensive references to the dao, the notion of dao is very different from that current among the Daoist philosophers. The version in the *Book* is of the multiple causes of change in the universe, and are the principles behind the various kinds of production and creation in the universe. What makes one thing distinct from something else is its dao, which accords with a particular name. When one applies this theory to a book of divination the result is to interpret the hexagrams and the individual lines of those hexagrams as representing the various daos that make up the world. The sixty-four hexagrams and their 384 lines constitute the entire structure of the universe, the complete list of daos. The structure has a normative value, so that if the combinations of lines or hexagrams are followed, we are obeying the structure of the world and will have good fortune. If we obey the lines, we are doing what is right, if we disobey them, we are pursuing immorality.

There are two classes of dao. There are many individual daos and one dao that controls the production and development of everything. When something is produced, there must have been something that produced it, and also something out of which it could be produced. The former is the active principle, the virile *yang*, while the latter is the passive *yin*. It would be simplistic to think that everything is just *yang* or *yin*, but this is not the case. For example, a husband is *yang* with respect to his wife, but *yin* with respect to his father. On the other hand, the original principles of creation are themselves unchangeable, and serve to represent the basic principles of change. Change is the basic feature of the universe, and the idea that the *Yi jing* values is that of balance and lack of excess. Each hexagram is generally followed by another that is opposite to it, and this is because everything in existence involves its own negation. Everything that happens consists of a natural process of sequence, and there can never be a final end to the evolution. This refers not only to the natural world, but to human nature also, so that the individual should not try to be too successful, and it is wise to have at the forefront of one's mind the possibility of failure and reverse. This leads to a theory of the necessity to find the mean position, the point at which one can hold on to what one seeks without pushing too far in the opposite direction. That successful position is the harmonious one, and is the careful blending of opposites to construct something new, and also something that manages to balance the opposites properly. The *Yi jing* can be seen as a recipe book, as it were, for the appropriate combination of these different harmonious wholes, which enable us to be so balanced that we manage to hold these positions for a long time.

There is a particularly important development of Neoconfucian thought on the *Yi jing* by the Korean philosopher Yulgok. He argued that *cheng* or sincerity is so basic to the meaning of the universe that it cannot just be seen as an aspect of our motivation. There is a hexagram in the *Yi jing* called the creative which has four aspects – the sublime, order, *li* where this is equivalent to **harmony**, and perseverance. These are themselves identified with the principles of **heaven**, and are representations of the sincerity of heaven. In so far as we manage to act in accordance with these principles, we at the same time act in accordance with heaven, which is equivalent to our real nature. Sincerity is just acting in accordance with the nature of a thing, doing what one ought to do given how one is, and in a sense this does not involve conscious effort. That is why Yulgok wants to deny that sincerity can be a motive, since that implies that it is something that one tries to do, or that it represents a way of acting. In fact, our actions should just flow out of our nature quite naturally and align our consciousness with that of the universe. This brings out nicely what highly complex uses could be made of the *Yi jing*, in that an analysis of one or more hexagrams could be taken to represent the basic structure of reality, the dialectical nature of the universe. Once one grasps those principles of structure one understands why and how change takes place in the way that it does.

Further reading: Chan 1972, Creel 1953, Lee 1993, Wilhelm 1967.

brahman The abstract and impersonal Absolute or principle of reality in Hindu thought. In itself the Absolute is pure and unchanging, and is completely incompatible with attributes. There is a more limited notion of the Absolute, though, and in this form it can serve as the cause of the universe. The term seems to have arisen from the chants of the brahman priests, which were taken to be powerful and so came to represent absolute power. In the **Vedic** literature there is the notion that prayers and ritual have the power to create and there is a category of Vedic literature called the *Brahmanas* which deals at great length with topics connected with ritual. The **Upanishads** urge a move from ritual to **meditation**, and made possible a shift in meaning of *brahman* from the priest and his power to the basic power or vitality on which the universe rests. The implication of the text is that *brahman* is a sacred power which is the basis of the world, and the cycle of rebirth comes about through the blending of *brahman* with the self, *atman*. There is only one reality, and also only one self, according to the **Advaita Vedanta**. The apparent differences between different selves is only apparent, in just the same way that the apparent differences between different objects are just effects of the one genuine notion of reality. We are taken in by appearance, and we should try to achieve **liberation** from the cycle of birth and rebirth (*samsara*) through turning away from **ignorance** and illusion. The **Purva Mimamsa** system treats *brahman* as the ultimate cause of all existence. In the **Vedanta** system there were a variety of views of its nature. Some argued that *brahman* is neither the same nor different from the soul, others suggested that the soul is different from *brahman* before liberation and identical with it afterwards. In his *Brahmasutras* Badarayana presents an analytical account of some of the main themes of the Upanishads, and in particular the concept of *brahman*.

He sets out some of the key principles of the Vedanta system of philosophical thought relating to the nature of reality, in particular that it consists of the absolute *brahman*, the individual soul (*jiva*) and material reality (*jada*). This division in terms of infinite **consciousness**, finite consciousness and the unconscious leads to a subtle model of the links between the different aspects of reality. Badarayana argues that we should not seek to create a strict dichotomy between the real and the unreal, since the absolute, independent and spiritual are distinguished from the material and dependent solely in terms of mode and not of essence. He looks at the precise nature of the relationship between this concept and the origins of the world, how dependent the world is on it, and what different ways there are of gaining knowledge of *brahman*. Finally, he deals with the results of knowledge of *brahman*, the nature of release from suffering without return. The thesis is that *brahman* is both the ultimate principle of the world, and also the material **cause** of what takes place. He argues that *brahman* is eternal, the cause of the universe, and participates in the universe's workings, but does not explain how something can change with the world while at the same time remain unchanged. On the other hand, he uses an interesting analogy when looking at the way in which *brahman* exists in the individual soul without being influenced by it. He suggests that this is like the way the sun remains unchanged despite the changes that occur to the light that stems from it. The soul suffers pain, has ideas and desires, and pursues pleasure, while the *brahman* which is the source of these changes remains itself constant and permanent. Although we can through moral behaviour acquire knowledge of *brahman*, and so liberation from the ignorance and suffering of the world, this will not enable us to share in the creative and destructive powers of *brahman* itself.

Bhartrihari has a different view of the concept. He links *brahman* closely with language, and criticizes the idea that it could be an indeterminate idea or equivalent to an **ambiguous** word. Since he argues that the unit of meaning is the sentence, not the word, he goes on to suggest that if we are to understand the nature of *brahman*, we must understand the whole system of the conceptual and cosmological scheme. This view was taken up by Shankara, who worked from the premise that there is no way of understanding the nature of reality unless we rely on the Upanishads. Since there is such a huge distinction between the nature of reality, and what it leads to in our world of generation and corruption, there is no point in trying to work back from where we are to the nature of *brahman*. On the other hand, he argues that every human being has a certain access to this reality through the existence of our consciousness. We can make progress in overcoming ignorance and achieve pure and immediate consciousness of *brahman* itself, and to do this we have to take seriously the different ways in which we tend to be taken in by illusions. Shankara also deals with the way in which *brahman* can be both the material and efficient cause of changes in the world, and yet also the unchanged source of change. He uses the analogy of the magician and his tricks to show how someone can make something appear in one way to the public while himself remaining undeceived by his sleight of hand. What we refer to separately as *brahman*, *jiva* (the finite self) and *atman* (the essential self) are really not three different things, but just different aspects of the one thing, the one reality or *brahman*. He suggests that in a sense there is no real difference between *brahman* and its effects, so that the apparent changes in the world are only apparent and not real. Believing anything else fails to acknowledge the real unity of reality, which could not really be differentiated into many forms in the world. We should recall here the thesis that pure consciousness, which we all possess to a degree, can give us a route to the understanding of the nature of reality. There is an important argument between Shankara and Ramanuja about the appropriate Vedantin account of *brahman*, and the former argues that we can stretch our ordinary **language** sufficiently to describe reality if we use it to deny that it has any positive or negative characteristics at all. Ramanuja, by contrast, suggests that language does have as its primary function the ability to describe reality, so if it is going to be used to describe reality it must reflect the simple and undifferentiated nature of that reality, which is a problem for language which has as its basis complexity and differentiation. He argues that we can use language to describe reality through purifying our concepts and applying them analogically to reality.

Although it might be agreed that the Vedantas present information about the nature of *brahman*, it is quite another matter to know how to extract this information from the text. As we have seen, Shankara and Ramanuja differed on how this could be done. According to the latter, reality is one, but it can observe itself in a number of different ways. First, it has the character of being transcendent, unchanging and perfect. Then it has a causal function, in that it is capable of bringing into existence the phenomenal world since it is itself the substrate out of which that world flows. Lastly, the produced world is equivalent to *brahman*, since nothing can come into being nor continue in being without contact with *brahman*. Does that mean that there is no difference between the finite world and *brahman*? This would be to go too far, since from a different perspective the role of *brahman* is like that of the soul to the body, the assumption being that the soul at least can exist without the body, but of course the body cannot exist without the soul. Ramanuja presents this theory to attack the Advaitin approach, which he interprets as going too far in defending an absolutist non-dual concept of reality.

The view that *brahman* can be seen in different ways is important for Ramanuja, who uses it to show that reality can be seen as both the substantial and the efficient cause of the world. In spite of the efficiency of the cause, there is no necessitation in it, and *brahman* in itself transcends and rules over the world. The world cannot have come about through nothing more than the operation of matter, but must have had some conscious direction, and **creation** is dependent on thought. We should recall that it is necessary for the creator of the world, if he is going to be a designer, to understand the nature of the future shape based on existing and future *karma*, and who but a conscious and omniscient *brahman* would be able to bring this about appropriately? It is important also that this creation is seen as entirely free, and did not emerge through some inner necessity given the material substrate of the world.

Gandhi developed this concept to argue that the finite souls of this world are united with the universal soul, which is itself united with *brahman*. The unity in multiplicity was a basic notion of his thought, so there was little difficulty in linking the overall cause of multiplicity and still insisting that it was in itself entirely one. According to Sri Aurobindo, *brahman* is both **being** and non-being, a combination of the dynamic and the static. There is a truth behind all the dualities, all the varieties with which we are apparently familiar, and this is the ever-present *brahman*. This ultimate reality develops in stages, from matter to life, then to mind, cosmic consciousness and finally transcendental consciousness of what cannot be known. At every stage of this process the ineffable *brahman* partly reveals itself, and also to a certain extent remains hidden. What is important in his metaphysics is the way in which every higher development of reality consists of a development of an earlier form which is then superseded, but none the less is still present to a degree. Along with all such changes the super-mind or *brahman* is present. This process is also acknowledged by Radhakrishnan, who claims that it represents the main difference between Indian and Western forms of philosophy. In the latter there is a dichotomy between **faith** and reason, while Indian philosophy sees humanity as an organic unity of natural and religious attributes. All aspects of our experience are significant, as represented by the concept of an all-embracing ultimate reality such as *brahman*. One aspect of the latter is that it is the breath of God, while another is that it is the human sense of the transcendent, and divine reality itself. There is no real difference between the existence of God and the reality of spiritual experience. They are all aspects of *brahman*.

Further reading: Bhatt 1975, Brockington 1996, Chatterjee 1983, Dasgupta 1975, Deutsch 1968, Patnaik 1994, Potter 1972, Radhakrishnan and Moore 1957, Raju 1985.

brahmanas, Hindu schools of thought – *see* **brahman**

Brahmasutras – *see* **brahman**

Buddha The title of Siddhattha Gotama (Siddhartha Gautama in Sanskrit), the originator of Buddhism. The normal translation is 'the enlightened one' or 'the awakened one' and represents the way in which enlightenment is achieved through waking up from the delusions that arise through uncritical trust in the senses, which is a stage on the route to finally understanding the real nature of existence. There are often taken to have been a number of Buddhas in existence, although they are rare beings. Buddhas are the highest form of creature possible, and they represent a very long process of moving along the path to self-awareness. Such a process is not limited to just one lifetime, but extends over many generations and incarnations. Siddhattha himself lived in India and was born around 563 BCE near the Himalayas into a privileged family background. He came to reject this, and many of the principles of **Vedic** thought, being impressed by the apparent omnipresence of suffering, and set out to discover a way of life that could overcome suffering and set mental tranquillity on a firm foundation. He argued that the source of suffering is human craving, and recommended a strategy of overcoming suffering by avoiding its cause, and replacing it with setting out on a path that can result in a complete bypassing of suffering.

There is an entertaining zen proverb that were one to meet the Buddha walking on the road, one should kill him! The idea is that since the Buddha is **empty** of real existence, what actually happens to someone's body is of little significance, and the notion of killing him is equivalent to the idea of seeing him as having no inherent existence and preventing him from becoming a source of attachment. In any case, what we see as important about being alive, the preservation of the self, is not a consideration for Buddhists, so there is really no importance in the continuation of the mortal life of the

Buddha, and the prospect of killing him brings this out nicely. The Buddha is more than a particular historical individual, but rather someone who exemplifies in his person the truth about reality. There is no particular benefit to be had from meeting him, what involves merit is following his teachings and making them part of ourselves. The notion of killing him implies going beyond his physicality to the inner truth that he encapsulates.

Becoming a Buddha is a task often seen as highly complicated, involving protracted **meditational** exercises and also, for the Mahayana, actions on behalf of others. There are a wide variety of ways in which this process is described, which leads to a path being followed along which varying degrees of 'enlightenment** are available to successful seekers after **knowledge** and enlightenment. The earlier stages involve becoming a *bodhisattva*, allowing oneself to be motivated by *bodhichitta*, and then gradually working up to the level of the *arahat*, which is equivalent to stopping at the level of establishing a personal *nirvana* (called a selfish *nirvana* by the Mahayana). Proceeding even further involves putting oneself in the position of being able to work out of **compassion** for the benefit of everyone else, and understanding the precise way in which the different routes to enlightenment are interrelated. Some, particularly those in the Tibetan tradition, would argue that to acquire complete Buddhahood involves **Tantric** practices, while on the *tathagatagarbha* view the whole complicated process is a misunderstanding of what needs to be done. Nothing needs to be done, since everything already has a **buddha nature** and so is already a Buddha.

See also: **anatman**
Further reading: Conze 1962, Dreyfus 1997, Eckel 1992, Griffiths 1994, Gyatso 1992, Warder 1980.

buddha nature This is the potentiality to become a Buddha, which is innate in all beings according to Mahayana teaching. Since everything has it, **enlightenment** is universally available. Since everything shares in the nature of the Buddha, which is itself completely pure, it follows that the buddha nature (*buddhata* in Sanskrit, *fo shing* in Chinese) is just another aspect of the absolute. The question arises as to why, if all beings have the buddha nature, do some see it in themselves while others do not. It depends on one's view of how to achieve enlightenment, which can be seen as either sudden or gradual. On the former view, the **mind** is essentially pure, and the impurities that seem to adhere to it are really illusory. They may suddenly be disregarded, and the real brightness of the buddha nature revealed. On the other hand, gradualism explains that effort is required to polish the mirror, as it were, and remove the impurities.

According to Dogen and his version of zen Buddhism, the buddha nature is not an innate potentiality nor a state we can realize, but it is rather part and parcel of the impermanence of a constantly changing reality. We should not distinguish sharply between **time** and **being**, since in reality these are fused together, and so what we think of as being in the future is in a sense already here, while what we think of as being here now is in a sense in the future, and in the past. This attempt to mediate contradictions is apparent in his account of the controversy between the Soto sect, who favoured gradualism as the route to enlightenment, and the Rinzai sect, who advocated the use of riddles, **koan** and sudden enlightenment. The latter use the riddle 'Does the dog have buddha nature?' and its answer 'No' (*mu*) to suggest that once we consider this riddle we can see that it brings to an end conceptual thought. Dogen suggests that what we need to do is to consider why this response is appropriate, and that means thinking about the nature of the question, contemplating the meaning of **emptiness**, and understanding the point of providing a puzzling response to a query. The character of the buddha nature is not something we can grasp without also grasping a great deal of the metaphysics of being and time, and our role in it.

See also: **tathagatagarbha**, **zen**

Further reading: Gregory 1987, Griffiths 1986, Guenther 1972, Heine 1993, King 1991.

buddhata – *see* **buddha nature**

buddhi, linked to awakening – *see* **yoga**

bushido, way of the samurai – *see* **death**

caste According to the doctrine of caste, which has arisen from social and cultural practice, only those from appropriate castes who are male can hope to achieve salvation. This does not mean that other groups cannot lead virtuous lives, nor that they cannot become wise, but as a result of *karma* the sort of person that they are in this life means that they cannot achieve **liberation**. Their condition in this life, that is, is a result of their behaviour in previous lives, so if it is not as well-formed with respect to liberation that is only their own fault.

Further reading: Brockington 1996.

causation Issues of how one thing brings about something else were much discussed in Indian philosophy. The Jain view is that the effect is to a degree something different from its cause, but also to a certain extent the same. One substance can bring into existence another substance, but when one quality changes another, the new quality is not necessarily part of its cause.

In the *Chandogya Upanishad* the problem of explaining how being can emerge from non-being is raised. It is argued that what is important and powerful is what cannot be seen, what is at the essence of reality is not visible in the world. Two different accounts of causation were developed. The **Nyaya-Vaisheshika** school treats causation as objectively real, countering the **Sankhya** view that the effect is already present in the cause, albeit not realized, so that there is an identity between cause and effect. There are different kinds of causes, but in every case the effect is something new. They employ this theory of causation to produce a **cosmological** argument for the existence of God, which starts with the premise that every effect must have an agent that brings it about. The universe is an effect, and so something must have brought it about. This cause is called God. They argued that we have constant experience of the ubiquity of causality, and also that when something comes into existence it must have been acted upon by someone who wanted it to be like that. But do not some changes take place without being directed by any being? And even if we agree that the universe is a product, we may well doubt whether the creator has the qualities of the God of religion. The sorts of examples this school liked were those where a pot is put together by joining its halves, and a piece of cloth by combining its threads. The causes of the new thing are brought into operation by some agent, in these examples, and the resulting creation is of something distinct.

We can contrast this with the Sankhya view, according to which causes and effects are really identical since they are just states of the same substance. What comes about is not something new, but just a different organization of what already exists. The reasoning for this surprising conclusion takes this form. If something cannot be produced from a cause, then nothing will bring it about through that cause, so if something happens, it must already have been present in the cause. There is a fixed relationship between the cause and the effect, since not just anything can follow from something preceding it, and both the cause and the effect must exist. The cause and effect must be linked since they have the same nature. The sorts of examples used are those of thread and the garment that is made of it. The latter is clearly the same sort of thing as the former, which is its cause. Therefore cause and effect seem to be merely different states of the same substance. The theory only gains in strength when we consider something that is apparently very different from its cause, such as butter being produced from milk. There is no milk to be seen in the butter once it is butter, but had there not been milk in the first place then there could not be butter finally. It does very much look as though the cause continues, in some sense, in the effect, and that in causation the same substance manifests itself in different, albeit linked, ways. Cause and effect are the developed and the undeveloped states of the same substance, so that from the basic matter of the world everything originates and then returns to its original form on the ending of the world. This leads to the objection that if the material cause is the only necessary condition for the creation of the effect, then we have to raise the question as to what the earlier material cause of the later material cause is. This gets us back eventually to some primary material cause, matter itself, and then the question arises as to what leads it to change from its pure state of matter to bringing about material objects. An answer is provided by Ramanuja, who also accepts the significance of matter as a cause, yet he makes it dependent upon God. Matter has to be controlled by God in just the same way that the soul controls the body. On the other hand, he does not create matter, only the things made out of matter, and matter itself is co-eternal with him. Creation leads to matter being transformed into things in accordance with their *karma*s. This was not the standard Sankhya line, which refers to the role of the *purusha* or spiritual self in affecting the matter or *prakriti* into evolving in particular directions. What we need to do to attain salvation is come to understand the process by which matter is informed by the spiritual selves, and once we do this we have identified a form of causality – **knowledge** – which does not transmit its force to its object, the object of knowledge. This knowledge consists of an understanding that the material aspect of our lives is not really what we are, we are really a spiritual self, and once we understand this we can set in motion the route to **liberation**.

Shankara has to explain how the diversity of the world can have its origin in *brahman*, absolute reality which is entirely one. He gets around this by arguing that there is no real difference between the cause of the world and the world itself. He uses this theory to criticize the Sankhya view of causation. They are right to think that the effect exists already in the material cause, but they fail to see that this means that the effect is then the same as the material cause. He strengthens the links between the cause and the effect by arguing that the effect cannot just exist within the cause, but there must be some explanation as to why it exists within the cause. That is, there must be something about it which makes such a form of pre-existence possible, since not just anything can lie in waiting within any cause. Yet it seems quite a jump from this position to the argument that the cause must be identical with the effect. Shankara suggests that there is a problem in saying that the effect is in the cause since it is unclear whether it is in all the cause, or just part of it. If it is in all of it, it cannot be in the former, since we do not understand by an effect something that has been created by the whole of its cause. For example, we may agree that cloth is caused by threads, but we do not need to be aware of each of the fibres of the cloth for this to be proved. The effect cannot lie in part of the cause, since then that part would be enough to bring it about, which might well not be the case. The conclusion that Shankara is looking for is really that the nature of *brahman* is the cause of the world of generation and corruption, so that it can lead to the creation of something entirely diverse out of something entirely unchanging and undifferentiated. This is no longer a problem, since one does not have to explain how some-thing so different from its effects can cause those effects. The cause and the effects are really the same, and the distinction between the ground of reality and the universe is only apparent. A problem with this view, and one with which Shankara wrestled in his work, is that it seems to identify the cause–effect relationship too closely with necessity. It also makes it difficult to understand how a person can achieve salvation, given the apparently rigid process of causation.

This theory is challenged by Madhva, who argues that God is only the efficient cause of the world, and not its material cause. God is so unlike the material parts of the world that he cannot be regarded as its cause. He accepts the Sankhya notion of an eternal and subtle matter, *prakriti*, as the basis of material change, and suggests that God sets off each cosmic cycle by getting this matter to evolve into progressively more complex forms. He is also seeking to overturn the Nyaya view that the world is a real effect of which God is the efficient cause. This is because an effect cannot come about through an efficient cause alone, but must also have a material cause. Then something that is unreal cannot have something real as its cause, since the latter could not be a material cause of something unreal. Unreal things do not have material causes. The world itself is neither entirely real nor entirely illusory, and so its cause must share this rather ambiguous ontological status.

Vedanta made a good deal of use of statements in the scriptures which seem to imply that the phenomenal world emerges out of *brahman*, which is both the basis of its production and also its location after the dissolution of the world. Ramanuja was clearly heavily influenced by the many scriptural passages that suggest that finite existence emerges from *brahman*, so that there is a continual link between the realm of infinity and the finite. The connection is established by the substantial cause, so that the nature of the cause brings about the effect, and also keeps the effect in existence while it is in existence. The effect is again believed to pre-exist in the cause, and the way in which change takes place varies. It can be accidental change, in which case the matter is shaped in a particular way, but it could have been shaped in any way at all, within certain limits of course. On the other hand, the change may be essential, as when milk becomes curds and a seed a tree (the standard examples). In both cases the cause is both identical and different from the effect. It is the same in the sense that the effect derives its being from the cause, while it is different because it is not the cause, and has a form that is either accidentally or essentially distinct from the cause.

Action or *karman* is generally motivated by the desire to satisfy one's selfish ambitions, and so continues to pull us along the path of *samsara*. These actions can be morally appropriate if they are in line with our *dharma*, the obligations and practices describing our station in life. It is up to the individual to decide how to act, and he has the advice of religion to help him determine the right path, but it is not only the agent who is responsible for his action. There is a role also for the original causal principle, *brahman*, for unless this operates, whatever our intentions, we shall be able to bring nothing about. Whereas this principle could go against the individual will, it never does, leaving it to us to make our own choices and suffer the consequences accordingly. Yet there is scope for the individual agent to claim with some plausibility that the most important factor in what he does is not in fact his intentions about what he is going to do, but rather the underlying causal dependence of what he wishes to do on the principles of action and matter. That is, there is an aspect of the individual as an agent which is moved by more powerful causal forces, so this aspect does not itself act, but remains unchanging and perfect throughout. On the other hand, it is itself the principle of action, and makes possible human behaviour in so far as it is up to us to formulate hopes and ambitions about action.

Causation is a problematic concept for Daoism, since the dao as a cause that can bring other things about (*sheng*) cannot really be identified with a first cause or originator. Since dao is said not to interfere or assert itself, how can it bring other things into existence?

According to Buddhism, the world consists of a system of causes and effects, and this came to be known as **dependent origination**. An effect is not really the result of a single cause, but of a number of causes in tandem, and there cannot be a constant relation between things, nor even stable things themselves. We need to grasp the momentary nature of this system of what looks like an explanation of how things are linked if we are to overcome **ignorance**, which can result in also overcoming suffering. The detailed breakdown of the system starts with ignorance (*avidya*), carries on with dispositions, forms of knowledge, the sense faculties, various forms of attachment, and ends in old age and death. This causal process has been in existence eternally, but it can be evaded, by replacing ignorance with knowledge. Causation is a crucial notion since it establishes the lack of substance and stability in the world. This might seem strange, since it is often argued by philosophers that causality is an indication of the objectivity and reality of the material world, given that it consists of a system of rules for the organization of experience and reality. For the Buddhist, causality gives us the idea of regularity, and that is an important idea. That idea permits us to construct habitual ways of thinking, which are useful to us in our ordinary lives, since they allow us to construct the notion of a personality and form some conception of an objective world. On the other hand, there can be no necessary link between causes and effects, since really these are just ways we have to view the world, there is nothing inherently real in this way of discriminating our experience and what we take to be external objects are not really persisting phenomena. The example they often give is what happens when a torch is used to create an appearance of a circle of fire in the air. We think there is an existing circular thing when we see it, but in fact this is just an impression which we form, nothing more.

The **Sarvastivada** school were more sympathetic to the notion of causation than many other Buddhist schools, arguing that while in reality everything only exists momentarily, the continuity of our experience can only be explained by the relative stability of at least some features of things and their links with other things. For instance, a particular seed can only produce a certain sort of fruit, so there must be something in the seed that obliges it to do so. The Sautrantikas, by contrast, replace that sort of language of material objects and constant conjunction with a terminology that interprets what look like things in terms of processes. Seeds are indeed generally followed by fruit, but there is nothing in the seed that makes this inevitable, and in principle there is nothing necessary in the link between cause and effect. Nagarjuna rejects all theories of causality that do not acknowledge the

way in which everything that we take to be reality is interlinked. Causation as understood by most of the theories he
attacked distinguishes between causes and effects in the sense
that one side of the relation, the cause, is more real than the
effect, since the latter emerges out of the former and might
be regarded as part of it. Dependent origination implies that
nothing has any stability or priority, and so leads to the notion
of **emptiness**.

The notion of causation generally accepted by classical
Islamic thinkers was Neoplatonic, being based on the principle of emanation. According to this everything comes about
through the mental activity of the First Cause, which in
thinking about itself creates an object of thought, and which
in turn creates further things and objects of thought through
following the processes of what follows logically from thinking. The structure of the universe is controlled by such a
mechanism, with the moon being the last stage along the line
of relatively pure emanations from the One until the earth is
reached. Here the baseness of matter interferes with the ability of thought to affect what it causes, and yet it is still the
case that what exists is necessarily connected to what brings
it about. As ibn Sina often puts it, the events in the world are
possible in themselves, and necessary given the existence of
something else, their cause, ultimately God being the only
thing that is both possible *and* necessary in itself. This theory
led to the objection by some thinkers like al-Ghazali that it
left no room for God to create freely, since the nature of the
universe seems to be specified right from the beginning by
the principles of rationality. They argued that the universe
did not emanate from the First Cause, but was created by God,
a God who could at any time decide to end his creation and
who is totally in charge of what takes place.

Most of the early thinkers in the Islamic world were **atomists**, understanding by this that there is nothing solid in the
structure of the world except the ways in which God holds
together its different atoms or parts. Later thinkers like ibn
Sina and ibn Rushd opposed this view, adhering to the broadly
Aristotelian view that it is not possible to analyse physical

terms like space and **time** into atoms. This enabled them to argue that causality represents the logical structure of the world of generation and corruption, and could not have taken a different form. Al-Ghazali tries to mediate between the Aristotelian philosophers and the theologians by arguing that there is such a thing as causal necessity, but this merely represents the way in which God wishes nature to be organized. If God had to go along with nature, then he would not have been free to act in the world, and if nature could take any form at all, it would be impossible to work our way through it. This opposition is reconciled by a God who freely decides to fashion a particular version of nature and causality, and once this is created it presents evidence of the thinking and planning that went into the natural pattern.

In Islamic philosophy the debate about causation generally takes the form of the controversy between those who argue that causal properties represent an aspect of the meaning of things, and those who claim that they are the effects of the will of God. Al-Ghazali is often identified with the latter (although this view has come in for criticism recently) and ibn Sina with the former view. According to the latter, there is a close resemblance between the course of nature and a logical process, in that what leads something else to happen is like the way in which the premises in a syllogism lead to the conclusion. Everything in the universe apart from God is both possible in itself and necessary through another (God by contrast is necessary in himself), and once the agent has affected the thing that it necessitates then the result has to come about. Al-Ghazali challenges this, arguing that God could alter the course of nature were he to wish to, and insisting that what makes something happen is God making it happen, whether we are aware of it or not. God could organize the world differently were he to wish to, and what we see as the smooth flow of natural law is in fact a reflection of the many decisions that he makes that allow the links between causes and effects to be possible.

In response ibn Rushd argues that were everything that happens to be the work of God as the direct agent then we should have no grasp of natural law at all, and we could not find our way around the world. Moreover, we should not know how to talk about that world, since the meanings of terms and their causal powers are linked, and if the latter are only contingently related to the terms themselves, those terms would lose or change their meanings. Ibn Rushd further argues that the natural structure of the universe reflects a rational order, and God could not but have carried out his **creation** in accordance with that order. This is not a limitation on divine action, but it is reasonable to expect that the most rational being in the universe will act, and has to act, in accordance with rationality itself. Both ibn Sina and al-Ghazali use the notion of God as the agent to bring possibilities into actuality, although in the case of ibn Sina God is involved in a rather distant way. For ibn Rushd, by contrast, God brings about the order that exists, but it is not at all clear how far God is the real agent, since ibn Rushd's cosmology seems to operate quite independently of individual decision, as a reflection of the rules of reason.

See: **Ash`ariyya and Mu`tazila**
Further reading: Burch 1976, Cabezon 1994, Carr and Mahalingam 1997, Chan 1972, Chatterjee 1965, Fakhry 1983, Kalupahana 1975, Nasr and Leaman 1996, Potter 1972.

chan, *ch'an* Buddhist school – *see* **zen**

Chandogya Upanishad – *see* **causation**

change – *see* **causation**

cheng – *see* **Book of Changes**, **enlightenment**, **human nature**

Chinese philosophy There are three main schools in Chinese philosophy – Confucianism, Daoism and Buddhism. These were also incorporated in religion, of course, and came to be practised as parts of folk religion, where there was often a good deal of syncretism in operation. The earliest thinker was Master Kong or Confucius, who lived in the sixth century BCE, and even at that comparatively early date he was able to refer to long periods of previous Chinese history to illustrate his arguments. He says that he considered himself as merely a mouthpiece of the classical Chinese tradition and wisdom. He paid particular attention to the idea that the ruler has the sanction of **heaven** if he is righteous, and has it taken away from him if he behaves badly. Although Confucius spends a good deal of time referring back to prior states of affairs, he is very far from being a conservative. He did use the concept of social relations as the basic building bricks of society, and emphasized the significance of respect for those in such relationships, but what makes his theory so interesting is that he does not just say that there is a lot of value in traditional ideas. These ideas need to be revived, he argues, because they symbolize the rules of the good society, the rules of social **harmony**. Those rules strengthen personal integrity and also rest on such integrity, and the cultivated individual is not just someone who is born a member of an educated class, but someone who seeks to be wise and benevolent, and who submits himself to authority where such submission is justified. **Education** involves respect for the past and for those superior to oneself, but once it has been achieved one ought to progress socially to whichever position one is most appropriate to fill on the basis of one's own talents and efforts. This idea led to the theory of the **rectification of names**, according to which it is important for those who are acting out a particular role to work in accordance with the real nature of those roles or names.

Confucius may well have written the *Spring and Autumn Annals*, and the *Analects* is a collection of his sayings and ideas. There are other books that incorporate Confucian ideas, especially the book by Mencius, the *Mengzi*, and there grew a number of commentaries on his thought. What might be regarded as the philosophical curriculum also included the

Book of Changes, the *Yi jing*, which deals with the principles controlling change.

Tradition has it that the founder of Daoism (Taoism), Laozi, was a contemporary of Confucius, and the main text of this school is the *Dao de jing*, or the 'Account of the Dao and its Power'. This is a text with a highly mystical flavour, advocating the advantages of the quiet and contemplative life, which also conveys political advice and ideas. It deals with the notion of the dao or the Way which structures the life and operations of the universe. According to it, the ultimate reality cannot be described, yet we can make some sensible statements about the operation' of the Way. It acts spontaneously and without intention, and so in a sense acts without acting. Through being as it is, other things are brought into existence, but not through anything it sets out to do. For example, the valley makes possible the mountain, but it does not do anything directly to bring about the mountain. It is just there, and since it is there it defines the mountain. Human beings should align their activity in similar ways, to act through not acting, to unite through contemplation with the harmony of the Way. The notion that the microcosm that is us can become identical with the macrocosm, and that the ultimate aim is harmony is strengthened by the use of the concepts of *yin* and *yang*, the two contrasting forces in the universe which pull in opposite directions and which have to be reconciled for balance to be achieved. The book should not be seen as part of a tradition of pure speculation, but as containing a great deal of practical advice and analysis.

Before the advent of Buddhism there were a number of other schools of philosophy, including **Mohism** and **Legalism**. Mozi lived around 400 BCE during a very turbulent period, and objected to the Confucian emphasis on tradition and ritual. He advocated a form of universal benevolence and the equality of all **humanity**, and the abandonment of the elaborate rituals and sacrifices that characterized so much Chinese formal worship. The Legalists, as their name suggests, argued for the important of **law** or *fa* as the central point of the state, since they suggested that anything weaker would not do as a method of social control. This became the official doctrine of the Qin dynasty between 221 and 206 BCE.

The leading schools of Confucianism and Daoism came in for a great deal of elaboration by later thinkers, and eventually developed into the theories of **Neoconfucianism** and **Neodaoism**. At the same time Buddhism arrived in north China from India from the second century CE, and gradually came to have a strong effect on Chinese philosophy. As one might expect, it had a stronger influence in north China, and it is only with the reunification of China between the sixth and tenth centuries that it really established a solid grip on China as a whole. The *tian tai* school emphasized the significance of the *Lotus Sutra*, and particularly its use of the idea of **skilful means**, *upaya*, in order to show how the Buddha adapted his teaching to the abilities of his hearers. This can be broadened out to think of the different periods of the Buddha's life as being those in which he produced different messages for different audiences. That is why we get a variety of different Buddhist schools, but they are all encapsulated in the *Lotus Sutra*, the greatest of the teachings. The most characteristic view of the theory is that everything already possesses **buddha nature**, so **enlightenment** is a matter of rediscovering that which we already are.

The *hua yan* school in the fifth century used the theory of **dependent origination** to argue that the universe is a system of interlinked *dharma*s. Each individual *dharma* or event is able to represent every other, although in itself it is completely **empty**, only able to reflect the others. Like the *tian tai* school, the *hua yan* was able to present a theory of the variety of Buddhist schools which explained that variety. The Hinayana or Lesser Vehicle school was right to emphasize the emptiness of everything, but wrong in its account of the emptiness of the whole system of *dharma*s. The Mahayana are right to defend emptiness and attack the ordinary ideas people have of what constitutes reality, but do not understand that the **mind** contains also great insight and knowledge.

The *tathagatagarbha* school correctly points out that the buddha nature is present in everything sentient, but used it to devalue the events of the everyday world which remains of importance only insofar as it is symbolic of a deeper reality. Finally, those who think that enlightenment can come about suddenly are right to suspect concepts and **language**, but they do not understand the importance of language and adequate preparation for the approach to enlightenment. The *hua yan* sees itself as being in the middle of all these interpretations, advocating both the particular and the universal, the empty and the real, the sudden and the gradual, the duplicity and yet the necessity of language, and the unreality of the world along with the necessity to regard it as real to a certain extent.

The chan form of Buddhism argued that it is possible to achieve enlightenment through sudden experience, and in this aligns itself more closely to Daoism than to Confucianism. The latter was horrified at the idea of a philosophy that sought to exclude rituals, tradition and all the trappings of religion. The idea of chan is that all that one needs is a direct experience of reality, and this can lead to sudden enlightenment, which is not difficult to understand given the omnipresence of the *tathagatagarbha* or buddha nature in us. The language of chan is frequently paradoxical, since it describes an experience that is literally indescribable, and uses language to account for what cannot be said. There is much use of riddles, the *kongan*, which stimulates our concepts in such a way that we are obliged to go beyond them. This form of Buddhism, *zen* in Japanese, became especially significant in Japan, as did the **Pure Land** school, which identified *nirvana* with a particular heaven and argued that salvation is attainable through worship and the grace of divine beings.

Different political regimes came to favour different schools of philosophy, and there were long periods during which one school or another was in official disfavour or even active persecution. It is often said that Chinese philosophy tends to share a practical orientation, in the sense that the main doctrines of all the schools seem to oppose the other-worldliness of Indian thought, for example. There is certainly far more speculation about social and moral issues in Chinese thought than one might find in other cultural areas. Even the Chinese Buddhist schools advocate a positive notion of the practical world. Perhaps the most antagonistic approach to the world is that of Daoism, but even this philosophy discusses how we should behave in the social world and bring ourselves into harmony with nature. Some of the principles of harmony and *yin* and *yang* seem to extend through many of the Chinese theories, and bring them into alignment with a conception of the unity of the practical and metaphysical world.

Further reading: Adelmann 1982, Chan 1972, Cheng 1989, Creel 1953, Fung 1952, Gregory 1987, McRae 1986, Peerenboom 1993, Tu Wei-Ming 1985.

chitta – *see* **mind**

Chittamatra – *see* **Yogachara**

communism   Mao Zedong created a form of communism or Marxism which is in some ways a synthesis of Marxist and Chinese thought. All Marxists have the problem of translating a universal theory of revolutionary change into the conditions of their own culture, and this was certainly an issue for Mao. Basic to Mao's system is the notion of contradiction, where the world consists basically of relationships of opposition and identity. There is a pattern to these relationships which takes a dialectical form, but the world as a whole consists of continual conflict, where nothing is stable or has existence outside its relationships with other contradictions. While this is the normal description provided by Marxism, the difference that Maoism makes is to resist the idea of there being some conflicts that are more important or crucial than others. The revolutionary has to navigate through the structure of contradictions by shaping them in a way likely to be most effective with respect to the goal of revolution. It is important that he has a grasp of the theory of contradiction, since otherwise he will be unable to operate successfully. But Mao also argues that the world is objectively real, so that our knowledge of it, albeit affected by our class position, is knowledge of something that really exists outside us. This seems to contradict the subjectivism of seeing the world as a construct out of the system of contradictions.

There was a protracted controversy in Chinese philosophy over the relative merits of thought and **action**. Mao comes down very much on the side of action, arguing that it is through political action and social practice that **knowledge** and action can be successfully linked into a correct view of the world and of our duties with respect to it. He criticized in many places the inappropriate division between theory and practice, arguing that it is only through practice that one can form an appropriate theoretical attitude. On the other hand, it is also the case that it is not enough to act, but one's actions must be informed by the correct theory if they are to bring about one's aims and objectives. But the criterion of a correct theory is its effectiveness in practice. Mao definitely aligns himself with the tradition in Chinese philosophy that emphasizes action over reflection, and the interpretation of dialectical thinking in terms of *yin* and *yang*. Economic forces and classes operate within the context of a wider superstructure, and Marxism is interpreted as fulfilling and explaining a pattern of behaviour and relationships that reflects a view of the world and humanity constructed over several millennia of Chinese philosophical thought.

Further reading: Carr and Mahalingam 1997, Creel 1953, Mao 1961, Schram 1989.

compassion – *see karuna*

conditioned arising – *see* **dependent origination**

Confucianism The system of thought stemming from Confucius ('Master Kong'), who did not actually write any directly philosophical works, but who expressed his thoughts in his educational and political work. His disciples collected his works in the *Analects*, He was largely concerned with social philosophy, and paid limited attention to **cosmology** or **knowledge**. He argued for the unity of benevolence and propriety, where the latter represents a hierarchical society in which the roles for each individual are firmly determined. Such a society should be run on principles of **benevolence**, which sought to achieve a mean in its navigation between the extremes of human behaviour.

The benevolent person is superior, and inevitably an aristocrat, and is obliged to act in accordance with his social rank. He must feel affection for everyone, or at least the degree of affection it is appropriate to feel for people of different social levels, and he must treat others as he treats himself. In politics the state requires a benevolent government which does not impose its authority by arbitrary force and punishment, but which establishes peace and **harmony**. His discussions of **education** have been very influential in Chinese culture, especially for their linking of the acquisition of knowledge and the development of virtue. Although the general tenor of Confucius' thinking is conservative, it is worth pointing out that his remarks on education suggest his support for a meritocracy at least in this sphere, albeit one designed to serve and preserve the feudal nature of society. A characteristic aspect of Confucianism is to analyse the individual in terms of society, since we act within a community and we cannot abstract from that community when we seek to determine our duties. The Golden Rule, 'Do not do unto others what you would not want others to do to you' implies that one's duties to oneself and one's duties to others are parts of the same thing. This should be linked with another of his sayings, 'in order to establish myself, I establish others; in order to enlarge myself, I enlarge others'. Neither of these principles is altruistic, but a description of how the self should seek to transform itself. Confucius was humble himself in his claims about how far he had managed personally to do what he ought, and this is how he should be followed as a paradigm. There are always problems with individuals who think that they have got the balance right between serving their own private interests and serving the interests of the public, but it is very difficult to get the relationship just right. Sometimes this is given a religious twist, as when it is suggested that self-cultivation leads to union with heaven. The point here is that becoming a real human being is both to transcend oneself, and also to concentrate on that with which we are very familiar, that is, ourselves. For Confucius, serving heaven is a matter of deepening our understanding of ourselves as human beings.

One of the revolutionary aspects of Confucius' approach is his rejection of the traditional notion of the gentleman (*junzi*) as someone necessarily of high birth. Anyone could be a gentleman on the basis of noble, unselfish, kind and just action, and such behaviour can serve as an exemplar to others of how to live excellently (*de*). The route to such a high level of behaviour includes *li* or propriety, following the rules of action that enable people as a whole to cooperate appropriately. *Li* is a combination of morality and etiquette, and the notion of combination here is important. It is not enough just to carry out rituals because they are traditional, since in that case they might not be heartfelt and, as a result, would be of limited moral import. Being a human being (*ren*) should be seen as more of a process than a product, a process of acquiring all the social virtues and reflecting in oneself the most well-developed 'traits that can result from life with others in a community.

Confucianism is the doctrine, or rather doctrines, that originated with the thought of Confucius, and it developed in a variety of different ways as variously interpreted by later thinkers. The two most important Confucianists were Mencius and Xunzi. The former emphasized in his philosophy the virtues of benevolence, rectitude, wisdom and propriety, and sought to broaden the scope of the doctrine, arguing that everyone had a disposition to behave in a virtuous and controlled manner. When people become **evil** this is a result of something negative twisting their natural goodness and distorting it. The state should establish a context within which good dispositions can flourish and evil dispositions wither. The best sort of political rule is carried out with the support and advice of those who understand the principles of supporting virtue and suppressing vice, but if the ruler does not want to listen to good advice, one must leave the state and seek a more compliant ruler. **Violence** is to be avoided at all costs. Xunzi differed in thinking that nature and society are in some ways in conflict, and that human beings do not possess innate characteristics. He also stressed the role of propriety and music as important in maintaining and deepening royal rule. The theory took an even more conservative direction in the thought of Dong Zhongshu, who built up the notion of loyalty to the ruler at the expense of the necessity to **love** everyone, and identified the ruler guiding the subject with the father guiding his son and the husband his wife. He identified the ruler with the **heavens**, and just as we should not think of rebelling against the heavens, so the subject should be absolutely obedient to the ruler. It is a waste of time for human beings to fight against the necessary pattern of nature, and against the sons of heaven, their rulers.

Further reading: Confucius 1993, Creel 1953, de Bary 1996, Fingarette 1972, Graham 1981, Tu Wei-Ming 1988.

consciousness **Materialist** Indian philosophy had difficulties in explaining consciousness in the sense of a soul or self that is essentially separate from the body. The Lokayata, for example, thought that the emergence of consciousness comes about from a particular combination of elements, although there were also a variety of views on this topic even within this school. On **death**, consciousness disappears as that combination of material elements changes. Buddhist approaches also criticize the notion of a particular consciousness, and analyse the notion of consciousness in terms of different groups of attitudes to experience. On the other hand, the **Nyaya-Vaisheshika** tradition distinguishes the self from the body, senses and **mind**. The body and the senses are clearly distinguishable, since they can change without the notion of the self changing. The mind might seem to be the same as the self, yet is not, since the mind is **atomic** and as a result cannot be the faculty that grasps a variety of objects all at once. It is in **Sankhyan** theory that consciousness (*purusha*) is explicitly contrasted with matter (*prakriti*), since the self as conscious is the subject of **knowledge** and is presupposed by the possibility of knowledge. Again, though, there is a distinction to be made between consciousness and the mind, since the latter is material. Consciousness, by contrast, is eternal and beyond the bounds of matter. Such an immaterial notion is important, since it only makes sense to talk about **liberation** from the world of suffering if there is a consciousness capable of release and which is more than a combination of material elements. Interestingly, consciousness is understood to contrast with the simplicity of matter by being multiple. If consciousnesses were not many, then everyone would have the same self, and there would not be changing selves after birth and rebirth. Ordinary consciousness, *jiva*, is consciousness irretrievably contaminated with the influences of matter, which does not appreciate the freedom and eternity of consciousness as *purusha*. Once *jiva* understands the distinction between matter and the purity of *purusha*, liberation is achieved.

Shankara identified the consciousness with **brahman**, reality. What we normally think of as consciousness is merely an effect of it, though, and the 'I' that lies at the basis of experience is in itself beyond apprehension. On the **Advaita** approach, this *brahman* or *atman* is the basic self of everything, and is the same for everything. As a result of **ignorance**, we tend to identify the self with objects in the world of matter, and we do not appreciate how distinct the real self is. It is easy for us to think that the empirical self which we can observe through and in our experience is the real self, but this is an error. We can appreciate the nature of the error by considering that the empirical self cannot understand itself, since there is always an aspect of self that remains outside the object of knowledge. This transcendental self is immediate, since if it were to be an object of consciousness itself an infinite regress would be created. Consciousness in itself is there all the time, and is not in the objects of that consciousness. Consciousness is completely independent, and does not need another consciousness to function, nor does its operation require the object of consciousness. The analogy of consciousness with light was often drawn, since light is not dependent on the objects illuminated by it, as compared with those objects themselves. Objects can only be noticed if they are lit up, as it were, while light itself requires nothing to light it up, since it is itself the basis for illumination. The Advaita and **Vishishtadvaita** schools both accept that the self manifests itself at the source of our knowledge, but they differ on its precise nature. According to the former, the transcendental self is equivalent to consciousness, while for the latter the self is an immortal and individual knowing subject. Vishishtadvaita argues that the self cannot just be consciousness, since consciousness requires something to be conscious. Consciousness also has to have an object it can be directed at, and this is a lower form of consciousness that exists at the level of *karma*. Once we achieve liberation this sort of consciousness disappears into the transcendental consciousness and we are left with a soul that knows itself and is concerned with nothing else.

There are difficulties about conceptualizing consciousness for Buddhists, since there are difficulties in accounting for the nature of what looks like a real self. According to the **Yogachara** tradition, the whole of the phenomenal world is a function of consciousness. There are eight types of consciousness. Five relate to the senses, one to the mind which mediates between ordinary experiences and psychic events, and then there are two other kinds. One is what is often referred to as the tainted mind, and the other is storehouse consciousness. The former has the latter as its object, and comes to the false conclusion that it is a real self. This variety of consciousnesses is designed to represent the variety of the interrelationships between subject and object, and the storehouse consciousness (*alayavijnana*) appears from this perspective to be the cause of the rest. It is sometimes referred to as like a great mass of water, which is always changing and yet which preserves its identity none the less, and it is often identified with the dependent aspect of reality. As a storehouse it is the repository for the elements that lead to phenomenal existence and personal experiences, containing the *karma*s of individuals and underpinning *samsara*. Now, one might wonder whether this in fact is not just a concept of the self. The answer is that it is not the self, although we may think of it erroneously as a self, since it is always changing and does not survive **enlightenment**. On enlightenment what disappears is the tainted self, and what survives is the stream of consciousness itself, albeit no longer seen from an individual point of view.

Further reading: Beidler 1975, Collins 1982, Larson 1969, Nagao 1991, Nakamura 1983, Pereira 1976, Potter 1988, Radhakrishnan 1966, Radhakrishnan and Moore 1957.

cosmology   Jain cosmology divides the universe into the non-living (*ajiva*) and the living (*jiva*), where the former includes **atoms** and the principles of physics. The realm of the living exists on three levels, initially in hell, then as plants, animals and human beings, and finally as gods.

The different schools of Hinduism took distinct lines on the nature of the universe. The **Sankhya** divided the world into the material (*prakriti*) and the conscious (*purusha*), where the former consists of two levels. The first level is matter that has not been made into anything else, and the second level consists of a number of primary entities. The differences between what exists come about as a result of the initial differences in the nature of the matter itself.

According to Buddhism, there are three spheres of **existence** where living things are placed. At the summit is the immaterial sphere, where pure spirits live, and as one might imagine since they have no matter they are not limited to existing in just one place. Then there is the material sphere where ethereal beings live, whose bodies consist of subtle matter, and they live in the highest part of the material world. Finally, on the sphere of desire the creatures of gross matter exist. This is more or less the natural world that we experience, subject as we are to physical urges and carnal desires. This world is made up of four elements – earth, water, heat and wind. The sphere of desire contains five kinds of creatures. There are heavenly beings or gods, human beings, spirits, animals and the damned. There are two interesting aspects to this cosmology; the gods live in the same sphere as we do, and so do animals. The cosmology of Buddhism represents the cycle of rebirth (*samsara*). In this landscape are the beings reborn as animals, ghosts, devils and jealous gods as a result of their bad actions. There are also those who live as gods as a result of their virtuous actions, and in a different place ordinary human beings. These different realms are the world of the five senses, and beyond them are the twenty realms of those gods who have been reborn as the result of varying **meditation** techniques. Although the descriptions of these realms is often highly graphic, they should not really be taken to exist in space or **time**, or even to be describable in terms of our ordinary categories, since really the character of the world sphere is constantly changing and has been in process for an infinite amount of time. What is remarkable about this conception is its blend of description of the world with the different mental states and levels of **consciousness**, and the thorough blend of the material and the spiritual. However, it is the levels of consciousness that really exist, and the apparently material phenomena are just misleading reflections of thought.

Early Chinese views on cosmology attributed to Laozi assert that everything under heaven comes from existence, and yet existence comes from nothing. The idea is that what has shape is derived from the shapeless, and originally there existed nothing that was in any way differentiated. Then there was a sudden change (*qi*) which started to shape matter and led to the structure of our world. This view developed into a theory of stages, each lasting for an extraordinarily long time. There are four stages, consisting of creation, existence, destruction and finally **emptiness**. The distinctive notion here is that there is no more basic being behind the beings of the world, and the dao is both what exists and how it exists. It operates in line with the principle of *ziran*, a way of coming about that is not caused by anything else.

See also: **prakriti**

Further reading: Cook 1977, Dundas 1992, Guenther 1972, Henderson 1984, Kaltenmark 1969, Needham 1956.

creation In early Zoroastrian thought, Mazda creates material life through thought. In later thought, there are vivid descriptions of how the evil spirit attacks the seven levels of creation, and so brings **death** into existence.

The *Rig Veda* presents creation in the form of a craftsman making things, or procreation. But as well as the highly poetic descriptions of creation, philosophical issues are raised about the nature of the process. This came to be much discussed in Indian philosophy in the topic of the precise relationship between **cause** and effect. The central problems of creation are how to explain the production of an impure material world from an absolute and unchangeable source, and how something that is completely real, **brahman**, can be said to be source of the world of illusion and confusion. A particularly sophisticated modern account is provided by Sri Aurobindo, who uses the notion of *brahman* as the unknowable source of the material world. On his account the spiritual sinks to meet matter, while the material rises to come into contact with the spiritual. The spirit is without form, and when it blends with matter it is shaped into the universe and into the individual. As it enters matter, it becomes progressively more concealed, until there is virtually nothing left of its original character. But this is not the end of the process of creation, since it at the same time regains its spiritual nature and withdraws from matter, thus leaving open the possibility of self-revelation. Creation is *lila* or play, since it is both self-revelation and self-concealment. On this view going down really is just another way of looking at going up.

Creation came to have enormous importance as a doctrine in Islamic philosophy. By contrast to most of the creation stories in the Hindu and Chinese traditions, the Qur'an implies, although does not clearly claim, that God created the world out of nothing, which is important in the sense that it would mean that he could do anything with the world, instead of being constrained by a world that has always existed, or which has to be created out of a particular matter or with a certain form. Many philosophers argued that this view of creation is inappropriate, since the world must always have existed, given that there could not have been a **time** before the time at which the world was created, since with the movement caused by creation time came into existence. In any case, if the world is worth creating, why should God wait to create it at a particular time? Unlike us, he is not constrained by limitations that might force him to pick his time. The Neoplatonic notion of emanation, according to which the world flows from the original oneness of the deity, does explain how the world remains in existence (through the continuation of the emanation from God) but does not give any support to the idea of creation in time. Emanation is an eternal process, so the world has always existed and could not have been created at a particular time.

See: **causation**

Further reading: Leaman 1985, McDermott 1987, Minor 1978, Sharma 1964, Zaehner 1975.

D

dahr – *see* **time**

Daoism A form of thought founded in the same period as Confucianism, during the declining period of the Zhou dynasty, by a thinker often known as Laozi (Lao Tze or Lao Tzu) or 'Old Master'. It has its origins in earlier shamanistic traditions and was later influenced by Buddhism. One of the bases of Daoism is the ***Dao de jing***, a cryptic text that has been subject to an extraordinary amount of study and reflection. Dao is the way in which things exist, the way in which things change in the world and how we should exist. It transcends the normal ways of talking about the role of the divine in relation to the world. One of the problems in trying to describe it is that we may then think that we know what the nature of reality is, and this is something we cannot know. The basis of the dao is a form of reality that is unnameable or *nothing* (*wu*), and this description is an attempt at transcending traditional distinctions between reality and unreality, substance and function, subject and object, **existence** and non-existence. The idea is that the nature of reality is unaffected by our ways of trying to grasp it, and although we may use concepts to make sense of that reality, we should be aware that reality in itself is completely undifferentiated. We see, hear and touch reality but in itself it is invisible (*yi*), intangible (*wei*) and inaudible (*xi*).

This difficulty in defining the nature of the dao did not, of course, prevent attempts to define it, and it is defined in various ways. As origin, it should be understood as an ontological rather than temporal cause, and as principle, it is the ultimate basis of change, although itself changeless. As function the dao advocates *wei wu-wei*, which is the avoidance of contrived **action**, especially action brought about through attempting to achieve an end. It is not so much what we do as the way in which we do it. As a system of virtue dao recommends absence of action, lack of effort, lack of desire, absence of partiality, resulting in **harmony**, simplicity, obedience. Morality should not be regarded as the attempt to recapture a form of social virtue that is under general threat, or a struggle with one's desires, but a natural and spontaneous identification with one's nature. This led to accounts of appropriate behaviour as rather aesthetic, something that is also the case with dao as a way of ruling, where the successful ruler is also the least noticed. The best ruler does not interfere with his subjects and allows them to act by themselves.

Zhuangzi is best known for a book of the same name, although he probably is not actually its author, or not of all of it. He provided a particularly clear account of Daoism, illustrated with some delightful images. There is the famous story of how he dreamt he was a butterfly, and when he woke he wondered if he was Zhuangzi dreaming he was a butterfly, or a butterfly dreaming he was Zhuangzi. This story emphasizes the constant flux of the world. He makes a sharp distinction between what is natural and what is social. The former is the source of all happiness and virtue, while the latter leads to suffering and **evil**. Everything is different due to their different natures, and the only characteristic they share is that their welfare is established if they are able to act naturally. The *Zhuangzi* is full of rather charming stories designed to illustrate this point. Yet the tendency of **law** and government is to seek to impose uniformity and ignore the differences between things, and in this one is involved in an essentially unnatural process. Even though the motives of the ruler may be of the best, his efforts are doomed if he tries to treat everyone the same. Hence the Daoist idea of governing through non-government, since government through the direct imposition of laws and authority is bound to fail. Such direct efforts at government involve trying to replace what is natural with what is artificial, and this can only end in tears. All we can hope will happen in society is that each individual will achieve the level of happiness appropriate to him or her, through following the natural path for that individual.

The Daoist sage has emotions, but does not allow them to distract him, since he realizes that they are part of the natural flow of life and neither to be welcomed nor resisted. The important thing is to understand why things change and what sorts of emotions we can expect to acquire, which leads to independence from external things. The perfectly happy person transcends the ordinary world altogether, and the distinction between the self and what is not self. He becomes one with the dao, with what is nameless, and so he has no name; and the dao governs without governing, so he may govern the world without taking any action at all. Zhuangzi spends a lot of time discussing the differences between the finite and the absolute point of view, and one of the features of the former is that it can be described using ordinary **language**, while the latter is beyond language. The problem with describing ultimate reality is its unity, since language only really gets to grip with objects that are various and embodies within itself the self/non-self distinction. All this disappears when we are at the level of the infinite, the dao. The sage perceives that **death** is nothing to worry about, since it is part of a natural process, and everything is part of a process of change. In a sense the sage never really dies, he blends with the dao which never comes to an end. To repeat one of those paradoxes so popular with the Daoists, the sage acquires **knowledge** through rejecting knowledge. In order to unite with the dao he has to transcend the ordinary distinctions we make between things, and it is these sorts of distinctions that make up what normally is regarded as knowledge. The more we forget these distinctions, the more we come to appreciate the unity of the dao, so we acquire that knowledge through turning our backs on ordinary knowledge. What the sage needs to do is first acquire knowledge and then set out to forget it, although there are also references in the *Zhuangzi* to the happy condition of those who never managed to acquire any knowledge in the first place. On this view what sages need to recover is the point of view of children and the ignorant.

See: **Neodaoism**
Further reading: Allinson 1989a, Capra 1976, Chung 1992, Graham 1981, 1989, Kaltenmark 1969, Kjellberg and Ivanhoe 1996, Laozi 1989.

Dao de jing The crucial Daoist (Taoist) text, reputedly written by Laozi (Lao Tzu), although it probably came into existence a couple of centuries after him. It argues that the nameless unchanging essence and source of heaven and earth can be called the dao (Tao) or 'way'. The book is literally 'the classic of dao and *de*'. The dao produces everything, and keeps everything in existence, but without wishing to do so or trying to achieve a purpose. The dao consists of non-being (*wu*) and **being** (*yu*), and from this mixture everything else emerges and stays in existence. The political implication of this is that the ruler should be without desires or purposes, since only through achieving a state of non-doing will he become tranquil and an appropriate leader of the empire. More generally, we are to reconcile our notion of excellence or virtue (*de*) with our role in the world (dao). This construction of a **harmony** out of difference is possible given the interrelated nature of *yin* and *yang*, the central concepts that describe how we may understand the relationships between people and things.

Further reading: Laozi 1989, Lau 1963.

dao zue – *see* **Neoconfucianism**

darshana Originally meaning 'seeing', the idea in Hindu thought is that once one sees the world correctly, one is firmly on the path to salvation. So the term came to represent particular views of the world. There are six orthodox darshanas in Hinduism – **Nyaya**, **Vaisheshika**, **Sankhya**, **Yoga**, **Mimamsa** and **Vedanta**. Although there are important doctrinal differences between the different schools of thought, they are in agreement on many of the social and ritual principles. All these schools accept that the **Vedas** are a source of scriptural truth, and that the sense of those texts can be interpreted and analysed through logical argument. It is important to realize that before one can understand these scriptures one has to be in an appropriate state of mind in which one distinguishes between the permanent and the temporary, where one controls one's cravings and has a wish to be **liberated**. The point is that the Vedas are not just collections of arguments to be understood, but also represent routes to experience of the ultimate truth.

Further reading: Hiriyanna 1985, Radhakrishnan and Moore 1957.

de A fundamental notion in Daoism and Confucianism. In the former it refers to the particular thing that is the source of its own potentiality, a thing that operates within the context of dao. Once *de* becomes embodied in practice, the distinction between it and dao vanishes, since the individual contains within itself its potentiality to develop in particular ways, and once it has developed fully there is no point in contrasting it with its environment. After all, that environment is nothing more than a way of interpreting the particular thing's potentiality to become what it really is.

In Confucianism the notion of *de* represents the significance of the individual linking personal behaviour with the community at large, so that through virtuous behaviour the individual becomes an example to others. *De* is often translated as 'virtue', but it is not virtue in the sense of Western morality, since the emphasis of the latter is often mainly on the individual actor. The Confucian notion involves both trying to become virtuous and also fitting that behaviour into an appropriate communal context which both supports it and leads others to share it, which in turn provides the background to nurture virtue. At a political level, the citizens identify with the ruler through observing and following his exemplary behaviour, while he embodies his activity in the culture understood by the people. The ruler's behaviour itself seeks to accord with the principles of **heaven**, which offer a paradigm to be followed. The important methodological principle here is to examine the ways in which the particular immerses itself in the general, the individual in the community, the people in the ruler and the ruler in heaven in order to express the full scope for **harmony**. The gentleman (*junzi*) has *de* in both its sense as virtue and power. It is through his virtue that he acquires the ability to induce others to treat him as a paradigm.

Further reading: Hall and Ames 1987.

death According to Zoroastrian philosophy, death enters the world with **Ahriman** or **Angra Mainyu**, the Evil Spirit. After death those who behave virtuously will be rewarded in an **afterlife** of bliss, while those who are **evil** will continue in the realms of darkness. It is not just behaviour that leads to a reward or punishment in the afterlife, even thoughts will be judged. Later versions of Zoroastrian thought clearly bring in more modern ideas, and Dhalla presents death as more a way of calling human beings back to themselves. The death of innocent children is explained on the grounds that they are so good that they cannot live on earth but need to return to heaven. Hell is not really a specific place, but a state of mind. This demythologizing process continues in the twentieth century with many Zoroastrian thinkers admitting problems with adhering to a personal Angra Mainyu, and as a result they identify him with the evil characteristics of humanity.

In Hindu philosophy death is described in a number of different ways. According to the *Bhagavad Gita*, those selves that have managed to free themselves join Krishna, yet remain distinct from him. Selves that are not freed are reborn repeatedly, until **liberation** is finally achieved, although there is a self that is not touched by this involvement in *samsara*, the cycle of birth and rebirth. There are two ways of looking at the self, *atman* or the self that is in contact with *brahman*, absolute reality, and *jiva*, or the temporal aspect of this unchangeable self. Death is really of little consequence, it is going to take place many times within the cycle of change, and the more that the person can disregard it the more likely he or she is to transcend the cycle eventually and attain *moksha* or escape. Of course, the **materialists** such as the Lokayata have few problems in discussing death, which is merely a rearrangement of the material parts of the human being, leading to the dissolution of the person.

One of the main differences between the role of death in Buddhist philosophy and Hinduism is that in the former there is taken to be no eternal self that continues through many changes of the material aspect of the person. On the other hand, Buddhist thinkers certainly do not want to argue that nothing remains after death. What lasts is *karma*, the consequences of our actions and the actions of others, and what we should do to try to escape from this process is to abandon our trust in the reality of the world and the existence of a real single self. We seem to remember aspects of our past lives, but these are not really aspects of *our* past lives, but combinations of moments that took place to something linked loosely with who we are now. Death is not very significant in that it is going to lead to the dissolution of the particular combinations of impulses and motives and replace these with another combination within a new form. If **enlightenment** is achieved, then death is a significant event, since it stops the whole process of rebirth. Death is always a significant event in the round of rebirth, since it is the point of transition from one body to another, but it has no importance in itself. The Buddha compares the body and the mind to a clay pot and the oil in it. When it is thrown into a pool of water, the pot breaks up and disintegrates, but the oil rises to the surface. The body is only the container of the *chitta* or **mind**, and the fact that we die is merely a reflection of the truth that everything that is created will come to an end. The Daoist thinker Zhuangzi is particularly interesting on the appropriate attitude to death. This is that we should liberate ourselves from the fear of death, even though there is no hope of life after death or salvation through a divine intervention, but just through an acknowledgement of the natural course of events. Zhuangzi is an exception to the normal Daoist view here, which emphasizes the pursuit of physical immortality and longevity.

Within Japanese Shinto thought death and the way of dying has been a much discussed topic. This has often been through the incorporation of Confucian ideals of regarding fear of death as a weakness to be overcome in the superior individual. A code of conduct, *bushido*, was constructed, based on a notion of honour that was entirely dependent on loyalty to a ruler or leader, so that the self itself was submerged into the code. Death becomes of little significance since all that is important is living one's life in a selfless and controlled way.

The zen thinker Suzuki contrasted Eastern and Western views of death. According to the latter, death is the end of life, and the individual needs to overcome death in order to gain eternal life. Yet Buddhist philosophy regards life and death as not contraries but aspects of the same thing, and the aim is to achieve *nirvana*, release from the cycle of life and death.

According to the Islamic philosophers al-Kindi and Abu Bakr al-Razi there is no reason to fear death. For one thing, it represents the release, in true Platonic fashion, of the eternal soul back to the realm of eternal ideas, and so is surely not to be regretted. Also, al-Kindi argues that for a human being, death is inevitable, since it is part of what is involved in being a human being, and we cannot wish that an essential part of who we are should not be as it is, since that is irrational. Al-Razi adds that death brings an end to suffering and pain, and so is to be welcomed. But does not death also bring an end to pleasure? It does, and this is also to be welcomed, since what we call pleasure is more or less identical with the absence of or relief from pain, so when we die we are saved from having to try to escape from such unpleasantness.

Further reading: Allinson 1989a, *Bhagavad Gita* 1994, Bowker 1991, Boyce 1975, Filippi 1996, Hiriyanna 1932, Nasr and Leaman 1996, Tsunoda *et al.* 1964, Zaehner 1975.

democracy Chen Duxiu. the founder of the Chinese Communist Party, put democracy firmly at the front of the aims of political progress in China. Only the introduction of democratic institutions could replace the old feudal system. But the connection between democracy and communism was to be explored in much more detail later. Mao Zedong's essay 'On New Democracy' suggests that the initial stages of revolutionary progress will involve an alliance across different classes and a mixed economy. This will foster national liberation, and is a feature of communism in semi-feudal and semi-colonial societies, which cannot just move to the stage of encouraging one class to take over from another. There are three features of this new democracy. The new culture was to be national and independent, scientific (very much a theme of Chen also) and part of a mass culture, serving all the people. It is important to grasp that democracy is not at all to be understood in the sense of liberal democracy, but in rule of the people by those who encapsulate the interests of the people, the revolutionaries. The liberal notion of democracy was defended by Sun Yatsen, but the failure of the 1911 revolution led to a lot of questioning of how appropriate such basically Western models of government are in China. Even Sun had problems in reconciling the ideals of democracy with the demands of nationalism and social upheaval. Often the discussions of liberal democracy within a Chinese context seem just to be a direct import from the West, as with Hu Shi's application of Dewey's argument that education is the best way of introducing and maintaining democracy. Zhang Dongsun pursued the notion of socialist democracy, where there is a combination of a political system that represents the views of the people and a system with social and economic ends in view.

Most of the Islamic philosophers in the classical period were highly suspicious of democracy, which they related to one of Plato's corrupt forms of society. It is a society in which the rational members are subdued by the power and numbers of the masses, representing the body overcoming reason, and this can only end in disaster. A problem with incorporating democracy within a religious context is that it is difficult to see how authority can really flow from the decisions of the majority if the religious authorities have independent access to the truth. Some Islamic thinkers have argued that the notion of democracy is implicit in the structure of Islam itself, and its institutions such as *shura* or consultation, but this is far-fetched.

Further reading: Adelmann 1982, Cheng 1989, Leaman 1985, Mao 1961.

dependent origination   According to Buddhist philosophy, the only thing that comes about without being dependent on preceding conditions is *nirvana*. Everything else, including the aspects of human **personality**, are part of the world of conditioned arising or dependent origination. This is far more complex than just referring to the fact that there are **causal** links in the world, it is a principle of the illusory nature of phenomenal reality. The basis of the whole process is what are sometimes called the twelve links of the causal wheel of dependent origination:

1 **Ignorance** (*avidya*) of the **Four Holy Truths**, which results in belief in the reality of what we experience. This is followed by
2 Conceptualization, where our self is shaped by karmic forces to make distinctions about that experience. Then we arrive at
3 Discernment

4 The combination of the **mind** and the body
5 The six sense organs
6 The fact that the mind can receive sense impressions
7 The ability to feel
8 Craving, which is the basis of suffering
9 Grasping and clinging to things
10 Becoming, or the continuing processes of change that make up life
11 Birth, and then the whole process comes to a temporary end when it reaches
12 **Death**, and all the experiences that we encounter on the way to this form of *dukkha* or suffering.

This sequence is an attempt at answering a series of connected questions, beginning at the bottom. We start off by wondering why we suffer death and old age. The answer is because we are born, and we are born because of a desire to be born. There is such a desire because we wish to become, and this is because we cling to the things of this world. We cling in this way because we crave to enjoy those things, and we have that craving because of our faculty of sense-experience. We have that faculty because we have contact with objects that stimulate the sense organs. We have these organs because of our physical constitution. We have that constitution because of the ways in which we have physically and mentally developed. What causes that form of development? The answer is our *karma*. That *karma* comes about through our ignorance, through our acting in ways that do not acknowledge the real nature of what exists.

The importance of this concept is that it is supposed to show that there can be no such thing as a real self, nor any permanence in the world of experience. All that exists is a flow of conditioned states, with no persisting self or object behind it. One thing becomes another in the way in which a seed becomes a plant, when the appropriate causes apply to it. The important point here is that the thesis is taken to be a middle position between the idea that new things come from nothing, and that they are merely new aspects of something that continues to persist. The only way to bring this cycle to an end is through cultivating the sort of **knowledge** capable of replacing ignorance.

See: **anatman**
Further reading: Conze 1962, Dreyfus 1997, Gombrich 1997, Hoffman 1987, Jayatilleke 1986, Kalupahana 1975, Williams 1989.

desire – *see* **love**

destiny – *see* **karma**

dhamma, order, morality, teaching of the Buddha – *see* **dharma**

dharma   A Sanskrit term for the notion of order in the universe. Each creature in Hinduism is regarded as having its own proper way of living. As for human beings, what is important is the **caste** one belongs to, whether one is a man or woman, and what stage of life one is at. In the **Bhagavad Gita** the term used is *svadharma*, and is equivalent to what is helpful socially and also leads to personal **harmony**. It is often used in the sense of treating other things or people as we would treat ourselves, hence the identification of this term with duty.

The notion is developed in very sophisticated and distinct ways in Buddhism, which tends to use the Pali term *dhamma*. If we fail to grasp our *dhamma*, we fail to act in accordance with reality, and so end up suffering (**dukkha**). One of the main purposes of the teaching of the Buddha is to help us understand the nature of our *dhamma* and then follow it, which results in **enlightenment** or **bodhi**. The precise status of *dhamma* has become an issue of great controversy in Buddhist ontology, given that some schools represent it as existing independently of our awareness of it, which has seemed to some thinkers to multiply entities unnecessarily. It is often referred to as representing the way or path that the Buddhist should follow.

Further reading: Gombrich 1971, 1988, Williams 1989, Zaehner 1969.

dhawq, taste, experience of reality – *see* **Sufism**

dhikr, remembrance, experience of reality – *see* **Sufism**

dhyana – *see* **meditation, zen**

dravya – *see* **Vishishtadvaita**

duhkha, suffering – *see* *dukkha*

dukkha A Pali term (*duhkha* in Sanskrit) meaning pain or suffering. It has a wider reference than the ordinary English term, in that even ordinary events which might seem to be quite pleasant are describable as *dukkha*, because they are unreliable and contingent, and relying on them for happiness is to ensconce oneself in suffering. Everything within the cycle of rebirth, **samsara**, is *dukkha*, since it is all impermanent and unstable. *Dukkha*, **anicca** and **anatta** are the three criteria of imperfect and contingent existence, and transcending them is necessary if one is to achieve perfection (**nibbana**).

Further reading: Griffiths 1994, Warder 1980.

Dvaita This Indian realist doctrine adheres to belief in a personal deity, in this case Vishnu, and is marked by its commitment to pluralism, 'Dvaita' meaning 'philosophy of the two'. God is the efficient **cause** of the world, and his existence is established by scripture itself, since it is beyond

reason to prove his existence. The material cause of the world
is matter, and Madhva rejected the idea of making God the
material cause, since this would interfere with his transcendence. There is a similar account of **creation** as with the
Sankhya, with the exception that the three *guna*s of *sattva*,
rajas and *tamas* are not regarded as parts of matter but are its
first effects. These are the fundamental qualities of the pure,
the dynamic and the immobile which characterize the
material world. Matter (*prakriti*) is not in any way illusory,
but is real and eternal, the object of God's knowledge and
creativity.

Why do the Dvaitins think that difference is a real phenomenon? The **Advaitins**, by contrast, reject its reality on the
grounds that it is a relative notion, relative on an understanding of the objects between which the relation is taken
to hold. Yet once one grasps the objects, there is nothing
left for the relation to show, since it is equivalent to the
objects which differ themselves. The Dvaitins counter with
the argument that the difference between two things is not
something else, but just a quality that is expressible through
the essences of the two things. Then when we say that there
is a difference between two things, what we mean is that
each thing is itself. Each thing is unique, and so each thing
has as part of its essence the quality of being different from
everything else. But this is not another thing, just another
way of looking at the essence itself. There are five main
examples of difference (*bheda*), and these are between God
and self, the different selves, God and matter, self and
matter, and between different forms of matter itself. Although
these things are different, this should not be taken to imply
that they are independent of each other, and the body is
obviously taken to be dependent on its soul, and the world
on God. There are ten categories of being, and there is an
interesting theory of substance. According to Madhva, a
substance may have qualities that last as long as it does,
but it may not. In the former case the substance is identical to its properties, while in the latter we would expect
him to say that it is not. In fact, he argues that in this sort

of case the relation is both identity and difference. It is identity when 'the property applies to the substance, but difference when the substance changes. If there were no difference, then when the property left, so would the thing itself that had been characterized by it. Take a piece of cloth and its colour. Is the cloth identical with its colour? We tend to talk of the colour of the cloth, which implies there is a distinction between them, and so not identity. This leads to the general thesis that it is acceptable to analyse things that appear to be identical as having differences that are not immediately obvious.

God is unknowable through even revelation, and certainly through reason, but it is possible to acquire some idea of him. God is the only really independent thing. There exist an infinite number of souls, **atomic** in structure and with their own qualities of imperfection and suffering due to their individual character. There are three kinds of such souls, those that are bound but can be freed, those that are eternally part of the cycle of birth and rebirth, and finally those that are eternally damned and in hell. The ultimate source of the phenomenal world is matter, which produces effects that are both existent and non-existent before they are produced. The material cause cannot be the effect, and when the effect has been produced, the cause is both existent and non-existent. It exists since it was effective in producing the effect, but it may be that it no longer exists in the way it did when it produced the effect. It exists through the effect, yet also to a degree does not exist any longer, since its role in the pattern of change has now come to an end.

Madhva is a thoroughgoing realist, arguing that there can be no knowledge without reference to an object, an object in space and **time**. Even illusions have a reality about them, in the sense that what observers thought they saw they did indeed see, all that they got wrong was the precise nature of the object which the experience purported to describe at a particular place and/or time. A rope that is mistaken for a snake does lead to an experience of a snake, albeit the snake is not actually where it appears to be.

The ignorance of human beings leads to their lives in *samsara*, this ignorance hiding from us both the nature of God and our own nature. Self-knowledge is important, but knowledge of God is even more important, and through study of religious texts and **meditation** one could achieve bliss and **liberation**, yet the self will remain distinct from other selves. It is only when we understand the nature of God that we can look forward to complete and infinite bliss. To attain this end involves constant **love** and devotion in our attitudes to God, resulting in divine grace possibly saving us. The processes involved here are the usual selfless devotion to duty and performing that duty in a spirit of complete detachment, through the study of scripture with an appropriate teacher, reflection on what one is taught and continual meditation. The final stage is the direct perception of God, which can only be achieved through God's grace, and is only given if the appropriate preparatory steps are taken. God in the Dvaita approach of Madhva is definitely a personal God.

Further reading: Carr and Mahalingam 1997, Hiriyanna 1985, Radhakrishnan 1966, Radhakrishnan and Moore 1957, Raju 1985.

dzogchen, great symbol or perfection school of yoga – *see* **Tibetan philosophy**

E

education Confucius concentrated in much of his thought on the nature of education. He insisted that the aim of education was not to achieve a practical end, but that it was an end in itself. The content of education should be literature, virtuous behaviour, faithfulness and sincerity, and education should be open to anyone who is capable of undertaking it. Interestingly, he did not seem to value science, and placed most emphasis on practical **knowledge**, knowing how to apply one's ideas to the social world. His ideas of education are very hierarchical, and there is constant emphasis on stability and **harmony**. Finally, there is to be a spiritual direction to education, and the material aspects of acquiring knowledge are relatively unimportant. Morality is both the basis and the primary end of education. There is no point in knowing anything unless one is first of all a morally upright person. Real learning has as its point the self. The Confucian scholar, *ju*, cultivates himself, but this does not mean that he turns his back on the rest of society. On the contrary, self-cultivation is necessary to bring into harmony our relationships with human beings as a whole. This should not be taken to suggest that the point of education is to harmonize social relations, since for Confucius the value of education is part of the process itself, not due to any effect it might have. The purpose of education is self-cultivation. The metaphor often used is of strengthening the root (self-cultivation) in order that the branches (the organization of the family and the state) flourish and grow. If we try to do it the other way round, by first imposing order on society in the hope that people will learn to live harmoniously as a result, we violate the natural process of moral education. This will be ineffective, since social harmony can only come about through individual self-cultivation. Although the descriptions of Confucian self-cultivation look rather elitist, in that only the privileged few have the opportunity to do it, this is not really the case. The point of education is to learn to be human, and even those who will not be able to acquire the skills of reading and writing are encouraged to pursue their education as human beings. Human relations will be in harmony if people have cultivated themselves. There is no way that the individual can cultivate himself and ignore everyone else, since we are part of a community. This idea was taken up with enthusiasm by Japanese writers on education, and was translated by Motada Eifu into a national policy for Japan. He argued that the essence of national education should be the precise nature of the duties that constitute the relationship between the emperor and his subjects. This brings out the fluidity of Confucian ideas about education, since it was possible to reorganize the principles of Confucianism to stress national duties as opposed to other moral aims such as filial piety. Motada also sought to add to the Confucian duties the necessity to pursue natural science and technology.

Like most Indian thinkers, Gandhi was very much in favour of education. He advocated a system that started early on in a child's life, based on the local language and directed very much to character development. The rationale is to unite the body and the mind, and so develop a genuinely human individual.

In Islamic philosophy a good deal of significance is given to education and knowledge, and the **hadith** (saying of the Prophet) 'Seek knowledge even though it comes from China' was often used to defend the acceptability of importing new knowledge from a non-Islamic source. It is very much part of the tradition of Islamic philosophy that a sharp differentiation is made between different kinds of learner, so that the language of instruction has to be made appropriate to the audience. In this way the Qur'an is said to be written in a variety of ways, with a high intellectual content for those able to understand it at that level, and with a very imaginative and evocative vocabulary for those who cannot follow the arguments that lie beneath the surface. This is appropriate since God has created everyone differently, and so he has provided them all with a route to salvation and comprehension of deeper realities.

In recent years there have been many discussions about what the nature of an Islamic education would be, how it would differ from other forms of education, in particular secular varieties. There are some issues such as evolution on which some Muslims would wish education to express a degree of caution, but apart from that it is difficult to see how an Islamic education would differ from any other form of education, apart of course from the inclusion of work on Islam itself. The important feature of it would be that it would seek to construct a form of education of which the student and teacher was an organic part, given the all-encompassing nature of Islam. Education cannot be segregated from the religion of the participants, since their religion and their relationship to God is the most important part of their lives.

Further reading: Chambliss 1996, Chatterjee 1983, Creel 1953, Gandhi 1969.

emptiness Although the notion of emptiness is significant in most versions of Buddhism, it is crucial to Mahayana Buddhism. The argument goes that everything is without a nature, and so is empty. *Nirvana* or **enlightenment** is also empty, since it is realized through the acquisition of an empty **consciousness**. If everything is empty, both the material world and the perfect world, then we are also empty from an essential point of view, and we each share in this quality of being *shunya* or empty. The Mahayana use this as an argument for the availability of the **buddha nature** to everyone, since everyone shares emptiness, and if the buddha nature is empty, then it is the same sort of emptiness that is present in and has to be appreciated by everyone. How can we attain an understanding of emptiness, especially when we are to engage in a process that in itself is far from empty, but involves a great deal of theory and argument which is designed to help us to appreciate the emptiness of everything? The answer is that the words of the teaching are distinct from the teaching itself, and the words can lead us close to the point where we have to rely on ourselves and our experiences alone, to blend with the emptiness of the essence of the world which is the source of our own emptiness.

The **Madhyamaka** ('middle') school, which is usually linked with Nagarjuna, emphasized the emptiness of the key ideas of philosophy, such as the self, **causality**, motion, **time**, *karma*, and even *nirvana* and the Buddha. It seems likely that the stress on emptiness was designed to oppose the views of the **Abhidharma** school which often implies that there is some reality in the basic categories of the universe, and of course it might be used to counter all the 'orthodox' Hindu notions of what essentially exists. Nagarjuna and his followers thought that compromising on the notion of reality was going against the principles of Buddhism. After all, they argue that to appreciate the emptiness of everything is the same as absolute **knowledge**, and the objective of religion itself. As one might expect, the doctrine of emptiness came in for a lot of criticism, which Nagarjuna tries to rebut in his works. For example, it was argued that if everything is empty, then the thesis that everything is empty is itself empty, and so has no force. On the other hand, if the thesis is not empty, then it is not the case that everything is empty. If everything can be negated, then so can the thesis presented by Nagarjuna. Many similar objections are marshalled against him, some linked to the problems of self-referentiality and others questioning the accuracy with which the thesis fits in with Buddhist principles. His general reply is that it is important to distinguish between relative and absolute reality. Everything, he argues, is absolutely empty, but relatively real, since we have evidence for the latter from our experience. Nagarjuna accepts that in absolute terms all arguments are empty, but on the relative level it is acceptable to use them to show that one cannot stay at that level if one is going to make progress. There is a nice medical analogy which points out that if medicine is used to cure an illness, the medicine itself must also leave the system after having carried out its restorative function. The doctrine of emptiness should be used to cure ourselves of belief in the absolute reality of what we experience, and then it also should be expunged from our conceptual system, in just the same way that the Buddha after enlightenment was reluctant to speak and teach any more. The paradoxical strategy of claiming that everything is empty is none the less impossible to state, since it is self-refuting. But its supporters have a point in arguing that although the argument cannot be proposed, it could still be valid, although not once stated. In any case, one could always hold the emptiness doctrine as applying to the nature of reality, but not as describing our experience of the material world.

There was a lively debate within Tibetan philosophy on this point also. This was put in the form of reconciling what were called the three turnings of the wheel of doctrine. On the first turn the Buddha taught that everything exists, on the second that everything is empty, and on the third that some things exist and some do not. There was a great deal of argument as to what if anything was the Buddha's final view, and which if any of these views were provided for those unable to grasp or work with the final view. Some held that emptiness was the fact that things do not exist in themselves and do not have a nature of their own. This is the radical view of the second turn of the wheel, and advocates understanding emptiness as a non-affirming negation. The qualification is important, since nothing else must be put in the place of that which is denied. Others supported the third turn of the wheel view, and argued that emptiness is a matter of degree, with some things existing and yet also being empty if they do not possess any impurities or limitations. They point to the descriptions in Buddhism of the buddha nature

as having very much the characteristics of something permanent and real, indeed, the most real thing of all. Their opponents claim that such language is merely a way in which
the Buddha expressed himself to those who are incapable of
grasping the true message frankly stated.

In descriptions of the **dao** the role of emptiness or nothingness features significantly. There are many descriptions
of things that are empty, such as a bowl, a window, a valley
(which is defined in terms of what it is not, i.e. a mountain), which are used to emphasize the power of the weak.
These ideas were developed into a complex system by Wanbi,
who made the source of being non-being or nothingness.

In Chinese Buddhist philosophy this view came to be
criticized once the works of Nagarjuna were made available
in Chinese. The main problem was then seen to be that the
Daoist view is dualistic, and it asserts the existence of some
basic immaterial thing as the cause of everything else with
no evidence at all that any such thing exists. Daoism seems
to offer an account of what can be known, which was criticized by Buddhist philosophy which advocated the replacement of knowledge as an aim with the way of knowing.

According to the Tendai (*tien tai*) school in Japan, we need
to emphasize the unity of the **mind** with the world by using
the doctrine of Three Truths, and these are emptiness, the
temporary and the middle. Everything has no persistent
constant being in itself, and so everything is empty. Of course,
there is temporary existence and occasional natures, and this
is actually part of what it means to say that everything is
empty. That is, it is the temporary nature of natures, as it
were, that points towards their absolute emptiness. The middle
or true state is an acknowledgement of neither emptiness nor
the temporary as final descriptions of reality. The charge might
be brought that even a conclusion of 'no state' or 'no truth'
makes a truth claim, which appears to go against the general
thesis. Tendai argues that this is not an objection, since it
is a conclusion that goes beyond conceptual thought, and
relies on attaining enlightenment. This conclusion was highly
influential in Japanese Buddhism, and various strategies were

adopted to prove the identity of the Three Truths. Nishida Kitaro also pursued the notion of nothingness as equivalent to absolute reality, which came to be the foundation of the Kyoto school of thought. The doctrine is given an existentialist flavour by Nishitani, who argued that the fact of the emptiness of the self and the world allows us to appreciate our total freedom and lack of essential dependence. Using concepts derived from Heidegger and Nietzsche, Nishitani brings in zen ideas to argue that the standpoint of emptiness leads us to question who we are and what the purpose of our lives is. It is the breaking up of the idea of the self that is important on the route to seeing the self as linked with everything else in reality, rather than as something individual and limited. From the point of view of emptiness opposites meet, including the self and non-self, being and non-being, the particular and the universal, and so on.

Further reading: Cabezon 1994, Carter 1989, Dilworth and Viglielmo 1998, Dreyfus 1997, Eckel 1992, Fung 1970, Garfield 1995, Huntington 1989, Inada 1970, Nishitani 1985, Streng 1967, Swanson 1989, Tsunoda *et al.* 1964, Williams 1989.

enlightenment What transformed the ordinary Siddharttha into **Buddha** was enlightenment, when he achieved *bodhi*. He often described himself as *tathagata*, the person who discovers and broadcasts the path to *nibbana*. There have subsequently been lively disputes about the precise nature of enlightenment. One reason why it is easy for there to be disputes is because Buddhism is not only a doctrine, but also a path, and there can be a lot of disagreement about what the path precisely means, and where it leads. A general theme is that enlightenment is reached when an appropriate attitude is adopted towards the world. Once we acknowledge our **ignorance**, we are on the way to enlightenment, and this is not necessarily restricted to those who withdraw from the world. According to the Mahayana tradition, we should distinguish between the form of *nirvana* achieved by someone like a monk, and the form of enlightenment available to everyone as shown by the Buddha and the **bodhisattvas**. There is a general Mahayana confidence that enlightenment is widely available, and can be achieved within one person's lifetime. This is often accompanied by a theory that all beings have the **buddha nature**, or even are Buddhas. This approach was taken to its logical conclusion in China by **chan** (zen), who argued that we are all Buddhas and all can achieve enlightenment suddenly. That is, we all have the buddha nature, and we can use it to adopt the correct attitude to the nature of reality, and once we do this we can break with **samsara** and immediately become enlightened.

According to **Yogachara** Buddhism, enlightenment can be achieved if we transfer unenlightened mental impulses away from ourselves through the following of religious practices. There are various approaches to how enlightenment may be realized, some arguing that what is required is gradual progress through many lives, while zen thinkers are in favour of sudden enlightenment, since only the present really exists. But their theory was more complex than this, and they also emphasized the importance for enlightenment of appropriate deeds. The point that Dogen made was that everyone had the buddha nature in the sense that everyone had it potentially. Everyone may at one time be the slave of illusion, but since they all innately possess the buddha nature, they can in principle and in practice throw off this ignorance and acquire enlightenment. The **Madhyamaka** school interprets enlightenment slightly differently, in that it tries to wean us away from our attachment to concepts, which it sees as a form of craving or desire. Of course, the route to doing away with concepts is through the use of concepts, and so this form of Buddhism is fond of self-subversive riddles and stories. Concepts only work at one level, and at a higher level of truth we have to transcend concepts if we are to achieve enlightenment. This form of enlightenment can never be expressed in **language**, which means that language can only take one part of the way to enlightenment. The final step has to be something that one does after receiving hints, in the form of paradoxical slogans and possibly even jokes.

A form of Buddhism that became popular in Japan is **Pure Land** Buddhism, which advocates reliance on the power of the Buddha who rules over the Pure Land (*Amida* in Japanese). Enlightenment is achieved through rebirth in the Pure Land as a result of the faith and actions that individuals have performed in their lives. Followers of this school differentiated between two paths to enlightenment. The sage could follow the very difficult path of spiritual exercises leading to enlightenment, and all that he or she had to rely on were the personal qualities and efforts of the individual. For the majority, though, there is concentration on the nature of Amida and the possibility of being helped by Amida's grace.

The possibility of enlightenment raises a large number of difficult but intriguing conceptual issues. Does enlightenment consist of degrees, or is it something that has to be realized all at once? Is the sort of ignorance from which enlightenment is the escape an error in perception, or is it part and parcel of the human **personality**? Is enlightenment more like opening one's eyes, or overcoming a bad and damaging habit? Is ethical, religious and social activity something to be cultivated as a necessary precondition of enlightenment, or is it something that flows automatically from it? Is enlightenment ineffable, or can we say something meaningful about it? What role does language have to play, and if the only role our concepts have is to say what enlightenment is not, how can students be taught the route to enlightenment? Finally, are **skilful means** of presenting the truth a necessary precondition of understanding the truth, or can they be disregarded in favour of direct experience of enlightenment?

The Confucian *xue* (learning) is etymologically linked to *jue* (enlightening), and brings out the close connection between **education** and enlightenment for Confucianism. It is possibly linked to the Daoist idea that in the search for dao we have to learn to lose ourselves. This is because there are aspects of the self that both Confucians and Daoists think we should lose, especially selfishness, possessiveness, material desires and attachment to mental and physical objects. This is not an argument in favour of **asceticism**, but rather the losing of these dispositions will open us to the experience of a deeper and more inclusive self. We do not require any outside agent to help us achieve enlightenment, what we need to do is find ourselves, the self that has been lost and which we want to bring home, as it were. The concept of *cheng* is important here, the idea that sincerity leads to enlightenment, and sincerity is just understanding the significance of the ordinary and banal acts of human life. Enlightening oneself involves enlightening others also, since to become properly self-cultivated one must pay attention to the needs of the community of which one is a part. Confucians use the idea of **harmony** through balancing the principles of change to argue that enlightenment is understanding the significance of our ordinary actions, which brings us into alignment with Heaven and Earth. In this way one can both transcend the world and remain part of it, by contrast with the Daoists and Buddhists who Confucians criticize for wanting to transcend this world completely.

There is a particularly interesting debate within the Buddhist tradition as to whether enlightenment can be sudden, as opposed to gradual. Some thinkers argued that for advanced *bodhisattva*s the Buddha taught the sudden method, while for everyone else he taught the gradual way, and this dichotomy provides a neat explanation for the diversity of paths that the Buddha mentions. It also incorporates the notion of skilful means (*upaya*) as part of the style of the teaching, which pays attention to the different levels of understanding and spiritual achievement of different audiences. The supporters of the sudden teaching suggest that enlightenment can occur outside temporal limitations and without our first having to look for it. There is a form of salvation linked to a synthetic notion of reality, which is a philosophy of the immediate, the eternal and the instantaneous, whereby things are grasped all at once, in an intuitive way. Gradualism, by contrast, is analytic and leads to the absolute through a gradual progression of various practices and techniques – moral and religious activities, **meditative** exercises, intellectual study – which are an effort to bring about salvation.

The term *tathagata* literally means 'thus gone' where this refers to someone who has attained the truth or who has the capacity to acquire the truth. He is a person who has detached himself from the burdens of life, in particular the things outside him and his own personality dispositions. He detaches himself from everything that limits us, and so his **mind** has expanded to infinity, but this does not mean that he has become a sort of self. It is precisely this issue that prevents the Buddha from wanting to say what precisely happens to the enlightened person after **death**. Saying he survives or does not survive implies the existence of a persistent self, in the first case one that continues, and in the second case, one that does not. Yet there is no self to be destroyed, so no self can be destroyed, nor can one persist. What falls away on death are the aspects of our personality linked to suffering, and what remains is free of dependence on anything else. The thinking itself that leads to enlightenment continues after death, characterized as it is by having no object and not being brought about by anything else in a **causal** manner. This enlightened thinking becomes equivalent to *nibbana*, and so is timeless, unique and blissful.

The Korean thinker Chinul presented an interesting synthesis of different accounts of enlightenment, which note the particular characteristics of sudden and gradual approaches to enlightenment. First, one can understand that one is a Buddha quite suddenly, which then prepares the route to the entrance of the Buddhist path. This initial achievement needs to be buttressed by gradual cultivation, since the sudden understanding requires continual refinement and improvement if it is to persist in the force it has to move the seeker in the appropriate direction. Finally, the experience of genuine awakening should be seen as the result of gradual cultivation.

In the Islamic world a movement in the nineteenth century came to be called the *Nahda* or enlightenment because it sought to incorporate some of the principles of the European Enlightenment within the Islamic world. This movement employed the rediscovered thought of ibn Rushd to argue for the significance of rationality and science, and the possibility of combining these with the basic principles of Islam. It led to the identification of enlightenment with modernity, and to a rejection of tradition. But the main discussion of mystical enlightenment is in **Sufi** thought, and the description of mystical progress is very similar to that of Buddhism and Indian thought.

See: *anatman, koan, moksha*
Further reading: Abe 1992, Angel 1994, Brockington 1996, Buswell 1983, Conze 1962, de Bary and Haboush 1985, Eckel 1992, Eliade 1969, Griffiths 1986, 1994, Heisig and Maraldo 1994, Jackson 1993, Karmay 1988, Nagao 1991, Nasr and Leaman 1996, Pye 1978.

eternity   Some of the accounts of the Buddha suggest that he is eternal, and rather like a deity. This is problematic, in that if he is eternal, then no one who is not already a Buddha could become a Buddha also. The eternity of the Buddha often came to be seen as one of the doctrines of what essentially exists, and so an appropriate object of attack by Buddhists.

Eternity is a highly controversial issue in Islamic philosophy, especially with respect to the creation of the world. Many philosophers within that tradition argued that the world must be eternal, which means that it is at best co-eternal with God, or that it flows eternally from his being, which means that God does not make decisions about what to do to **create** the world. On **illuminationist** views according to which God is the Light of Lights and the world radiates from him like light coming from its source in an eternal way, once again is some way from the traditional God of religion. Al-Ghazali claims that the arguments for the eternity of the world are unconvincing even if one defines time in terms of motion. If God creates the world at a particular moment, then the world started at that time, and there is no need to claim it is eternal. The time at which the world began was the time that time started, and God existed before that time eternally.

Mulla Sadra has an interesting way of resolving these difficulties about eternity. He argues that the world is eternal in the sense that it is in a constant state of change, and existence is always undergoing substantial change, so every new form of existence takes place in time. The world then comes about in time, and is also eternal in the sense of having no beginning or end, since time is not something independent of the existence of the world.

See: **time**
Further reading: Nasr and Leaman 1996, Ward 1998.

ethics   In Zoroastrian philosophy the requirement to do good will benefit one's soul. There is also a stress on the effect that evil actions can have on the world as a whole, and on other human beings. Early Zoroastrianism is constructed around the idea of a basic moral dualism between good and evil, and the world is taken to be the site of an enormous struggle between the forces of good and evil.

Some Indian theories of ethics are hedonistic, in particular that of the Charvaka or Lokayata, which advocates action in accordance with whatever brings most pleasure. 'Evil' means what brings suffering, and there is no transcendental level of ethical value. **Materialists** such as these will, of course, have no time for the idea of survival after **death** or spiritual exercises in order to achieve salvation. They could see no principle worth following except that of setting out to enjoy oneself as much as possible. This is a rare view, though, and the Jains by contrast see the soul as potentially transcendental albeit linked to the body by *karma*, represented by matter. We can free ourselves of this servitude by following a moral life, the Three Jewels (*triratna*) which are right conduct, right knowledge and right faith. The most important virtue to acquire and practise is *ahimsa* or non-violence, which is both the principle of not harming others and also helping others. This by itself will not lead to *moksha* or **liberation**, although it is important as part of the path. As is well known, the Jains are so intent to avoid harming other things that they will

111

often sweep the path in front of them to avoid stepping on insects, and when turning in their sleep will try to avoid crushing insects by brushing what they are lying on with their hands.

On the theory of *karma* in the Indian tradition, it looks very much as though there is no scope for free will and autonomous ethical decision-making. After all, one's actions affect not only one's future in this life, but in future lives also, so the intention to act in a particular way in a particular life is determined by what happened in a previous life. The **Nyaya-Vaisheshika** tried to get around this with their fruits of action theory. This suggests that while what happens at any particular time is the result of what happened in the past, the present can be controlled by one's will, and so the future will be directed by the will also. Thus there is scope for autonomous ethical decisions. Within the boundaries set by *karma* there is plenty of scope for ethical action, especially when one considers that there is divine help in the form of the scriptures. These set out which actions are to be followed, and which to be rejected, and if we follow them we can be confident that we are setting ourselves in the right direction. Also, it is worth pointing out that the fact that we are confined within the bounds of *karma* is a reflection of divine **justice**, merely reflecting the fact that we are responsible for our decisions and actions, and these will resonate through our lives. God makes available to us salvation, and it is for us to select the virtuous path to bring this about. The theory based on ethical action is **Mimamsa**, and it analyses ethical language in terms of our possibilities to act in particular ways. Our ability to change our character is dependent on the ways in which virtuous action may compensate for the effects of past bad actions, and its consequent *karma*, and the Mimamsa have a well-developed and interesting account of how ethics and the human character are interrelated.

According to Buddhism, the aim of morality is to get rid of *karma*, which links us with the natural world and which leads to suffering. The path to *nirvana* has eight aspects: right faith, right resolve, right speech, right thought, right action, right living, right effort and right concentration. Although the soul is not permanent, it is still capable of initiating **action**, and the more it fits in with an ethically valuable way of life, the more surely will it approach *nirvana* or salvation. **Meditation** is certainly not enough to achieve salvation, but an ethically acceptable lifestyle has a vital part to play also. This contrast between the virtues of the solitary and **ascetic** life, and the more social life of ethical behaviour runs throughout Buddhism, and acquired enormous theoretical elaborations in later developments of the theory.

In Chinese philosophy there are basic distinctions between the ethical views of the **Confucians**, **Daoists**, **Mohists** and **Legalists**. According to Confucius, morality is the most important theoretical topic to be analysed. Morality is the basis of all philosophy, and consists of a combination of a conception of **humanity** (*ren*) and righteousness (*yi*). The notion of the morally self-cultivated man plays a crucial role in Confucius' system, the individual who acts in accordance with his social status, loves all humanity, treats others as he treats himself and adheres to objective principles of justice. Righteousness is acquired through education in the ways in which the community manages to bring its varying interests into harmony. An aspect of this is the pursuit of *li*, the rituals of the community, which generally, but not always, embody how humanity ought to behave. Mozi, the creator of Mohism, has a slightly different understanding of humanity, which he interprets as universal **love**, and which by contrast with Confucius he understands in a non-hierarchical way. He presents a kind of utilitarian view of ethics, although with its basis being the interests of the community at large, not individual pleasures and pains. The Legalists had a rather pessimistic view of **human nature**, and emphasized the role of **law** in regulating society so that people can pursue their interests and avoid harm. The supreme moral principle of some varieties of Daoism is detachment from the world, and so one might imagine that there would not be much in the way of an ethical system. The Daoists are often suspicious of the whole notion of the individual who sees himself primarily as a moral agent, since he is setting out to intervene in society, a crucial error for Daoism. The appropriate end for human beings is personal serenity, so what we ought to do is accept things as they are. There is also the point that since the basis of reality, the dao, is itself nameless and undifferentiated, morality rests on nothing, and right and wrong have no foundation in anything except the arbitrary behaviour of people. On the other hand, Daoist writings and traditions are full of worthy sentiments and instructions on how to live decently, and these are often very similar to those of the Confucians.

In Islamic philosophy there was a prolonged argument about whether ethics is objective or subjective. If the former, then God commands us to do what is good in itself, and he is as constrained in giving those commands as we are by the nature of the good itself. On the other hand, if ethics are subjective then what 'good' means is what God commands, and there are no constraints on those commands at all beyond his will.

See: **Ash`ariyya and Mu`tazila**, *atman, de*
Further reading: Aronson 1980, Basham 1971, Brockington 1996, Carr and Mahalingam 1997, Chatterjee 1996, Hoshino 1997, Hourani 1985, Keown 1992, LaFleur 1992, Leaman 1985, Peerenboom 1993, Watson 1967.

evil   According to Zarathustra, one's evil actions and thoughts can be transformed in our lives by good ones, and so need not be the basis of future punishment. There is also the future possibility that **Angra Mainyu**, the evil forces, will be finally defeated by the good, and then there will no more evil in existence. The material world derives its meaning from its role as the site of the struggle between good and evil. Evil is the opposite of good, and only the latter really exists in the sense that evil has to be defined in opposition to good. The basic principles of religion are the awareness of the distinction between **Ohrmazd** and **Ahriman**, the good and the evil forces, and in practice it is important to treat the cosmic struggle between good and evil as an aspect of the individual's struggle against wrongdoing and impurity in everyday actions and thoughts. What makes evil so potent is the fact that it is not initially based in the body, and so finds it easy to move from body to body, invading any matter that does not deny it place. What makes evil ultimately vulnerable is the fact that since it is immaterial, if everyone were to purify their bodies and minds to forbid evil access it would be completely destroyed.

In the theory of what might be regarded as evil presented in the **Upanishads**, it is firmly identified with error, and in particular with the error of misunderstanding the nature of *atman*, the self. Really this self or soul is the same for everyone, eternal and only accessible through *moksha* or **liberation**, when we transcend our individuality and contingency. When we regard ourselves as different selves, which then encourages us to seek to benefit ourselves at the expense of other selves, we sink into error and evil, become selfish and turn away from what we have in common with the rest of humanity and creation. An advantage of the doctrines of rebirth and *karma* is that they bypass the traditional problem of evil. The fact that suffering in one life can be explained on moral faults in a previous life looks fair, as does the fact that sufferings in this life might be rewarded by joys in a future life, provided that one acts in such a way to help bring this about. The **materialists** argue that on the contrary there is nothing to justify the distribution of pleasures and pains in this life, and there is nothing after this life that could take on this justificatory role. In Buddhism there are extensive lists of particular forms of evil, taken to their greatest sophistication perhaps by the **Sarvastivada** school which presents a highly complex theory of the human mind in terms, partially, of the different forms of evil dispositions that we can acquire.

In Chinese thought there is clearly no point in human beings blaming **heaven** for the existence of evil, since this is equivalent to blaming someone else for one's own failings. Evil is not something independent of us which sometimes affects us, on the contrary, it is a feature of humanity and arises when we fail to realize ourselves completely. We in practice never do realize ourselves completely, and so evil is

115

always there, but in principle we could, since **human nature** in itself is good. The reason evil manages to get working is due to the way human nature is embedded in concrete life, and this brings with it a whole range of difficulties in our access to the real essence of that human nature.

Many of the Islamic philosophers identified being with good, and evil with non-being, so that the way the universe is constructed is good while the actions and the results of the actions of human beings are often evil, since these result from our desires and mistaken ideas, and go against the rational constitution of reality itself. They often identified evil with matter, since the material aspect of our world is taken to resist the imposition of the rational and ultimately divine form that changes everything above our world, and our material side gets in the way of the full sway of reason over our lives. We progressively liberate ourselves in so far as we concentrate on the spiritual and abstract aspects of our lives, and remove ourselves from our material needs and desires.

Further reading: Chan 1972, Creel 1953, Fakhry 1983, 1997, Karmay 1988, Ling 1981, 1997.

existence   A doctrine of existence is an important part of any theory that describes a particular notion of reality. **Materialist** theories tend to accept that the everyday objects of the world really exist, albeit possibly only in **atomic** form. Theories that see the world as in a radical sense misleading are going to question the real existence of what we see before us in different ways. According to the **Sankhya** school, for instance, when we perceive something in the external world it really exists, and its real existence is what **causes** it to appear to us in a particular way. However, this view of what really exists is only a limited grasp of what really exists from our point of view, since at a deeper level anything that comes from matter is quite superficial and in fact we approach nearer to what really exists when we transcend the ordinary attitude which we have to the world of experience and regard it as *maya* or **illusion**.

The relationship between essence and existence is a controversial one in Islamic philosophy. While most philosophers agreed that there is a logical distinction between the concept of a thing and the existence of that thing, the precise nature of their interrelationship was a topic of much debate. According to ibn Sina and al-Ghazali, there is no ontological connection between them, and something has to move an essence into existence if it is to be instantiated. For ibn Rushd, by contrast, it is part of the essence or meaning of a thing that it either exists or does not exist, and this is not a feature that can be arbitrarily added or taken away from it without affecting what it means. **Illuminationist** philosophy also generally accepts the priority of essence over existence, claiming that it is existence and not essence that is a derived mental concept. If existence has a reality outside of the **mind**, the real must be the principle of the reality of existence together with the being of existence, which involves a reference to something outside of the mind. Its reference outside the mind must itself consist of two things, and so on in an infinite regress. So if existence refers to something that exists, there must be another existence that is connected to it which makes it real, and so on ad infinitum. We can only avoid this absurdity by regarding existence as a derived mental concept and not an actual being. This fits in nicely with an ontology based on light, of course, since existence is then nothing but an idea that may be indicated, but not defined, by a gradation of light. This approach to the priority of essence was later challenged by Mulla Sadra who argued that existence is equivalent to reality and essence is only a mental concept. He tried to avoid the charge of setting up an infinite regress by arguing that existence can be an accidental aspect of an essence, but it can also be an integral part of the latter, in which case the regress does not get started, since if it is an essential attribute then one need not look for some further form of existence to which it refers.

This theory produced by Mulla Sadra is a creative development of the illuminationist account of al-Suhrawardi, who had analysed essences in terms of ranges of intensities, given their

117

ultimate dependence of degrees of light. For al-Sunrawardi it is the same essence that comes to be characterized in different ways. Mulla Sadra used this theory, replacing essence with existence, and thus concluding that it is the same existence that takes place, but it has different characteristics. Reality is pure existence, and that existence is experienced in different ways, describable in terms of different essences. When reality is experienced by the mind it is described in terms of essences, and we tend to confuse the reality of existence with the mental constructs we form about it.

See: **being**
Further reading: Hiriyanna 1932, 1985, Larson 1969, Leaman 1997, Nasr and Leaman 1996.

fa This means law, and was a term much used by the Chinese philosophers called **Legalists**. It covers not only legislation, in particular the commands and punishments of the ruling authorities, but also the central institutions of the state. The idea that what is required for social and personal stability is a strong state with rigorously applied law was a reflection of turbulent times, when older ideas of how one ought to live, in particular *li*, were in abeyance. Legalists are critical of past norms of behaviour, arguing that new rules need to be established. They hold that human beings are essentially egoistic, and require strong sanctions if they are to be prevented from serving themselves and disrupting society. The notions of the **Confucians** and the **Mohists** that people can be encouraged to behave well through the pursuit of learning and the following of exemplars was rejected.

This theory might seem to be based entirely on respect for power, but it became more complicated when developed by Han Fei. He gave the theory a Daoist turn. At the level of **nature**, everything is structured in terms of opposites (there is an obvious application here of the *Yi jing*) and people try to establish a natural position after creating a particular balance between the opposites. Everything changes, and when one thinks that they are stable, this means that they are about to change yet again. Once things become extreme, it means that they are about to collapse, and what we ought to do is stay

119

in control of ourselves so as to prevent the development of an extreme. Finally, we ought to appreciate how prudence and wisdom regulate our behaviour by getting us to use opposites to moderate our dispositions. The information we require is that which tells us what laws are in operation here, so that we can predict what is going to happen and control change. We need to follow the dao and fit our lives into the objective pattern of events. This is an interesting use of **Daoism**, which one might think would be incompatible with Legalism, especially given the Daoist doctrine that more is less, that one should do everything by doing nothing. Particular rulers would no doubt find it very difficult to follow the dao, since they are likely to be overcome by their emotions and ambitions. On the other hand, there is no reason why the notion of law should not seek to fit in with the general pattern of how one sees everything developing, and in fact if there is a dialectical law of transformation, then law should be part of it. Law is taken to represent the criterion that distinguishes between right and wrong, and so it is a clear and perspicuous guide to action. By contrast, the Confucian doctrine of private morality and obedience to ritual is criticized for being ambiguous.

Further reading: Chan 1972, Creel 1953, Watson 1967.

faith   The notion of faith is dealt with entirely differently in Buddhism as compared with the Judaeo-Christian tradition. The dichotomy between faith and reason is not applicable to Buddhism at all. Reason and faith cannot really be in conflict, since what is proved to be true in accordance with the Buddhist canon is also provable in accordance with reason. To a certain extent this is because neither faith nor reason gets us to the truth itself, but only part of the way on the path to the truth. Since what constitutes **enlightenment** cannot be put in words, there are no propositions that need to be assessed on the basis of faith and/or reason. Only two kinds of Buddhism stress faith, **Pure Land** and **Nichiren** Buddhism. The former is based on the worship of a particular conception of the **Buddha**, while the latter emphasizes the *Lotus Sutra* over every other text, and they do seem to call for faith if salvation is to be possible.

The apparent contrast between faith and reason is much discussed in Islamic philosophy, often as a result of the rather embattled nature of many of the philosophers in their dealings with the forces of religious orthodoxy. Ibn Rushd argued that it does not matter that philosophy came from non-Islamic sources, in the same way that it does not matter where a tool comes from, so long as it is used in an acceptable manner from a religious point of view. He goes on to suggest that philosophy and religion are merely two sides of the same coin, as it were, with religion being the more popular version of the truth which philosophy describes in more abstract terms. This was very much of a theme of philosophy, that religion and philosophy are different ways of approaching the same subject matter. Such a view came in for a good deal of criticism by those who were worried at the apparently irreconcilable differences between faith and reason, and what is interesting about such criticisms is that they are often produced from a philosophical view. That is, they do not argue that philosophy contradicts faith and so must be rejected, but argue that the sort of philosophy that contradicts faith is bad philosophy and should be replaced by better philosophy which can be shown to fit in with faith. So, for example, al-Ghazali uses the metaphysics of ibn Sina to criticize the conclusions that the latter drew from it, and ibn Taymiyya used the Aristotelian logic of which he disapproved in order to show how unsatisfactory it is.

Further reading: Hick 1997, Leaman 1985, Rodd 1980, Yampolsky 1990.

falasifa, philosophers – *see* **God**, **Islamic philosophy**

falsafa, philosophy – *see* **Islamic philosophy**

fatalism   Some of the teachings of Indian philosophy are fatalistic. For example, the Ajivika school argued that fate (*niyati*)
governs both the cycle of birth and rebirth and also individual lives. Suffering is not attributed to past actions, but
just takes place without any cause or rationale, as does relief
from suffering. There is then nothing that we can do to
achieve *moksha*, we just have to hope that all will go
well with us. The **materialists** also reject the possibility
of release, since we are part and parcel of the process of
causality, and what is due to happen to us will happen
to us. There is no such thing as free will, and everything is
at the disposal of fate. This was criticized by Buddhism as
implying that there is no point in achieving self-control or
virtue, since what will happen will happen. So one might
as well live a riotous and sensuous life. But the Ajivikas
were committed to **asceticism**, and they justified this in
terms of its practice being just as determined by fate as
anything else. The Lokayata tended to argue against fatalism,
impressed by the idea that things act freely according to
their natures. Yet is it not the case that the normal theory
of *karma* suggests that our actions are controlled by causality
not only in the natural world, but in the moral world also?
Then how free are we to make our own decisions about
how to behave? It might be argued that this theory is not
fatalistic in an objectionable sense, since all that it suggests is
that our moral character is affected by earlier decisions that
we take, some of which may even come from previous
lives. To be free does not necessarily mean that our actions
and thoughts are entirely unconstrained, but rather that we
are able to make decisions within a context that has already
been fixed for us. Human action sets up dispositions that are
to a degree under our control, and it is for us to decide how
far we are going to control them. For example, being charitable may make us feel good, and it may also make us think
that we are better people than in fact we are. We cannot do
much about the first feeling, but we can operate on the
accompanying feeling and try to prevent it developing into
a character trait.

The Buddha described his doctrine as being the middle way, and one of the dichotomies that it is supposed to fall between is that between fatalism and freedom. The doctrine that represents this middle position is **dependent origination** (*pratityasamutpada*), according to which every event is caused by some preceding event, but in such a complex way that there is scope for choice and even chance. In the ordinary world everything is governed by causality, everything is then relative to something else. It is not absolutely real, since it is subject to **death** and decay, nor is it absolutely unreal, since it takes place at some level of experience. At the source of all the causal links in the world of experience is **ignorance**, which leads us to make judgements about the world and pursue our desires. Our present world has the appearance it has because of the impressions of the *karma*s of previous lives, which will shape our future life. The notion of shape is important here, though, and distinguishes the position from that of fatalism. Our ideas are shaped by the past, but not in such a way that we have no choice as to how to think or what to seek. We should remember that this is supposed to be a middle position between extremes. We are not entirely free to do what we like, since what we are and what our environment is like is shaped by the past. On the other hand, we are not entirely unfree either, since it would be wrong to think of the self or the things of the world as having stable natures which force agents to move in certain directions. Fatalism is avoided if the Buddha is correct in thinking that he managed to describe a more moderate interpretation of the limitations of human thought and action.

See: **afterlife, ethics**, *samsara*
Further reading: Basham 1971, Conze 1962, Dundas 1992, LaFleur 1983, Nagao 1991.

fo shing – *see* **buddha nature**

Four Holy Truths – *see* **Four Noble Truths**

Four Noble Truths The contents of enlightenment in Buddhism (*ariya saca* in Pali; *arya satya* in Sanskrit) and the end of the process of seeking to attain **enlightenment**. The truths are suffering (*dukkha*), what leads to it, what can prevent it, and how to achieve the latter. It is not clear what the nature of these truths is until the state of enlightenment is reached, at which point all becomes clear about the precise nature of what is involved in suffering and what the nature of desiring (Pali *tanha*; Sanskrit *trishna*) is. There are various ways of describing the truths. They start with the idea of constant rebirth as part of the cycle of birth and rebirth, albeit with no permanent soul being reconstituted. Suffering through participation in the cycle starts off as dependence on causes which lead to desire and so, of course, ignorance. *Nirvana* is available if we manage to free ourselves from the bondage of *samsara* and ignorance. Finally, the last truth is that there is a path to *nirvana*, and to get on to this path we must acknowledge the absence of a real self and the **momentariness** of everything.

The basic idea is that life is frustrating and subject to *dukkha*, and that every aspect of the human **personality** consists of suffering, so that everything is really of dubious value. We get into this situation through the phenomenon of desire, which leads to the cycle of birth and rebirth, but if we manage to bring these desires to an end, we can destroy suffering and enter *nirvana*. Finally, the route to ending suffering is the Eightfold Path, which involves cultivating various types of virtue, **meditation** and wisdom. At the end of the process of meditation and charitable action, the *bodhisattva* comes to know the Four Noble Truths as they really are, and on the Mahayana tradition at the same time learns how to make a useful contribution to society.

See: **afterlife, dependent origination**
Further reading: Conze 1962, Dreyfus 1997, Guenther 1972, Smart 1964.

friendship In Islamic philosophy the discussion of friendship was heavily influenced by its treatment by Aristotle, regarded by many of the *falasifa* as 'the first master'. Miskawayh is the thinker who wrote the most developed work on friendship, and he provided an account that gives friendship an important social role, given its function in cementing conventional relationships in the state. Friendship is the rationale for many of the institutions of religion, which are designed precisely to use our social links with each other to strengthen our disposition to act in the correct way from an Islamic point of view. So the institution of gathering in the mosque on a Friday, for instance, is designed to bring different people together and make a pleasant social occasion support a religious obligation. By contrast, al-Ghazali argues that friendship is not of primary importance in the structuring of our religious duties, which have as their rationale solely that they have been demanded of us by God.

Within **Confucian** thought the value of friendship is restricted to the bonds that hold groups of scholars together, or similar groups of like-minded individuals. Within such a group, though, friendship is very important and the rules that it observes are strict and comprehensive. The arrival of **Neodaoist** thought added a more emotional understanding to the notion of friendship, which had previously been largely based on ritual. On the other hand, within Chinese thought as a whole it is difficult to find a notion of friendship that transcends the overriding social links between individuals.

Further reading: Leaman 1996.

fundamentalism   The basis of Islamic fundamentalism is the attempt to revive and reformulate the force of Islam in the modern world. It sees the world of Islam as in constant opposition to *jahaliyya*, the term for paganism that has come to include everything that can be seen as antagonistic to Islam. There are two basic views on how we should organize our lives. According to one, God is the sole source of political and moral authority, and we must submit ourselves to his will. We are put in the world to act as the *khilafa* or representatives of God, and we need in every time to work out

125

how to return to the principles and practices of original Islam. As one might expect, such an approach values a literal understanding of the truth of religion, and sees **human nature** as being essentially religious.

It might be thought that science and Islamic fundamentalism would be in conflict with each other, but in fact many fundamentalists are scientists, possibly seeking in religion the same certainty that they may find in science. None the less, there is often criticism of the positivistic assumptions of natural science, and especially the attempt to discover the principles behind nature in a non-divine source. Like al-Ghazali, fundamentalists insist that God is given the main role in any sort of natural action, and miracles are merely the actions of God that run against the course he normally follows. One of the principles of modern science that is objectionable to the fundamentalists is the way in which it often seeks to reduce nature to a few basic theoretical principles which operate by themselves, and the way in which science often does not regard the human being or nature as a whole, but just concentrates on one aspect of them. Reality is an organic whole, formed and sustained by God, and unless we take this into account we seriously misunderstand its nature. When it comes to organizing the state, the notion of the state as an organic unity comes to the fore, and there is no room for private, and certainly not public, deviation from the will of God, as expressed through his representatives. For the **Shi'ites** this is often arrived at through the decisions of the *imam* (the intermediary between God and humanity) or a representative of the *imam*, the latter possibly being seen as not at the moment on the earth. In **Sunni** Islam the sources of religious authority are more diverse, but the principle is the same. Once the decisions of the religious authorities become known, they must be followed, and there is no role for any institution able to oppose the wishes of God.

See: **causation, justice**
Further reading: Nasr and Leaman 1996.

God In Indian philosophy the notion of God is often a complicated one. There are theories that are determinedly atheistic,
while others refer more to a creator than to a deity. The
references to God in the **Upanishads** are to *Isha* or *Ishvara*,
who is taken to be immanent and absolute, very much the
personified form of *brahman*. The Hindus tend to believe in
one God, but not always to the exclusion of others. The Jains
think that *karma* does not require a personal God to distribute
rewards and punishments. On **atomistic** theories such as
that of the **Nyaya-Vaisheshika** God arranges the atoms in
such a way that the world that we know comes about. He
is only the efficient **cause**, since the atoms do not depend
for their existence on him. They defend a cosmological
proof of the existence of God, which works from premises
in terms of the purposive nature of the world to the existence of a creator with the characteristics of God. Since the
phenomenal world is made up of composite things, it must
have been constructed by a being capable of bringing the
imperceptible atoms together. There is also a moral proof,
based on the notion of the infinite numbers of selves, which
means that a being is required to allocate rewards and punishments justly to those selves. The author of the **Vedas** displays
knowledge of both the phenomenal and the hidden world,
and this can only be God. Since they are reliable texts, and
since they refer to God, God must exist. Revelation can be

accepted as valid since it is the work of an omniscient author, and we can establish his existence by using the principles of reason. The **Mimamsa** manage to do without a God in their system, arguing that the material world was always as it is now, and the existence of *karma* is sufficient to explain the way in which things turn out. According to the **Vishishtadvaita**, God, the souls and matter constitute an organic whole. He is both an efficient and a material cause, he brings into being not only the objects with which we are familiar but also the material aspects of those objects. God is the only completely independent thing in existence, and everything else is dependent on him. Everything, even **liberated** things, exist in a state of complete dependence on God, and if God did not continue to will their existence, they would immediately be destroyed. Ramanuja criticizes the traditional proofs for the existence of God, since these are not strong and we should base our belief on him solely on revelation. He did not accept the Nyaya argument that the universe is like an effect, and so must have a cause, nor that since it is made up of parts, the cause must be intelligent. This argument was rejected by the Jains also, who pointed out that it applies to space too, which is made up of parts. Yet the Nyaya school regards space as eternal and uncreated. Another criticism was that if God is taken to have created at a particular **time**, then he must have changed, since at an earlier time he did not create. This implies that he himself would be an effect and so require a cause. The Nyaya response was that space cannot be identified with parts. A part is something that can combine with other things, and can change its position. This is not the case for what we sometimes refer to as the parts of space. As for the argument from the nature of creation to a creator, they argued that a change in what God brings about does not imply a change in God. He can change things without himself moving. Such arguments are rejected by Ramanuja. It is true that we can infer the existence of a creator since we understand from our experience how some artifacts are produced, but this is not the case for the world itself, which is brought into existence in ways of which we have no experience. There is also no reason to think that if the world has a creator, it has to have just one creator. In any case, how could a spiritual being affect matter, and so be responsible for the imperfect character of events in this world? The Nyaya thought that such objections did not work, because God can operate on matter just through the use of his soul. It is also not much of a disproof to say that the universe is a lot bigger than a particular artifact in the universe, and so we cannot infer to its cause. After all, even within our own experience we may come across something very large and are justified in working out what or who brought it into existence. God is even more transcendent for the **Dvaita** school, and is beyond the limits of our comprehension. He controls all aspects of the universe, but not in order to satisfy some purpose that he has. He is perfect and needs nothing from his creation. Madhva argues that while the proofs for the existence of God are weak, they become strong once we accept revelation.

Buddhist thought does not use the notion of God. Many arguments were produced to suggest that since the process of *samsara* and *karma* do not require any external force or principle to operate, there is no need to accept the hypothesis of such a creator.

Although Confucius does use the notion of the divine in the sense of **heaven**, this is heavily criticized by the **Mohists**, who see it as an unnecessarily uncritical adherence to past beliefs. On the other hand, the latter also think that there is a use for the concept, since the majority of the population will be able to accept the necessity to act **benevolently** if they think that virtues will be rewarded and vices punished.

The Qur´anic notion of God is immediately problematic in that it describes a being who is both in the world, and at the same time above it. There is a lot of anthropomorphic **language** in the text, language that describes God using language appropriate to describing human beings, and this led to the controversy in Islamic philosophy of how this language is to be understood. The God of philosophy is rather different, in that he is for the *falasifa* the unmoved First Mover, and for those who use Neoplatonic language, the source of the emanations out of which the universe both comes into existence and remains in existence. This is very different from the idea of a deity who creates the world at a particular time out of nothing, for whom there are presumably no constraints as to how or what he will create. The God of the philosophers seems to have an agenda that he has to follow regardless of his own desires, an agenda set by the nature of the rational order in the universe. Existence flows from his essence quite automatically, there is no ordinary notion by which he can even know what is taking place in his universe, and God's contemplation (out of which everything ultimately flows) is entirely a self-contemplation. This view led al-Ghazali to charge the philosophers with using the concept of God while at the same time emptying it of any real religious meaning.

Further reading: Chatterjee 1983, Dasgupta 1975, Fakhry 1983, Hick 1997, Kitagawa 1966, Leaman 1985, 1997, Ward 1998.

good – *see* **ethics, evil**

guna, attribute, property – *see* **Dvaita**, *prakriti*

guru In Hinduism this term was originally used for a person deserving respect, and has come to mean more specifically teachers who are providing religious instruction for pupils. Most accounts of how to progress spiritually emphasize the importance of an appropriate teacher guiding the student, and this is not surprising given the very complex variety of knowledge and actions that are a necessary condition of liberation from the bondage of the phenomenal world. There is a similar role, albeit within a different religious context, for the *shaykh* in **Sufism**.

Further reading: Radhakrishnan and Moore 1957.

hadith   Arabic for a Tradition of the Prophet, which refers to a story or quotation that the Prophet or someone close to him is supposed to have produced, and which has been transmitted along a reliable oral route until it was compiled. The importance of the Traditions is that they supplement the text of the Qur'an and provide a rich resource of interpretational material.

Further reading: Nasr and Leaman 1996.

harmony   One of the main criteria of Zhou society that impressed Confucius was its harmony, and this notion is an important part of his concept of *li* or propriety. This was a kind of feudal society, but it should not be thought that it is essentially feudalism that Confucius identified with harmony, but rather the way in which everyone in that society had a role complementary to each other role, where everyone had an understanding that their welfare was linked to the welfare of everyone else, and where government was carried out by people who had as their intentions the preservation of the balance and stability of society. Hence Confucius links *li* with *ren*, the notion of **benevolence**, the idea that everyone has a nature that deserves respect and so we should practice the virtue of loving humanity. This virtue should be developed in everyone, but only to a moderate degree, since an

131

exaggerated notion of benevolence would disturb harmony. When the Confucian virtues are practised, they will result in harmony. In the twentieth century Sun Yatsen used this notion of balance to argue for a specifically Chinese approach to social and political progress, involving in particular the principle of nationalism. One of the points of creating a free and independent China was to create a harmonious state in which there would be a balance of different types of people, different virtues and a varied economic base.

The *Zhou yi* has harmony as much of its theme. The world is a place in which change takes place all the time, and this operates on the pattern of **yin** and **yang**. These principles cannot always be opposite, but they must complement each other also, so that change can be seen as either the destruction of the previous state of affairs, or the replacement of one state of affairs by another. Each state of affairs may be seen as a harmony, or if not as a step on the route to ultimate harmony. We are capable of participating in this process, and what we need to do is work out what pattern of events is likely to occur given the rules of transformation as either harmonious or on the path to harmony, and then we can most effectively seek to act within that context.

In Japan Prince Shotoku stressed harmony as the most important human principle, but this time from Buddhist principles. Everyone can revere the Buddhist truths, and so there is no reason to think that there could not be harmony between everyone in the state, intent as they should be on following the same spiritual ends. The sorts of factionalism that normally flourish have to be restricted, and society needs to be run on the basis of consensus, as a result of general agreement on the best way to proceed. Although much of the language of this approach appears to be Confucian, Shotoku orients it in a Buddhist direction, pointing in particular to the *Lotus Sutra* as demonstrating the Buddha's willingness to make doctrinal compromises, and so the general desirability of consensus.

See: **human nature**

Further reading: Chan 1972, Maruyama 1974, Moore 1968, Peerenboom 1993, Tu Wei-Ming 1985.

hatha yoga A variety of yoga that emphasizes techniques of physical training. Sometimes a prerequisite for the physical training is regarded as necessary in terms of spiritual types of yoga, and sometimes the physical training is regarded as a useful end in itself. What is developed is not so much speed or muscular development, but suppleness, flexibility and control over physical processes. It consists of postures, the tensing and relaxation of parts of the human physique, breath control and the use of mental control to achieve mastery of the body. While there is often an emphasis on mastery of the body, this should not be taken as the aim of the technique in itself, which is generally control over the emotions and all that is implied by that.

Sometimes **tantric** ideas are involved, which lead to the development and controlling of sexual energy.

Further reading: Eliade 1969.

heaven – *see* **human nature**, *tian*

himsa, violence – *see* **asceticism**

Hinayana A term from Mahayana Buddhism used to refer to what it regards as incomplete or secondary methods of achieving a form of **enlightenment** that is merely particular and personal, and which bypasses the complete enlightenment of a Buddha. According to the Mahayana version of Buddhism, the real end of Buddhism is the complete enlightenment of all sentient creatures, and seeking to achieve enlightenment in just a few creatures is a selfish and limited end. Sometimes the Theravada Buddhist school as a whole is called *hinayana* by its detractors, but in fact the Theravada school is just one of the variety of non-Mahayana schools.

Further reading: Gombrich 1988.

hoben – *see* **skilful means**

hongaku, enlightenment – *see* **Tendai**

hua yan, Garland School – *see* **Chinese philosophy, Korean philosophy**

human nature For Confucians, Daoists and many Buddhists, human nature as it is experienced by us is the launching pad for our eventual emancipation and self-transformation. Human nature is in principle able to be transformed and perfected. This is a theme of much Chinese philosophy, that although we may often be misled through self-deception about the nature of humanity, if we sincerely examine and cultivate ourselves in the right sort of way, our true nature will make itself known. This is something that we have to do ourselves, nothing from outside us is necessary, since human nature is itself not only able to hide itself, but can reveal itself also. In a sense, we need to learn to be human, although we all are human.

Mencius analyses human nature in terms of innate properties, and these involve **compassion** and the ability to discriminate between good and **evil**. It is not enough to have these dispositions innately, though. It is incumbent on us to develop these dispositions, and the sage will cultivate his human nature to its ultimate degree. By contrast, Xunzi argued that there is no such thing as an innate human nature where this is equivalent to moral behaviour. The **Neoconfucians** divided human nature into the nature of heaven's will and the nature of human life. Some ordinary human behaviour is acceptable since it reflects the principles of heaven, but what is required is a generally critical attitude to any behaviour based on human desire. What ought to be preserved is *tianli,* the social principles that are in line with feudalism, the laws of heaven. Once human nature is made to fit in with these principles, **harmony** in the state and in the individual is restored. This is a point that the Confucians make in response to the rather optimistic orientation of Mencius' thought. Against the idea that nature is good, Confucians such as Dong Zhongshu accepted that there are good aspects to humanity but that these are only likely to be elicited if we align our natures with heaven (*tian*). This view provided a theoretical justification of kingship, since the relationship between the king and his subjects resembles that between heaven and lower beings affected by it.

Further reading: de Bary *et al*. 1960, Chan 1972, Creel 1953.

humanism   One of the key terms in Chinese philosophy is *li* (*i* in Korean), which represents the standard human reactions to life, in the sense of propriety. The question that was raised was how human beings ought to live, what place human beings have in the world, as a consequence of the fundamental question as to how social **harmony** is possible. Chinese philosophers answered this in various ways, and they all had an idea of what this appropriate form of life would be. Within Marxism the notion of humanism is given a social and economic dimension, as compared to a religious interpretation. Within Chinese thought humanism was often linked with the Neoconfucian notion of single-mindedness (*jing* in Chinese; *kyong* in Korean). This disposition involves the process of constant moral effort and self-cultivation, and embodies the idea that what a human being becomes is largely a matter of his own efforts. The Korean thinker T'oegye argued that it follows that everyone is able to become a sage, which means becoming fully human, through serious thought, correct self-cultivation, study and appropriate moral conduct. His compatriot Yulgok developed this point by arguing that single-mindedness is a stage on the route to sincerity (*cheng* in Chinese; *song* in Korean). Such sincerity is the source of self-cultivation and the basis of our links with other human beings.

Further reading: Chan 1972, de Bary and Haboush 1985, Fung 1952.

hwadu, riddle – *see* **Korean philosophy**

I

i, ritual, idea, order – *see* **humanism**

I Ching – *see* **Book of Changes**

ignorance A key notion in Indian philosophy, where as *avidya* it is closely linked with *samsara*, the cycle of birth and rebirth. According to Shankara, our ignorance of the real nature of *brahman*, reality, leads to our mistaking aspects of reality for reality itself. The **Advaita Vedanta** follow this approach, according to which our experience of diversity is precisely a factor of our ignorance and the illusions that stand between us and reality, the one reality that is not diverse at all. Although ignorance leads us to mistake the unreal for the real, it is none the less itself to a certain extent real, and to a degree unreal. It is real because it actually takes place, but it is unreal in the sense that it is part of our mistaken way of accessing the real by concentrating on phenomena that are unreal. The Advaita use a lot of examples of illusions according to which one thing looks like something else, and the point of these examples is to suggest that something that is illusory may none the less have a powerful effect upon us. The interesting thing about these examples is that the 'real' object that the illusions are linked to is often regarded by the theory as being itself unreal, and believing in its reality is a factor in bonding us to the world. On the other hand, realizing that illusions are around us can be a step in freeing us from the illusion that we are not generally ignorant, and since the bondage is itself not real, there is no difficulty in principle in freeing ourselves of it. Once we start to appreciate the oneness of reality through **meditation**, we can start to throw off ignorance, although, of course, this is hardly something that can be done quickly, and even after having made the appropriate moves, we are still within the sphere of our **karmic** past, and have to wait until this comes to an end. Our bondage is an effect of ignorance, and **liberation** will only come through **knowledge**.

A similar move is made in Buddhism, where the cause of suffering is ignorance, and one can abolish suffering by abolishing ignorance. This is given an interesting twist in the Chinese *Awakening of Faith (Dashang qixinlun)*, according to which suchness is identified with substance and ignorance with the wind. The wind of ignorance blows up against the water of suchness and brings about the waves of *samsara*. Ignorance stimulates the innately enlightened mind. Fazang took this simile to show that it is the coming together of ignorance and suchness that brings about the world, since after all it is the meeting of water and waves that creates *samsara*. Since the relationship between ignorance and suchness are rather like a **yin–yang** relation, it looks as though we are never going to rid ourselves of ignorance, since it is one of the features of a constantly changing world.

See: **mind**, *tathagata*, **Yogachara**
Further reading: Creel 1953, Dasgupta 1975, Radhakrishnan and Moore 1957.

ijma`, consensus – *see* **law**

Ikhwan al-Safa' This can be translated as either 'Brethren of Sincerity' or 'Brethren of Purity', and refers to a group of Islamic philosophers who lived in the tenth or eleventh century CE in Basra. There has been great controversy about their precise names and affiliations, but their work, which consists of fifty-two epistles, is encyclopaedic in nature, dealing with mathematics, theology, magic and science as well as philosophy. It is a mixture of Platonic, Aristotelian, Neoplatonic and Islamic ideas, and has ever since played an important role in Islamic culture. This variety does occasionally lead to problems, in that several competing notions are sometimes employed in different parts of the text, but on the whole the approach is Neoplatonic, with a notion of the universe along the lines of emanation. There is a hierarchy of levels of being, ranging from the Creator, the Intellect, the Soul, Prime Matter, Nature, the Absolute Body, the Sphere and the Four Elements to the Beings of our world. Unlike the normal Neoplatonic view, matter is viewed positively, not as a force for limitation and **evil**. Our understanding of God is mediated through the different levels of being as he descends towards us, and is necessarily limited.

The point of the arguments of the epistles is to save their participants, to escape the claims of matter and join the 'Ship of Salvation' (an expression they use) through the practice of **asceticism**, cooperation and virtue. What is particularly interesting in their approach is their openness to alternative systems of thought and religions, which they attempted to incorporate in their compendium of wisdom. In some ways their work is representative of an important tradition in Islamic philosophy of presenting summaries of the thoughts and practices of a long line of great thinkers, and then discussing what relevance their ideas have to contemporary conditions.

Further reading: Nasr and Leaman 1996, Netton 1991.

illuminationist philosophy A form of philosophy whose name comes from *ishraq* which means 'rising (of the sun)' and is also linked to the Arabic for 'east'. It is often contrasted with Peripatetic thought and the importance the latter gives to deductive reason. Illuminationist thought uses a notion of immediate and intuitive knowledge, and is often identified with ibn Sina's oriental or eastern philosophy, which may not actually have existed, but which is taken to be his deeper teaching as opposed to his work within the Aristotelian tradition of philosophy. The real creator of illuminationism is al-Suhrawardi, a Persian thinker from the twelfth century CE. In his extensive work he sets out to replace Peripatetic philosophy with an entirely new form of logic and ontology. He rejects the Aristotelian account of definition which is in terms of genus and differentia since he argues that it is a process of explaining something in terms of something else that is less well known than itself. He also criticizes the list of categories, claiming that they can be reduced to five and still encompass the same conceptual range. His key epistemological notion is that of **knowledge** by presence (`ilm al-huduri) which is taken to be such an immediate relationship to the truth that it supersedes propositional knowledge. It is knowledge about which one cannot be mistaken, and the light of our self brings to our awareness important aspects of the truth. The notion of light is used to replace the traditional philosophical vocabulary of Islamic philosophy. Light flows through the universe and brings to **existence** and awareness different levels of **being**, so that the differences between distinct things lies in their degrees of luminosity, not in their essences. Later thinkers within the tradition often identified God with the Light of Lights, from which all light emerges and which does not itself receive light, and which is completely one. Although clearly this sort of philosophy does use language that fits in nicely with mysticism, it is worth noting that a good deal of illuminationist philosophy deals with technical and analytical aspects of philosophy.

Further reading: Nasr 1996, Nasr and Leaman 1996.

`*ilm al-huduri*, knowledge by presence – *see* **illuminationist philosophy**

imagination In Sanskrit *kalpana* or *vikalpa*, imagination plays a major role in Indian philosophy. Buddhists often disapprove of imagination, since it extends the sense of our experience and gives it an illegitimate link to something outside that experience. We have experience, and we use concepts to organize and categorize that experience, but this is to import concepts into our experience and unjustifiably so. What we perceive is what we perceive, and should not be muddled up with concepts and ideas that are not the objects of our **perception**. This view leads unsurprisingly to a suspicion of **language** and its role in confusing us and embedding us even more firmly within a world of illusion. Their more realist Indian opponents see the world of experience as actually embodying concepts and even language, so that experience would be impossible unless we brought our concepts to it in the first place.

In Islamic philosophy imagination is generally seen as the popular and persuasive way of expressing the truth which can be understood by the elite in the form of philosophy. Imagination is thus contrasted with the strict application of reason, since the former makes us turn away or be attracted towards particular things that may be very different in reality from how we imagine them to be. Imagination is closely linked with the physical parts of the soul, and so is attracted by physical examples and poetic language. It enables us to think and talk about things in language that does not fairly represent how those things really are, or at least it describes those things either better or worse than they actually are. It is here that conceptions of **aesthetic** value start to become detached from objective principles of beauty, since we may come through imagination to value and enjoy images that we really should not think about, or give the importance that we do. It does not even really matter whether the object the imagination describes exists at all. We may still experience the image as beautiful even though it bears no relationship at all to a factual reality.

Further reading: Leaman 1997, Nasr and Leaman 1996, Radhakrishnan and Moore 1957.

imam, spiritual leader of the Muslim community – *see* **fundamentalism**

immortality – *see* **afterlife**

indeterminacy of meaning – *see* **ambiguity**

Indian philosophy By 'Indian philosophy' is meant the philosophy of the Indian subcontinent. The obvious place to start is with the *Rig Veda*, an ancient hymn possibly as old as 1000 BCE, which defined the notion of the Brahmins, the priestly class. A number of **Vedic** texts were produced and some of the characteristic doctrines of Hinduism such as reincarnation and the cycle of birth and rebirth. The **Upanishads** went on to raise issues about the meaning of religious ritual, and also created certain themes such as that of the *brahman* or sacred which is implicit in everything, the notion of an eternal self or *atman* within us and within the universe as a whole, and finally the idea of **liberation** from the cycle of birth and rebirth.

The earliest philosophical Hindu school is that of **Sankhya** and it bases its view of reality on a mixture of eternal souls which are spiritual (*purusha*) and a material (*prakriti*) world. The souls are constantly reborn unless they manage to achieve liberation. All life is suffering and liberation can come about through **knowledge** of the real nature of the world. This real knowledge involves a grasp of the distinctions that exist between **soul** and nature. So the theory is strongly dualistic, since there are two entirely different kinds of thing in existence, many souls and one nature. It came later to be linked with **yoga**, on the basis that the sort of understanding of the nature of reality could be best attained through the sorts of practices involved in yoga. The other orthodox schools are the **Mimamsa-Vedanta**, which bases itself on the interpretation of the sacred texts, and the **Nyaya-Vaisheshika**, which is particularly interested in **logic** and an **atomistic** view of reality. These schools have their unorthodox equivalents, largely the varieties of Buddhism, Jainism and **materialism**. Although it is traditional to connect the schools in particular ways, it is worth pointing out that some of these combinations seem rather forced, and there is often far more disagreement among adherents of the schools than between the schools themselves and supposedly rival schools.

One of these rival schools is Jainism, which like Buddhism and Sankhya rejects the notion of God. This school envisaged many souls dying and being reborn but these are not spiritual, but are things that enter the bodies they inhabit. The path to liberation is via strict **asceticism** and preventing harm, *ahimsa*. Jainism had particularly interesting views on the nature of different points of view, according to which there is no absolute perspective from which truth may be seen.

Another unorthodox school, in the sense of a school that does not accept the authority of the Vedas, was the Charvaka or materialists, about which very little is known except through reports from its enemies, which may not be entirely reliable. Its main problem was dealing with the nature of phenomena that do not seem to be material, such as consciousness, and it used the analogy of putting together material things and getting something entirely different to explain consciousness. By far the most significant of the unorthodox approaches is Buddhism, which traditionally originated with the Buddha who was born in Nepal in the sixth century BCE. His pursuit of the ultimate truth that would end suffering resulted in the doctrine that the source of suffering is craving, identified with suffering (*dukkha*), whose termination can be found in the path to *nirvana* which results in 'the ending of the cycle of birth and rebirth. A particularly important doctrine was that there is no essential or eternal soul, which went right against the Sankhya theory. Buddhist philosophy became especially creative, and split up into many different schools. The two main divisions are the Theravada, which predominates today in Sri Lanka and South East Asia, and the Mahayana, which spread throughout the rest of Asia. The Theravada were called *Hinayana* by their detractors, the Lesser Vehicle, since they emphasized the importance of the individual seeking **enlightenment**, which their opponents interpreted as a selfish and limited objective.

The Mahayana or Greater Vehicle saw the enlightenment of everything sentient as the appropriate aim.

From the tenth century Buddhism fell into decline in North India, when the Muslim invasions became significant, while the Theravada version continued to flourish in Sri Lanka.

Further reading: Carr and Mahalingam 1997, Conze 1962, Gonda 1970, Hiriyanna 1932, 1985, Potter 1988, Radhakrishnan 1966.

inference According to the Lokayata, the main error the idealists make is over the nature of inference. They think that one cannot argue from the nature of the world to something ideal that lies at the source of what is visible. They base their arguments on empirical premises, but this falls foul of the familiar difficulty that a general principle of inference that claims to respect only empirical premises is itself not an empirical premise. On the other hand, their main point was that if **perception** is the principle of **knowledge**, then it is true that one has no perceptual evidence of the universality of the connection between types of events, so our judgements about what is likely to happen in the future is always likely to be speculative. The **materialists** accept perception as a route to knowledge, but reject inference, since inference depends on accepting a range of connections between events that are not observed. This means they are accepted without reason, and what looks like a solid and valid reasoning process is in fact based on the uncritical acceptance of general relations between things. Universal propositions cannot be established by inference, since we cannot observe every instance of a universal proposition. As the materialists point out in true empiricist style, it does not matter how reliable general connections between things have been in the past, what we need is a proof that they will continue to work in the future, and this we cannot get through perception.

By contrast, the **Nyaya-Vaisheshika** value inference (*anumana*) as a route to knowledge. The basis to such a route is their acceptance of **universals**, which means that it is easier to link general propositions to each other. In inference the

143

ambition is to establish links of invariable relation, to show that if one term or judgement is present, then so must another related term or judgement. In that case one can prove that if one starts with particular judgements, one is entitled to accept further and linked judgements. This theory was developed in very complex ways to explain a wide variety of valid argument forms. An object is qualified by five concepts – universality, particularity, relation, quality and action. The object is given in perception first as an item of sensation and then in some form or another, which involves the application of a predicate. This theory of perception leads to a theory of inference, since we start with a perception which leads to the inference of its qualities. The syllogism has five stages, a thesis, a rationale, a description of the inseparable connection or concomitance, the application of all three to a particular topic, and finally the conclusion. The theory was extended by the **Sankhya** school, who added to it a principle of analogy. This principle makes it acceptable to move from the visible to the invisible, something for which it was heavily criticized by Shankara, given his determination to stick closely to the letter of scripture and not use inference to extend the meaning of the text. Mahdva objects to this prioritizing of revelation over perception, and he argues that there is no order of priority between the different routes to knowledge. This is because if something is an item of knowledge it cannot be transcended and replaced by something higher. Also, there exists some perceptual knowledge that is completely secure, which enables the self to be entirely sure of what it thinks is true. Some of this knowledge relates to pains and pleasures, where we cannot be wrong about what we are feeling, and it can be extended to perception of space, which also may be immediately grasped by the mind. He argued that if we perpetually seek for deeper principles to justify our knowledge we shall set up an infinite regress, which shows up the Nyaya theory as unsatisfactory.

Buddhist theories of inference initially followed the path of investigating the relationships between the different aspects of the reasoning process, in particular what rules of reasoning obtain in connecting propositions with each other. Dignaga and Dharmakirti developed these earlier ideas into new and exciting directions, adding a great deal of sophistication to the understanding of the key logical concepts. A strong distinction was made between connections in **language**, and connections in actuality. In inference we have a connection that strictly speaking applies only to concepts, and no conclusion may be drawn from it about the nature of anything that actually takes place, or about what is real. The point is that it is acceptable to infer that where there is smoke, there must also be fire, since we know that there is a necessary connection between fire and smoke (or that was assumed). Can someone who sees smoke on a hill then conclude that there must also be fire on the hill? Some logicians would agree to this conclusion, while others would not. The Nyaya-Vaisheshika would accept that we could conclude that there is a fire on the hill, while Dignaga would only permit the conclusion that the hill is fiery. The difference is that this latter is taken to be a weaker conclusion, and refers to the way in which the hill is apparently reflecting the presence of an object which cannot be seen, yet not one that we can infer with confidence since we are only dealing in inference with associations of ideas, not reality. Dignaga only regards the object of perception as acceptable in a reasoning, and this has to be limited to how it occurs in experience, without those predicates that cannot be observed as part of the immediate experience of it. Inference is only valid for him if it involves the example of inseparable connection and its application in a particular case. Inference only operates within the confines of the world of experience, and can derive no knowledge at all of the real world that lies behind the phenomenal world. Inference is only valid within this world, and is the exclusive preserve of human thought within this world. There is often a suspicion of inference in Buddhism given the rejection of the reality of universals, since it follows that there are difficulties in explaining how reality can be grasped by thought.

Ramanuja defends a view of inference that makes it powerless to establish by proof anything of relevance to religion.

145

We cannot argue that the world must have a designer even though there is evidence of design, since we can form no idea of how the parts of nature were formed or why. Even if we could argue that it was designed, there would be no reason to ascribe this to only one designer. Agents of which we have experience are physical, but surely we should not want to argue that God has a body. Also, the more like us God is, the less appropriate it is to worship him, since such worship is for someone who entirely transcends the ordinary world. Ramanuja attacks all the arguments of his predecessors to suggest that we could make an acceptable inference from the nature of the world to the nature of its creator. It is not that Ramanuja mistrusted inference, but he argued that religious belief should rest on faith, and if we are to use inference to move us from the visible to the invisible, we should ensure that the grounds for connection between these two realms are sure.

See: **Advaita Vedanta**, **Dvaita**, **universals**, **Vishishtadvaita**
Further reading: Basham 1971, Bhatt 1975, Chatterjee 1965, Chi 1969, Dainian and Cohen 1996, Dravida 1972, Dreyfus 1997, Graham 1978, Matilal 1968, 1971, Randle 1930, Stcherbatsky 1962.

isha – *see* **God**

ishraq – *see* **illuminationist philosophy**

ishvara, *see* **God**, *jiva*

Islamic philosophy   The religion of Islam raises a number of important conceptual issues, and these are dealt with in Islamic philosophy. Islam arose in the Arabian peninsula in the seventh century CE, and rapidly spread throughout the Middle East and beyond, encountering along the way the civilizations and cultures that had flourished in those regions for a long time.

The early Muslims tried to persuade followers of other religions that they should embrace Islam, and for this they required arguments that were generally acceptable. Greek philosophy was translated into Arabic, often via Syriac, in order to provide an appropriate vocabulary and set of rhetorical techniques to convert the local populations, and also to convince Muslims of a particular sect that they should change their views. One of the main uses of philosophy was to explore some of the issues that arose within theology (*kalam*), and these were often more than merely theoretical issues, but related to major political and religious divisions within the Islamic world.

Within the first few centuries of Islam a rich mixture of Aristotelian, Platonic, Neoplatonic and other Greek-inspired ideas and theories were present in the Islamic world, and these were taken up and used by a series of outstanding thinkers in the construction of highly original and interesting philosophical systems. Every aspect of philosophy, ranging from ethics to logic, was explored, and there was a close connection between the development of philosophy and natural science, which was also especially impressive in the Islamic world during this period.

Certain issues were discussed very frequently in this form of Peripatetic thought (*falsafa*). There was the apparent conflict between reason and **faith**, between what the Qur'an appeared to claim and how those claims stood up to philosophical analysis. Much effort was expended, in particular by al-Farabi, ibn Sina and ibn Rushd, in showing that there was no real conflict between faith and reason, so that philosophy deserved to have a place within the Islamic world. The sort of philosophy dominated by Greek thought did not survive much after the twelfth century among Muslims, but flourished instead among Christians in Europe and Jewish communities. Another type of philosophy, that based on mystical principles, continued to be popular, though, and has continued up to now to be practised in the Islamic world, especially in the Indian subcontinent and Persia. This philosophy is often called **illuminationist** (*ishraqi*) or 'oriental philosophy', since

147

it uses the concept of light to explore the nature of the connection between God and his world, and finds in this notion a useful and rich conceptual tool. Although some forms of mystical philosophy or **Sufism** put the emphasis upon the personal experience of the individual, much of it is just as theoretical and abstract as Peripatetic thought, and often uses the same Greek principles. Today it is this variety of philosophy that has become quite popular, especially in the Persian-speaking world, but the earlier Peripatetic variety has made something of a comeback, especially among Muslims who are looking for theoretical ways of combining their faith with modernity.

Further reading: Leaman 1985, 1997, Nasr and Leaman 1996.

J

jada, material reality – *see* **brahman**

jahaliyya, ignorance – *see* **fundamentalism**

Jain philosophy   A series of unorthodox teachings often linked with the **materialist** Ajivika, and named after the term for spiritual conquerors (*jina*). Jainism is a variety of optimistic determinism, which advocates attainment of liberation through the rigorous pursuit of non-violence (*ahimsa*) as part of right action, together with right belief and right knowledge. This results in our escaping the consequences of earlier actions (*karma*) and when we are liberated (*moksha*) we end our journey through the cycle of birth and rebirth (*samsara*). There exist a number of substances, which are in themselves immutable but they also have changeable aspects. The most important substance is soul or *jiva*, and in itself this is perfect, eternal and undifferentiated. *Jiva* is identified with the deeper sense of self, *atman*, in the state of bondage, while in **liberation** both notions of the self are actually identical. There are an infinite number of selves, and no need to believe in a God, since it is the selves themselves that bring about the world due to their action on matter. However, when it is affected by the ordinary world, it takes on a shape and attributes due to previous actions and becomes a wanderer (*samsari*).

through an enormous number of existences determined by those actions and thoughts. Liberation is only possible when the soul transcends involvement with actions and the previous actions that form part of the itinerary of the individual have been exhausted. Good actions help to construct an acceptable life in *samsara* but do not really help attain liberation, although the converse, **evil** actions, merely prolong and deepen our immersion in the phenomenal world.

An important and distinctive concept in Jain philosophy is that of a point of view. Everything may be seen from a different point of view, and everything has more than just one meaning. When it comes to, discussing the origin of the world, it can be seen as one from one point of view, as many from a different point of view, and so on. Everything has an infinite number of modes or ways of existing and relates to other things in an infinite number of ways. So everything is both the same and also different from everything else. This gave the theory scope to criticize other schools for illegitimately prioritizing a particular attitude to the truth of its propositions, whereas they should have been more open to different understandings of the same proposition. The implication is that one should tolerate those with different views, since they are to an extent true. Their opponents swiftly pointed out that this suggests that the Jain doctrine is itself not something that one can firmly say is true, since from a particular point of view (that of another theory, perhaps) it is false. It also leads to difficulties with **inference**, since the premises on which one relies are to be regarded as false from a particular point of view. However, given the Jain permissiveness about different points of view, it is hardly surprising that they defended in their **logic** the largest variety of methods of inference as compared with other schools.

There are some features of our life that are objectively true, and for which points of view do not enter into their description, and these are the key notions of *karma*, *moksha* and *samsara*. To attain liberation one ought to practise **meditation** and so develop a disposition for dispassionate feelings. It is possible through *asceticism* to strip the material aspects of *karma* from the soul. This will result in the termination of new *karma*, although one will still have to work through one's former *karma* before liberation finally becomes feasible. The Jains developed a very complex model of the route to salvation, which involves breaking the connection between our actions and our self. We need to exercise restraint, prudence, obedience to rules, strength and appropriate behaviour. An active form of penance may then bring about the working out of our already acquired actions, and so prepare the way for liberation. This involves a thoroughgoing asceticism, and Jains will sometimes starve themselves to death in their desire to avoid acting in such a way as to increase their *karma*. This latter is often characterized as being a material and sticky substance, **atomic** in nature, which adheres to the *jiva* or life force and prevents it from ascending to liberation. There are different kinds of *karma* linked to different sorts of **personality**, varying in accordance with the degree of violence that the individual displays (on some accounts, there are 148 different material or *prakriti* forms of *karma*, which represent a continuum from black to white as individuals are characterized as destructive or non-destructive).

See: **creation**
Further reading: Basham 1971, Dundas 1992, Radhakrishnan and Moore 1957.

Japanese philosophy　　Japan has been subject to cultural influences from China and Korea, and in recent centuries from the West. Buddhism arrived in the sixth century CE, and developed in a number of interesting ways. There were Japanese versions of Chinese philosophical movements, especially of Confucianism and Daoism, and in particular the Tendai (from the Chinese *tian tai*) and Shingon (*tantra*), and later the **Pure Land** movements, **Nichiren** Buddhism, and two varieties of zen, Rinzai and Soto. Confucian thought was also often important, and then, of course, there was the native Shinto tradition, which sometimes blended with other philosophies and sometimes tried to maintain its purity. Daoist theories were also often popular. Shintoism represents a view of the way of the gods, and was easily integrated with other religious views, and in popular approaches to the nature of reality there has been a good deal of blending of Shinto deities with important figures in Buddhism.

A particularly muscular variety of Buddhism was created by Nichiren, who valued the *Lotus Sutra* over all other texts. Salvation is to be achieved by reciting this and in worshipping the transcendental beings it describes. Nichiren advocated the use of force to defend Buddhism, and indeed the school of Buddhism he created, and saw nothing strange in the persecution or killing of those with different views. It is difficult to get further from this position than that of zen Buddhism, which entered Japan from China at around the same time as the other schools. Rinzai zen was introduced by Eisai, and it put the emphasis on the individual pursuit of enlightenment, as opposed to looking for it from elsewhere. Rinzai zen adhered to the principles of sudden enlightenment, believing that we are already enlightened and just have to come to realize it, often as a result of a shock or sudden understanding of what we are. Dogen takes the opposite view, that **enlightenment** can only come about through a gradual process, in particular through sitting **meditation** (*zazen*). His Soto zen school argued that the **buddha nature** is in fact a changing thing whose very impermanence defines it. Anyone in principle can come to see that this is the case, but the difficulty of the methodology of seated meditation in fact left it available to only a few. Both schools have had a tremendous effect on Japanese philosophy, and have taken a specifically Japanese orientation with their emphasis on austerity, aesthetic representation and the capacity of religion to merge with the practical aspects of life.

A particular aspect of Japanese philosophy is its ability to combine different theoretical positions taken from a variety of religious traditions and shape them into a creative whole. Political events often led to the popularity of some forms of philosophy among the powerful, and there were occasional nationalistic attempts to emphasize Shintoism at the expense of the rest. Each of the major systems of thought which had come from China and Korea, and of course in the case of Buddhism originally from India, had supporters and antagonists, and during different political circumstances there came to be arguments between the different philosophical schools over their comparative value. It is often argued that one of the characteristic features of Japanese philosophy is that it is firmly connected with the world, in the sense that it values the ordinary features of our world and advocates a form of philosophy that fits in with the social and economic roles of the Japanese people. This generalization is only partly true, though, since the modern Kyoto school has developed an interest in Nietzsche and Heidegger for apparently entirely metaphysical reasons. The thinkers in this school sought to present distinctly Eastern perspectives on traditional Western philosophical problems by using Buddhist concepts, and at the same time they were interested in gaining a new understanding of those Buddhist concepts by examining them through the ideas of Western philosophy.

Further reading: Dilworth and Viglielmo 1998, Heine 1989, Heisig and Maraldo 1994, Hoshino 1997, Kitagawa 1966, Piovesana 1997, Tsunoda *et al.* 1964, Yamasaki 1988.

jian, universal – *see* **love**

jianai – *see* **love**, **Mohism**

jihad, war – *see* **violence**

jina, spiritual conqueror – *see* **Jain philosophy**

jing, reverence – *see* **human nature**

jiu – *see* **time**

jiva A Jain expression for the soul, which is possessed by every
living thing, however small or even invisible. In themselves
all these *jiva*s are identical, changing within each thing in line
with the different body that has been karmically formed
(*karma* being acquired through the actions during previous
lives). It is only when liberated (*moksha*) that the individual
jiva really becomes different from the others, since then the
effects of *karma* on the qualities of energy, bliss and omni-
science are lifted. This represents one of the main distinctions
between Jainism and many other Indian theories, which
conceive of the **soul** as either **atomic** or **eternal**. On either
theory, it is immutable. The *jiva* is impeded by the organs
of the body, in the sense that they prevent it from transcending
the limitations of treating the world as though it were a place
of importance. Another contrast is that the Jains do not find
a place for God in sorting out rewards and punishments along
the karmic path. *Karma* is all that is required, and God has
no role in such a process. *Karma* is not immaterial, but rather
consists of a type of subtle matter which manages to affect
the soul and drags it down away from the absolute. Some
writers make a technical distinction between *jiva* and *atman*,
where the latter means the permanent soul which is equivalent to **brahman** or reality, and the former represents how
we see the world from a contingent and limited point of
view. *Jiva* is real in so far as it is identified with *atman*, but
illusory in so far as it is identified with the body. According
to the Vivarana school, the *jiva* is a reflection of the *atman*
in the mirror of **ignorance** or *avidya*, and so it is just as real
as its source, which is undeniably real. Vacaspati argued by
contrast that *brahman* cannot reflect anything since it is itself
without qualities capable of reflection, and a better view is
that the notion of the individual self arises as a result of our
ignorant attempts at grasping the nature of reality. Once we
achieve liberation, through **knowledge**, we come to appreciate how limited what we regard as the ordinary self is, and
we can then transcend the notion of *jiva* for that of *atman*.

A strong connection is made between *jiva* and atoms by
Ramanuja, who often uses the term *jivatman*, playing on the

links between atoms and the notion of being part of a whole. In *samsara* the individual self has a particular relationship with matter which enables it to interact with the phenomenal world as a part of a whole. There is also the idea of there being a tiny element of **immortality** and perfection within the individual, by contrast with the decaying and changeable nature of matter. What makes the self so persistent is not its status as a thing but the way that through its faculty of **consciousness** it seeks to know everything. There must be something immutable about it, even though the object of its consciousness consists of changing things. The potentiality to have knowledge is itself constant, while the objects of that faculty obviously change.

A particularly controversial issue arose concerning the interpretation of the *jiva* after liberation. Does it become one with God (*Ishvara*) or reality (*brahman*)? According to Shankara, there are two possibilities here. We can create either a reflection or a limitation theory. On the former, *jiva* is as real as the reality that it reflects, while on the latter it is less real.

Further reading: Bhatt 1975, Dundas 1992, Hiriyanna 1985, Radhakrishnan 1966.

jivanmukti   The state of freedom in this life, in the sense that the body continues to exist but the individual who inhabits it is no longer deceived by the **illusory** nature of what the world of experience regards as real. It represents the attainment of *moksha* or **liberation** before **death**, while still alive, and this should not be regarded as a surprising achievement, since *moksha* is always there, it is always a part of us in the sense that it represents our potentialities as a human being. This concept brings out nicely the way in which liberation can be seen not as a solitary ideal, but rather as a form of life in which the liberated individual does his or her best to help others reach the same goal.

Further reading: Carr and Mahalingam 1997, Radhakrishnan and Moore 1957.

jivatman, mind – *see* **jiva**

jnana – *see* **knowledge**

jnana yoga One of the routes to spiritual development or yoga which are generally accepted in Indian philosophy. This is the way of **knowledge**, and represents the approach through which grasping the nature of human experience can bring about a transformation in basic motivation. This is based on a distinction in the **Vedas** between passages that directly insist on particular kinds of religious performance, and those that refer to the ultimate nature of things (in particular in the **Upanishads**). Seeing, hearing, contemplating and **meditation** on this text are a route to salvation. As with the other forms of yoga (*karma yoga* and *bhakti yoga*) the crucial point is that the activity of the individual should remain free of desire, and his concentration on a subject should be a means of severing his attachments to the world. It might seem that if one thinks about something, then one is necessarily attached to it, and so linked in an objectionable way to the **material** world. The argument against this is that the appropriate attitude that can be achieved by the individual is one in which he understands the nature of his self without being distracted by the contingent features of that self, and so comes closer to **liberation**.

Although many Indian philosophers argue that the different paths to liberation are equal in status, some, such as Shankara, suggested that there is a hierarchy between them, and *jnana yoga* is at the summit. This is because the route to liberation is through the understanding of reality, *brahman*, and this is essentially an intellectual enterprise.

Further reading: Carr and Mahalingam 1997, Deutsch 1968, Puligandla 1997, Radhakrishnan and Moore 1957.

ju, Confucian term for scholar – *see* **education**

jue, enlightenment – *see* **education**

justice According to Confucius, justice represents the way of life we ought to seek to follow, as opposed to private gain and advantage. This idea was developed in some complexity by the **Neoconfucians**. Mencius argues that justice is a natural disposition of **human nature**, and only requires cultivation in order to flourish both in the individual and in the state.

Many of the Islamic philosophers used Plato's *Republic* as their model of the just state, combining it with Islamic features to create a theory of how the state ought to be ruled by a philosopher who is at the same time a prophet and divinely appointed religious authority. The head of the state has a theoretical understanding of how the state ought to be run, since he is in tune with the real nature of things, while the community as a whole has a looser grasp on that nature. None the less, the ruler is able to convey to the masses the nature of their duty through using the **imaginative** language of religion (hence the significance of the link with prophecy). Justice is providing everyone, regardless of their role in society, with an indication of how they ought to act and what they should believe.

See: **democracy, fundamentalism**
Further reading: de Bary 1996, Nasr and Leaman 1996.

K

kalam, theology – *see* **Islamic philosophy**

kalpana – *see* **imagination**

kamma, action – *see* **karma**

karma A Sanskrit term for 'deeds' (Pali, *kamma*) which represents intentional **action**, acting on the basis of a motive and a desire. This determines the actor's fortune in this life and possibly the next, and links the actor with *samsara*, the cycle of death and rebirth. Some of the accounts in the Hindu literature portray the effects of action in very deterministic fashion, so that once one has performed a particular action, the consequences are inevitable. Yet there are also many accounts of reducing the **evil** effects of *karma* through good actions, or even doing away with those effects altogether. In Buddhism the future can be alleviated by good actions, and in both Buddhism and Hinduism there is scope for virtue to be transferable from one person to another, replacing evil *karma* with good *karma*. Jain philosophy takes a slightly different line, arguing that *karma* is similar to a material essence that is part of each soul (*jiva*) via the vibrations that occur through activity, and that *karma* attaches to the soul, clouding the soul's individualistic differences from other souls. This complex theory replaced an earlier account from the earliest years of Jain philosophy according to which all actions, both mental and physical, set in train a series of negative consequences. The only escape from these was to follow an **ascetic** path which means restraining all normal activity, both physical and psychological. Later Jain theory became very sophisticated in separating harmful from non-harmful *karma*. The former interferes with the soul's understanding, perception and energy and results in error, while the latter is the basis for the reborn soul's physical and mental condition. Non-harmful *karma* leads to the preservation of the soul over **time**, its spiritual possibilities and experience of a range of both welcome and unpleasant sensations. Of great significance in the preservation of as perfect a soul as possible is the pursuit of non-violence (*ahimsa*).

Karma is the source of our error in thinking that the world consists of many different things, according to the **Advaita Vedanta**. Our experience of the world turns out to be experience of many things, as opposed to **knowledge** of the single principle of reality (*brahman*), and this is because we want to do a lot of things and enjoy many physical pleasures. If we were not thus driven to see variety in that which is not really various, if we could abandon *karma*, then we should be well on the way to **enlightenment**. *Karma* is intimately related to our notion of the self, and it is important to appreciate that if we manage to transcend *karma*, the self remains. But it is now the real self, the self that is capable of being entirely independent and eternal. *Karma* tends to drag this self into the world where it becomes confused by what it experiences, yet through **liberation** we can untie the knot that limits us to the world and its pains and pleasures, and leave *karma* behind us.

The main goal is to work out how to bring the process of *karma* to an end. It is true that there is both positive and negative *karma*. Positive *karma* involves the agent directing her actions in a favourable direction, but even so there is no escape through such actions from *samsara*. After all, any sort of *karma* involves passion, and so cements our bondage. In any case, *karma* might well be taken to presuppose taking the self seriously, which on a Buddhist point of view is always a mistake, and prolongs the **illusions** of the phenomenal world as a real site for action and thought.

Returning to non-Buddhist ideas of *karma*, the Vedantist Ramanuja raises the question as to whether *brahman's* creative links with the world are at all necessitated by *karma*. There is certainly an understanding of the force of *karma*, since the world is constructed in the way in which it is to make room for the developing and impending *karma* of everyone in it. But is the force that created the world affected by *karma* itself, in the sense that it had to create in a particular way? Since *karma* restrains the freedom of the creator, this is ruled out, but the creator does voluntarily take into account in his creation *karma* and its implications. This accounts for the nature of the world, given its dependence on *brahman*, as a realm of suffering. A world entirely in accordance with *brahman* would not include the features of **ignorance** and suffering with which we are familiar, but these are due to our actions, and we are responsible for the world turning out in the way it has. Of course, *brahman* could ignore existing and future *karma*, and it freely decides to embody these in its creation, with the result that there is nothing we can rationally seek to blame for the sufferings of the world apart from our own actions and decisions.

According to Mahayana Buddhist thought, it is possible to relieve the *karma* of others by transferring whatever merit one might have acquired to them. The **bodhisattva** seeks to live entirely for the sake of others, and it is natural that part of this motivation would find an outlet in the saving of others from the negative *karma* they might have acquired. This is an interesting possibility, since it assumes that the effects of *karma* on the individual are not as determined as one might otherwise think. When people are evil, their actions affect the balance of nature, since the natural world is affected by the moral and spiritual level of human beings. Some aspects of *karma* make it difficult to understand how **personality** can be said to continue from one life to another, since although we can understand how there can be a **causal** link between different lives, it is not clear that the new person is really rightly affected by the actions of a prior person, unless they are in some way the same person. There is in Buddhism no real self, so it cannot be argued that this is what persists, but there are personality traits that could be continuous and connected. In the **Madhyamaka** school of Nagarjuna, *karma* is treated as something only provisionally relevant, since it is tied in with the notion of the self and should not really be regarded as a means to an end, the latter being *nirvana*, of course. Really, **karma** is as empty as the soul (*atman*) itself, and understanding this is itself an aspect of liberation.

Further reading: Cabezon 1994, Carr and Mahalingam 1997, Collins 1982, O'Flaherty 1980, Pereira 1976, Puligandla 1975, Reichenbach 1990, Sharma 1964.

karma yoga   One of the routes to spiritual development in Indian philosophy, the route to perfection through **action**. This can be either through the performance of religious and ritual activities, or through the carrying out of actions without any direct interest in their consequences. The latter means the action of doing one's duty without any ulterior motives apart from the desire to do one's duty, the carrying out of one's moral obligations without any desire to benefit oneself directly.

This notion of *karma* is discussed by Krishna in the **Bhagavad Gita**, where he justifies action as compared with inactivity provided that the motivation of the action is disinterested. The important aspect of this path is the use of action to attain non-attachment, which might seem to be a contradiction. The **Vedas** refer to three kinds of action. Some are optional in the sense that they can be expected to have beneficial results, some are forbidden because of their **evil** results, while others are obligatory, since they are virtuous. One route to perfection is to concentrate on the third type of action and abandon the first two, which means carrying out the religious rituals prescribed by Hinduism.

Further reading: Eliade 1958, Bhagavad Gita 1994, Zaehner 1969.

karuna Compassion, which along with wisdom (*prajna*) is one of the two virtues pursued by the **bodhisattva** and perfectly attained by the Buddha. It can be reached through **meditation**, a particular mental process in which one purifies one's thought to change it from its normal delusory direction towards the truth. Compassion is achievable once one considers that given the fact of infinite rebirth every sentient thing must at one stage have been one's mother. It is a characteristic of mothers to be compassionate, and in the normal state of things these beings are themselves all suffering, and so it is incumbent on us to feel compassion for them. We come to think of the whole of the sentient world as an appropriate object of our compassion, a feeling only perfectly attainable by a Buddha. Becoming compassionate means submerging one's individuality into the generality of suffering being, turning away from one's personal wants and feelings towards identifying with the needs and emotions of others.

The doctrine of **skilful means** is based on the idea that the Buddha presented his doctrines in ways appropriate to the understanding of the audience of the time, out of compassion for the relatively limited capacities to understand of the people.

See: **samsara**
Further reading: Aronson 1980, Guenther 1972, Ling 1981

khilafa, God's deputies – *see* **fundamentalism**

knowledge The term commonly used for knowledge in Sanskrit is *jnana* (*nana* in Pali). In the **Bhagavad Gita** Krishna praises both worship and knowledge, but worship seems to occupy a superior rank. The relationship between these two activities was much discussed in Indian philosophy, as was the source of knowledge (*prama*) itself given the widely held theory that it is through knowledge that **liberation** from suffering and the cycle of birth and rebirth is possible. A *pramana* is the route to the knowledge, *prama*. Many Indian thinkers set out to refute the sort of scepticism about knowledge produced by Nagarjuna, the main exponent of **Madhyamaka** Buddhism. He argued that however we try to define knowledge, whether in terms of reason or sense-experience, we are wasting our time if we think we can establish it on sure foundations. Whatever criteria of knowledge we accept are unsatisfactory, since they require further criteria, and so on ad infinitum, while if we insist on a particular criterion as being obviously right and so try to bring the series of justifications to an end, we are being arbitrary. Buddhists argue that the basis of knowledge consists of inference and experience, but the idea of some essence or substratum existing behind our experience is illegitimate, rather like the idea that a soul exists behind our experiences of the world. The **Nyaya** system is broadly realist, and takes a valid claim to knowledge to be about an actual object which has a **causal** relationship with the knowledge claim. In contrast to the scepticism of some Buddhists, it suggests that what we directly perceive are actual objects and their properties, not the impermanent flow of sensations. If it really is a knowledge and not just a belief claim, then it must be incorrigible, that is, it cannot be mistaken. A distinction is made between knowledge and truth, since we can be in a position to know that p is true without p actually being true. There are four ways of knowing. **Perception**, **inference**, verbal evidence and analogy represent the four methods. Perception is the basis of them all, and provides us with our initial data, while inference establishes the rules for working from that data to more ambitious judgements about the precise nature of what is being observed. Comparison is knowledge based on understanding the relation between a term and its meaning together with observation of the object denoted. As with inference, there are strict rules that circumscribe comparison as a means of knowledge, since there is always a danger that we shall be misled by customary associations of ideas which do not on a particular occasion actually concur with the truth. Verbal evidence is a form of knowledge based on **language**, and depends on people using language correctly and in a reliable way.

The **Sankhya** school omits comparison from the list of criteria of knowledge, but apart from that they are close to the **Nyaya** position. The **Purva Mimamsa**, by contrast, argued that knowledge is self-evident and when one has it, one knows that one has it. This leads to problems in explaining **illusions**, since we might think that we have knowledge, but we would be wrong. None the less, the 'knowledge' we think we have appears to be self-evidently knowledge while we are being deluded. A version of this theory was produced by Bhartrihari, who argued that there is no non-verbal knowledge, and the knowledge we get is based in *brahman* (reality), which we cannot actually describe. He was suspicious of the project of seeking knowledge outside the **Vedas**, something he shares with the later **Vedanta**, who hold that ordinary ways of knowing are appropriate to the objects of our world but have no purchase on the real world. Both **Dvaita** and **Vishishtadvaita** accept perception, inference and verbal evidence as the means of human knowledge. The first two are applicable to empirical matters, while the latter is appropriate for deeper issues, and is based on the interpretation of scripture. While **Advaita** appeals to the principle of the absence of negation to test the validity of knowledge, Dvaita criticizes such an idea on the basis that an example of opposite experience may always arise, which would mean that there could be no knowledge. Dvaita seeks to get around the possibility of future counter-evidence by claiming that we have an intuitive faculty which is brought into play when we have knowledge, and once it operates it can tell unerringly what is knowledge and what is not. The **Yogachara** school argues that consciousness is the basis to knowledge, and that all that is real is the stream of experiences that we can have. It was objected that this implies that there can be no spatio-temporal distinctions, but they replied that what we take to be spatio-temporal could just be a reflection of how we divide up our experiences, having nothing to do with real things themselves. Similarly with the phenomenon of shared experience, it arises because of collective intentions due to shared *karma* but there is no reason to think that it establishes a distinction between the real and the illusory. We just take certain experiences to be more solid and real than others, but there is nothing within those experiences themselves to make this more plausible or less plausible. It is just something we do. Indeed, this school argued that since what we call real objects are just collections of partial experiences, we never experience something as a whole.

In Chinese philosophy there is much discussion about the importance of knowledge socially and metaphysically. There is a protracted debate over the relative virtues of knowing with respect to doing, and vice versa. Confucianism puts heavy emphasis on the importance of **education** and the acquisition of theoretical knowledge. By contrast, the Daoists reject anything that interferes with our natural capacity to be spontaneous, and traditional knowledge, in particular what might be seen as conventional knowledge, is seen as an obstacle to living a life of natural spontaneity in **harmony** with the way of nature. Knowledge is often criticized in Daoism as being a repository of dead information, no longer relevant to the present situation, since each situation is unique. It follows that trying to imitate someone else, which is often the basis of education and learning, is damaging to one's integrity and leads one away from the dao.

In much Buddhist thought knowledge tends to be given a practical orientation, and before one acts one is obliged to find out what the true situation actually is. Knowing is being in accordance with the object, and is either intuitive and sudden, or discursive when it involves the sense faculties and the **mind**. One of the interesting features of Buddhist theories of knowledge is that these do not make a distinction between the mode of knowing and the knowledge itself. That is why on their view there is no difficulty in claiming that once we have the appropriate epistemic experience, we know, and there is no additional possible question about whether what we think we know actually is as we think it is. Compared to the correspondence view of knowledge, the Buddhists have a coherence (*sarupya*) view, where

165

the criteria of knowledge are found within the system of knowing itself. This fits in with other aspects of Buddhist theory, in particular the doctrine that all our experiences are basically **momentary**. Then if as well as the experience we do not also have a cognitive grasp of the experience, we shall be unable to say we know the experience, since if we think about its epistemic structure afterwards we shall have missed it. The process of knowing (*pramana*) involves being in agreement with its object, and must share the form of the object.

What are the objects of knowledge? These are of two kinds, either real objects or those formed through mental construction. The former exist only momentarily, they are part of a process of constant change, and although they are causally linked to each other, there is no way of linking them as far as we are concerned. Each momentary event is radically unique, and since it has nothing in common with anything else in character it cannot be named. What we normally talk about as objects of knowledge, by contrast, are ideas that we ourselves put together from the basic building bricks of our experience, and these we can name and identify easily since we have criteria of identity for them, in particular references in space and **time**. As a result of this distinction we can talk about two kinds of knowledge, perceptual which is directed at the momentary events, and inferential which has as its object the generalized forms we construct. They need to be distinguished, since the bare perceptual grasp of the momentary events is not enough to give us anything we can use in a proposition, and the judgement we make cannot involve entirely discrete particulars. Both methods are valid, and provide knowledge, but both are very different from each other. Perception itself defies conceptualization and language, and is free of error, since error only comes in with the introduction of our own ideas and generalizations. This theory of knowledge is a reflection of a Buddhist view that everything based on human thought is fictitious, while the real can only be a moment that coheres with pure sensation, a thing in itself. This does not mean that we cannot analyse what are on ordinary interpretations human knowledge, but we should be aware that the subject of discussion here does not really exist.

Islamic philosophers were generally agreed that knowledge is a matter of grasping the immaterial forms, the essences of things. There are two routes to knowledge, a philosophical and a prophetic route. The former process is one where we move from the known objects of conceptualization (*tasawwur*) to the unknown, using the tool of syllogistic reasoning. **Logic** is the way in which this is done, and it results in a demonstrative understanding of reality. Another form of knowledge is prophetic, in that God or the **active intellect** inspires an individual through affecting his **imagination** to acquire a great deal of knowledge, and not only knowledge of essences but also knowledge of how to put over that understanding to a wider public, how to make speeches and present truths that are difficult in easy and attractive ways. Philosophical and prophetic knowledge is the same knowledge, it is just presented to the knower in different ways. Knowledge of both kinds passes through discrete stages. First of all it moves from potentiality (potential intellect) to actuality (actual intellect), from actuality to an awareness of that actuality (acquired intellect), where the latter is the highest stage we can reach. This is called 'acquired' because the assumption is that it is achieved through connection with something outside of itself, a linking of the human with the divine. This brings out nicely the importance of knowledge not only in the practical running of our lives but also in helping us link up with the eternal forms, where such a link is the route to complete happiness, complete since the object of knowledge is **eternal**. Given the thesis that the knower and the object of knowledge are the same, if the object of knowledge is **immortal**, then so is the individual who manages to have the knowledge. Sometimes this is taken to mean, as it does with ibn Rushd, that in so far as we manage to grasp such knowledge, we are part of an eternal system of ideas. At other times it is taken by ibn Sina to argue that our intellect must be eternal since it is capable of understanding eternal objects, and he uses this idea to present a notion of an individual spiritual **afterlife**.

See: **action**, *samsara*

Further reading: Chatterjee 1965, Dasgupta 1975, Datta 1972, Garfield 1995, Jayatilleke 1986, Kalupahana 1986, Leaman 1997, Matilal 1971, 1986, Puligandla 1997.

koan, kongan In chan (zen) Buddhism use is made of critical phrases or puzzles which lead the seeker after **enlightenment** to reach a nonconceptual level of understanding that is helpful in his or her quest. The point of the perplexing nature of such sayings is to make the student experience doubt, since he cannot resolve the riddle. Doubt forces the **mind** to escape from the complacency of its normal way of thinking, and it becomes evident that the ordinary rational processes are incapable of understanding the problem that has been set. Anything that threatens the security with which we hold traditional ideas about the mind and the intellect is welcome to Buddhism, which tries to deconstruct such concepts. Creating mental stress is designed to change people, and some chan Buddhists valued ordinary life for its proclivity to raise issues that lead to frustration and doubt, by contrast with the security of the life of the **ascetic**. But the important thing is both to live in the world and remain detached; if one concentrates on the events of the world and regards them as significant, no progress will be made. A way of doing this is to allow doubts to build up to such an extent that they destroy the dichotomies involved in thought, as well as the notion of the individual self.

Further reading: Abe 1985, Gregory 1987, Heine 1993, LaFleur 1983.

kongan, riddle – *see* **koan**, **Korean philosophy**

Korean philosophy The Korean peninsula has tended to be under the control of China culturally, and often politically also, as well as suffering occasional invasions from Japan and Mongolia. Its philosophy has been just as heavily influenced by Confucianism and Buddhism, and the varying political powers in the country tended to support one form of religion over another. Both *tian tai* and *hua yan* forms of Buddhism became important, as did the chan (zen) version. A Korean thinker, Wonhyo, even played a part in the structure of *hua yan* Buddhism. Wonhyo sought to reconcile the different traditions of Chinese and Indian thought, and made a clear distinction between those texts that are mainly about explaining the idea of **dependent origination** and those that discuss the nature of ultimate reality. The former texts are rather negative, in that they present a critical interpretation of ordinary experience in terms of the illusions that we generally have about it. The latter texts are more positive, describing the nature of higher **consciousness** and the **mind** that lies behind or within ordinary events. This led to a version of the *dharma* nature (Popsong) school of Buddhism. The attempt at syncretising different philosophical trends was something of a theme in Korean philosophy, and there were many efforts to reconcile the chan approach to **meditation**, with its emphasis on sudden **enlightenment**, with the more gradual meditation approaches.

This was particularly important in the thought of perhaps the most important Korean philosopher, Chinul, the creator of a specifically Korean version of chan Buddhism. Enlightenment can be achieved suddenly, but it also involves a gradual process, and on both routes it is important to pay suitable attention to scripture. He developed the *hwadu* or *kongan* (Korean versions of the *koan*), spiritual riddles designed to replace conceptual appraisal and stimulate going beyond concepts and words in order to concentrate on the kind of mindlessness that leads to sudden enlightenment. What is important about his approach is that he stresses the reconciliation of such sudden enlightenment with the appropriate religious texts, so that it is clearly not enough for enlightenment to try just to abandon our everyday concepts. We need to use Buddhist texts to get to this position in the first place, and then we can explore the paradoxes that those texts throw up. The point of the riddles is to purify the mind and prepare it for enlightenment.

There was also an important trend in Korean Confucian thought. Yi T'oegye generally followed the approach of Zhu-xi, and developed the latter's thought in particularly interesting ways on the connections between *li* and *qi*, that is, between the notion of a principle and matter. The former is taken to be superior to the latter, but it is not made clear why. It is difficult to see how *li* could exist before *qi*, since if there is no matter there is nothing for the principle to define itself in. The solution Yi produced suggests that these notions go together at all times, and that *li* is the force capable of bringing about the good, while *qi* resists it and unless the *li* affecting it is strong enough, produces **evil**. We ourselves are capable of living our lives in line with *li*, but we are often confused by the forces of matter (here identified with our desires and egoism) in ignoring this or forgetting it, and so we sink into evil. What Confucian self-cultivation is designed to do is to help us reassert the original *li* and improve on the characters that we have acquired through turning away from it. This does not mean that we must magnify the significance of *li* as opposed to *qi*, quite the opposite. They should be applied together, as opposed to the situation in ordinary life, where the *qi* tends to overwhelm the *li*.

There is undoubtedly a certain amount of dualism in this interpretation of the struggle between our ethical selves and our material selves, something that was criticized by Yi Yulgok. Where his predecessor goes wrong, he argues, is in not understanding the basic metaphysical unity of reality. The universe is a unity made up of **yin** and **yang**, and the opposition of these forces constructs its **harmony**. The essence of the world is change, and this occurs in *qi*, but is shaped by *li*. When *yin* is the dominant force, the universe is empty, but matter is still there. The sage can fall into align-ment with the changing structure of the universe, and even more, he can affect the universe, as the universe affects him. What he needs to study are the basic principles of the harmony that makes up universal balance. On this view, there is nothing innately bad about matter, and it is a dualistic error to think of there being matter without shape, or shape without matter. These only operate together, and there is little point in thinking of nature and morality as being separate and independent forces. Rather, they are parts of the same thing, aspects of universal change and development. The sage actually operates in much the same way, as a sort of linking of heaven and earth, since he manages to direct his material force in virtuous directions.

Further reading: Buswell 1983, de Bary and Haboush 1985, Lee 1993, Park Sung-bae 1983, Swanson 1989.

kyong, single-mindedness – *see* **human nature**

language According to the **Nyaya-Vaisheshika**, there is a
type of knowledge based on language, and on the reliable
use of language to transmit information and ideas. They
stressed the role of language in the possibility of acquisition
of **knowledge**, and although their basic unit of meaning
was the word and not the sentence, they emphasized that
the link between a word and its meaning is conventional and
not natural, although there was disagreement as to whether
it is God or human beings who give words their meanings.
This theory is to a degree extended by Bhartrihari who also
insisted on the significance of language for the possibility of
knowledge, which he uses to criticize the idea that we can
have words that are indeterminate or indescribable linguis-
tically. He no doubt had in mind here terms like *brahman*,
reality, which some philosophers like Shankara and the
Advaita Vedanta held to be indescribable. For Bhartrihari
the sentence is the primary semantic unit, and if we can
understand a sentence, which is itself an aspect of the
manifestation of *brahman*, then it must provide some guide
to a clear understanding of *brahman* itself. One aspect of
his theory of meaning that makes this more plausible is his
inclusion of the speaker's intention as part of the meaning.
This rescues many sentences from obscurity, and suggests
that the meaning will be something quite determinate and
unambiguous.

One of the main sources of debate was over the primary unit of meaning, that is, is it the word or the sentence of which the word is only a constituent? The **Purva Mimamsakas** tend to opt for the sentence over the word, although not always. The **Vedantin** philosopher Ramanuja criticizes the view that the language of the **Vedas** is largely directed to **action** and not to the description of facts, and so should not be taken to be trying to describe reality. He criticizes the idea that what lies behind language is the intention with which it is produced. The theory he is discussing is one in which we establish the meaning of terms through ostensive definition, through someone uttering a word and then pointing to the object it describes, with the intention that we connect the term with the object. Ramanuja suggests that the intention here could not really be to describe an object, since it is accepted that the point of language is to inspire action, so it must be some subjective feature in the agent that makes him interested in the object. Yet the only subjective feature we possess that is generally acceptable is that which is pleasurable, and surely the key term in the acquisition of language and meaning cannot be pleasure. Pleasure as a guiding principle might be acceptable for a **materialist**, but not for an orthodox adherent of the Hindu texts. Ramanuja argues by contrast that the primary point of language is to describe facts, and its prescriptive use is a secondary consideration which is only possible once there is agreement about the facts. Of course, language can be extended to go further than the facts of the phenomenal world, and the ultimate referents of words are *brahman*.

Ramanuja accepts that Sanskrit is the model for language itself, a common assumption of Vedantins, and that language consists of words and sentences. The word consists of a root and a suffix, the former being the element that makes it possible for it to keep the same basic meaning, while the latter enables it to vary slightly in different developments of the root. The point of being able to differentiate such developments is to pick out different objects, albeit related ones, and the sentence brings words together in even more complex ways to refer to a variety of things. This leads to the acknowledgement of a serious limitation in language, since it specializes in dealing with the complex it cannot describe the pure, simple and undifferentiated essence of *brahman*. One way around this, which is adopted by Shankara, is to argue that while the language we use implies differentiation, this is to be understood as only being a subjective feature describing our own limited point of view. We can then undertake to purify the concepts we use to bring about an understanding that is more accurate of the nature of reality. *Brahman* is absolutely undifferentiated in itself, but the only language we have to describe it is our familiar unsatisfactory language, and the best we can do is to describe it in negative terms, so indicating its reality as entirely indeterminate. For Ramanuja, by contrast, the structure of language purports to be an objective representation of reality, and so this sort of solution cannot work. There is a problem anyway with the attempt to stretch language in directions it will not extend to, as when we deny that something has particular qualities like **being** or **knowledge** by claiming that it is 'not non-being' and 'not non-conscious'.

Does this mean that there is no possibility of using language to describe language, according to Ramanuja? This is not the claim, but rather he suggests that when we extend our ordinary language to describe reality we have to purify words of their empirical associations, and yet retain their root meaning. We can do this by arguing through analogy, which enables us to end up with a concept of reality that is both distinct from the constituents of our world and yet to a degree comprehensible as the ultimate meaning of that world.

Buddhism tends to be critical of the notion of language as representing the truth, since language treats phenomena as though they are real and worthy of our attention, and also suggests that a permanent and significant self exists. This critical attitude may have been very much a reaction to the realism of the Nyaya-Vaisheshika and Purva Mimamsa schools. Language is a matter of conceptualization, and as such it deals with a mental extrapolation of the **momentary** and changing experiences we have. Much use was made of the notion of

specifying meaning through contrasting it with negative properties, so that we are told what something is by being told
what it is not. There is a sort of dialectical relationship
between affirmation and negation, according to which neither
is primary and both have to be in operation for a sentence
to have meaning. Words represent concepts rather than real
things, and this representation takes place through the exclusion of opposites. Once one understands the meaning of a
word, one can disregard the word itself, according to both
Daoists and Buddhists. The meaning of a word is tied up
with many formal structures, and these can be left behind
once that meaning is grasped, in the same way that once one
has caught an animal in a trap, one can disregard the trap.
Another Buddhist example is that when one has reached the
farther shore, one can leave the boat behind. But will one
not wish to use the boat or the trap again? The answer is
no, since these tools have served their purpose, and they will
not be required again. The purpose of a word is to embody
a meaning, and once that meaning is extracted, the form of
the meaning is useless. So although language is conventional,
this cannot be its entire meaning, since such a description of
language is only a description, not an explanation. Dignaga
and Dharmakirti reject the Nyaya idea that language refers
to real **universals** as its meaning and replace it with the
theory that language describes reality in a negative way,
through excluding objects from being in a class to which
they do not belong. A name has meaning in so far as it refers
negatively to an object within a domain.

Nagarjuna has a particularly interesting account of language
in his defence of the **Madhyamaka** (Middle) version of
Buddhism. He argued that we tend to use sentences that make
sense only because of the combination of terms, and then
separate the terms as though they could exist on their own.
For example, the sentence 'Nina writes' uses names that are
fused together necessarily, since unless there was a subject of
the action there would be no particular action, and unless there
was an action to characterize the subject, the description of
the subject would be very different. Yet we tend to pull the

parts of the proposition away from the whole, imagining that there is a 'Nina' who exists apart from writing and a writing that exists independently of Nina. Of course, we can grammatically separate the different parts of a sentence, and this is acceptable provided that we do not go further and assert that the parts of the sentence are themselves separable. This seems to be wrong, since surely we can imagine Nina not writing, and doing something else, even when we produce that description of what she is doing. Not according to Nagarjuna, since our actions (*karma*) are constantly changing who we are, and thinking of the subject as someone who could now be writing, but who could also be doing something else instead is to fall into the notion of the independent self (*atman*) to which properties occasionally adhere, perhaps even a permanent and unchanging self which goes from life to life remaining constant. This is one of the primary illusions Buddhism warns us against, and Nagarjuna argues that it is an illusion fostered by confusing a grammatical separability of the parts of a sentence with the logical separability of the concepts involved.

Confucius argued that at the basis of any significant social reform lies what he calls the **rectification of names**. What he meant by this is that the nature of the leading concepts in a culture should be defined and clearly understood, and it will then follow that people will understand the place in society that they ought to fill. Zhuangzi regards language as a major problem in understanding the nature of the dao. What we should concentrate on are our experiences of it, and language just gets in the way of that experience. And yet, of course, there is a need to use language in order to communicate what the dao actually is. The answer is that language has to be used, but should not be taken as anything more than a rough approximation of the nature of reality. Daoism and Confucianism contrast here, in that the latter sees names as the route to achieving **harmony** in society and the world, while the former regards them as necessary evils, to be discarded once it is possible to link up with the main principles of reality. The **Legalists** follow the Confucianists in arguing for the importance of clear links between terms and what they represent, Han Fei in particular claiming that order is only possible when names correspond to actuality. When this happens everyone in government and society knows precisely what their duties are and so what is expected of them, and so harmony and control are then achieved.

The significance of language in Islamic philosophy is intimately connected to Arabic, the language in which God spoke when he transmitted the Qur´an. Interpretation of the holy text was made possible by those who studied the language and understood its grammatical structure. This view came to be challenged with the arrival of **logic** in the Islamic world in the tenth century, since the logicians argued that the grammarians only dealt with the superficial aspects of language, by contrast with the logicians' ability to investigate the deep structure of what is expressed in all languages. A famous debate took place in Baghdad between ibn Matta, the advocate of Greek logic, and al-Sirafi, a theologian defending the traditional Islamic ways of analysing language. The latter argued that it is impossible to separate language from logic, so that to understand Arabic texts one has to grasp the language and the culture of which it is a part. This debate was to continue in the Islamic world for some time afterwards, and was clearly highly significant since it deals with who is the appropriate person to interpret a text, the philosopher or the grammarian.

Two approaches to the nature of meaning dominated Islamic philosophy. According to one, followed by ibn Sina and al-Ghazali, the meaning of a term 't' does not include the **existence** of whatever 't' actually is, so for 't' to come into existence something has to happen to move it from potentiality to actuality. On the other, more Aristotelian, view defended by ibn Rushd the cause of 't' is part of what 't' means. It follows then that there are restrictions on what we can say about 't', since we cannot put it in an entirely different physical context as compared with where it normally resides. It is not possible for God to change the basic constituents of the world, since if he could do so he would also be changing the meanings of the concepts involved, and so not changing 't' at all, but something that to a certain extent resembles 't'. Al-Ghazali argues that God can do anything that is logically possible, so he can change the behaviour of 't' without changing the meaning of 't' itself, while for ibn Rushd if the behaviour of 't' changes then the meaning of 't' itself is different. Ibn Rushd accuses al-Ghazali of treating God as someone much like ourselves, except with more power, whereas ibn Rushd argues that the meaning of predicates when applied to God are very different from their application to ourselves. God is the exemplar or perfect example of these predicates, and they only apply to us in a derivative and weaker sense. Al-Ghazali, by contrast, insists that if our language about God is to have the significance that religion insists it should, we must use more or less the same language with the same meanings as we apply in the case of our ordinary lives. He argues for a view of language as univocal, where each term has a simple and basic meaning, by contrast with the equivocal approach of ibn Rushd, for whom there are a variety of layers of meaning which are loosely interconnected. The trouble with the theologians, ibn Rushd argues, is that they make religious language even more complicated than it is originally, and lead people to doubt their religion given the wide variety of interpretations that they produce. Language should by contrast be regarded as rich enough to embody **ambiguity** and indeterminacy, which mirror the differences that exist between different people. Al-Ghazali insists that language should be seen as simple, and argues that the notion of the indeterminacy of language is merely a way of disguising the fact that no real opportunity is given to God to participate freely in the universe. We know what it is for someone to act, and if we cannot accept that God acts in a similar way, then we do not use the language of action and God appropriately.

See: *anatman*, **creation**

Further reading: Allinson 1989b, Bhatt 1975, Cabezon 1994, Carr and Mahalingam 1997, Chung 1992, Creel 1953, Dravida 1972, Griffiths 1986, Hansen 1983, Kaltenmark 1969, LaFleur 1983, Leaman 1985, Matilal 1971.

law Islamic law (*shari'a*) is the collection of beliefs and rules that stem from the Qur'an, the **hadith** (sayings of the Prophet and his Companions) and the perfect practice (**sunna**) of the community of Islam. Out of this basis a variety of different approaches to the nature of law emerged in the sunni community, especially dealing with how one could work out what actions are legal or otherwise. Some accepted the use of analogy, while others put severe restrictions on it, and the notion of a consensus (*ijma'*) which represents an agreement among scholars, or the community at large, was also interpreted in a variety of ways. The Shi'i school tended to replace the notion of analogy with that of reason ('*aql*) and put more reliance on the judgement of an individual legal authority, who is regarded as standing in the role of intermediary with the *imam*, who in turn is the intermediary between God and his believers.

See: *fa*, **fundamentalism**, **justice**, **Legalism**
Further reading: Nasr and Leaman 1996.

Legalism The most systematic of the Legalists was Han Fei, who came at the end of a variety of Legalist schools. Legalism, as the name suggests, is concerned largely with organization, although not really legal organization. It deals with the principles of leadership and social control. There was a long-standing controversy in the movement as to what was the leading principle of Legalism, whether it is *shi* (power or authority), *fa* (law or regulation) or *shu* (the methodology of making friends and influencing people in politics). Han Fei resolved the argument by suggesting that all three are criteria of effective government. The intelligent ruler has authority, and uses it to establish a law which is carried out, and because he knows how to put over this law in such a way that the population does not even realize that it is being controlled, he is capable of being an efficient politician.

One of the unusual features of Legalism in contrast to other forms of Chinese thought is what is sometimes taken to be its lack of respect for the past. The Legalists suggested that in the past there was no need to worry about material success since there were few people and many resources, but in modern times the situation was far less happy. Now, they argued, there is a need for strict legislation to control the population, and what the ruler needs is power, not necessarily the ability to lead by the example of his moral character (the Confucian model). He does not need himself to incorporate these virtues since he will be able to get others to do this for him, since he is able to manipulate others to serve as the exemplar for moral conduct in his stead. He can know this through his political ability, and will be able to control people through the sticks and carrots of punishment and reward. In acting in this way he fits his policy to **human nature**, which is affected by pains and pleasures, and he uses his understanding of this nature to develop laws and policies that accord with what are in the interests of the people.

There is an interesting agreement between the Legalists and the Daoists when it comes to the best means of ruling. According to the both, the policy ought to be one of doing nothing, yet with everything being done, the principle of *wu wei*. The successful ruler should follow the principle of non-**action**, allowing others to act for him. This is based on the notion that human beings are part of the natural world, and so should be governed in accordance with the natural order (dao). The principles (*li*) of reality are to be followed by the wise ruler, who at his best manages to control everything by getting others to behave in accordance with his wishes. He not only controls others, but also himself in this way, by restraining his personal interests and bringing these into line with the dao and *li*.

Further reading: Creel 1953, Graham 1989, Han Fei 1964, Peerenboom 1993, Wang and Chang 1986, Watson 1967.

li There are two concepts of *li* in Chinese, with distinct characters. One means 'principle' and could well have come first from the **Book of Changes**, while the other means 'ritual' (coming from the word for 'sacrifice'). The latter is often translated as 'religion' or 'morality'; its original meaning is 'rites of propriety' and it denoted part of the ritual of sacrifice. It came to mean the rules of conduct and the right behaviour in particular circumstances. It played a part in the worship of ancestors in the Zhou dynasty, and has come to represent notions like stability, respect for people at different levels in society, and links between different periods of time, and so has become equivalent to the idea of what leads to **harmony** and stability. In modern Chinese philosophy the other notion of *li* has come to mean principle or form in the sense of the Platonic idea and the Aristotelian form. What makes it so important is that it marks the significance of differences, and also the significance of incorporating those differences within a unity.

Moral *li* involves the emotional reactions of people to the difficulties that arise in life, and when institutionalized appropriately will result in a just and successful polity. On a more metaphysical level, it deals with the links between heaven and earth. Confucius advocated the rediscovery of the principle of *li* so that there would be moral and cultural norms to bring about social harmony, norms that could be embodied in political institutions. This would result in the attainment of harmony and the possibility of individual moral and spiritual growth. What is required for this to happen is a limiting of the desire for personal advancement and an orientation towards the welfare of society as a whole. The metaphysical notion was even given a Daoist twist by Han Fei who links it with the way in which something becomes the thing it is. The dao then is the totality of *li* and while the former changes all the time, the latter remains relatively stable. Within all change, something remains the same, and *li* represents the particular that remains constant, while dao is the changing universal.

The **Neoconfucians** took *li* to be the metaphysical essence of the world, and used it as part of their argument that there is a basis of reality, perhaps the idea of something physical like gas. Once one agrees that the basis of reality is something, one then needs some argument as to why that common substratum was capable of producing different objects in the world. After all, in the substratum itself there is nothing to differentiate between one type of thing or another. All there is is a common form of material. The answer is in the existence of the principle (*li*) which ensures that the something out of which an object develops is shaped in terms of the principle of the particular object that in fact results. The notion is normally taken to relate more to moral than to metaphysical reality, though, and is very important for Confucianism with its concentration on ethics. The **Legalists**, by contrast, were critical of the moral concept, arguing that it was never going to be sufficient to bring about a **just** society. They stressed the links between notions of propriety and the economic conditions of the time, and doubted whether moral **education** would bring about positive social change unless the economic context were appropriate.

The Neoconfucians use the concept of metaphysical *li* to attack Buddhism. The latter denies the reality of *li*, and although there is truth in the argument that the phenomenal world is **empty** given its propensity to change and lack of permanence, this certainly does not extend to the principles behind the appearances of the world. That is, there are good arguments for the existence of eternal and permanent principles that lie behind the world. This argument from Zhuxi is supplemented by one from Wang Shuren, who suggests that the Buddhist claim to reject attachment to the world displays just such an attachment. The fact that Confucians do have an attachment to the world is compatible with acceptance of the dangers of such attachment, since the Confucians are able to combine connection with the world with an insulation of the self from attachment. The Buddhists are concerned about the problems associated with human relationships, and so try to escape them, but this is because they are already attached to them. Confucians, by contrast, are attached to the principles and relationships that are important and that provide an opportunity for virtuous action, but they do this in such a way as to avoid permanent attachment to the objects of the world.

The metaphysical concept of *li* plays an interesting part in the *hua yan* Buddhist ontology. Matter lacks its own essence, since it can be shaped into anything that a designer envisages (within certain limits, of course). When it is shaped into something it acquires a form or power, a *shi*, but as matter it is *li*, the basis from which forms are constructed. It is an easy step to identify *li* with the dao as the absolute principle behind change, and also to identify it with the **buddha nature**, which is an essential transcendent entity. But there is no point in strictly differentiating between different ontological levels of what brings about change and what the substratum of change is, since whatever is material must have some shape, and whatever has some shape must have a material basis. This brings out how the notion of ultimate reality is part and parcel of the world of experience, the ordinary world with which we are all familiar, and there is little difficulty in linking this conception with the Daoist conception of nature and **enlightenment** as living in harmony with nature and the natural processes of change. However, although the *li* has to have some shape or another, it does not have to have a particular shape, so the matter is always matter, but it is only matter if it also has a shape. It follows that when the shape is constructed, the matter comes into existence, in the sense that it takes on a particular shape. We might say that the matter remains matter throughout, and this is true, but the matter has to be shaped into a particular form if it is going to remain matter. The matter itself as matter does not change, and in a sense it remains dormant, since unless something changes it will not change by itself. Is *li* equivalent to emptiness, in the **Madhyamaka** sense of being bereft of real existence? This is a possibility, but the notion of *li* also has more positive connotations, which would involve identifying it with the buddha nature doctrine. Since all the things in our world are just matter with a particular form, and the form does not really exist, all things are the same. Matter, as matter, is the same and does not change; it is only when it is shaped in some way that it appears to be different from other shapes.

183

Since the matter itself does not change it remains the same throughout, and so all things that we experience are in themselves the same thing.

Further reading: Chan 1972, Confucius 1993, Creel 1953, Fung 1952, Griffiths 1994, Kaltenmark 1969, King 1991, Tu Wei-Ming 1985, Watson 1967.

li xue, School of Principles – *see* **Neoconfucianism**

liberation   A key notion in much Asian philosophy, since the world is regarded as a site of bondage, from which liberation through **enlightenment** is the only ultimately acceptable solution. It is linked closely with the concepts of *moksha* and *nirvana*.

lila   In **Vedanta** thought God creates the universe at various times, through *lila* or 'joyful play'. This does not imply that it is done in a casual or capricious manner, but were the creation to come about through the desire to satisfy a want or achieve a personal end it would involve *karma* and so not be free. God does not need to satisfy any needs or attain any ends, he is free from such imperfections in his actions, and so creates freely and spontaneously out of a pure pleasure in the capacity to act. The concept of *lila* is designed to escape the following apparent dilemma. God could not have created the world out of a desire to satisfy some need of his, since he has no needs. On the other hand, if God created the world in order to benefit his creation, he would surely have created it very differently, since it is now so full of suffering. The cause of the world cannot be reality or *brahman*, it appears to follow. When Ramanuja responds that *brahman* creates out of a spirit of sport or play he is pointing out that intentional action may be carried out without thought of gain. That is, it is entirely spontaneous and free, performed wholly out of a motive of the delight of acting and creating. The spontaneity is important here, since it brings out the fact that the activity is entirely unnecessitated, and so not part of the realm of **samsara**.

In his commentary on the *Brahmasutras* Shankara brings out his distinction between two notions of God. The *saguna brahman*, qualified reality, is often referred to as **ishvara** or Lord. This contrasts with the *nirguna brahman*, the notion of a creator with no properties, an indescribable creator. Saying that God created the world out of *lila* brings out the way in which he creates and sustains the world out of the sheer enjoyment of it, without any need to satisfy a desire on his part. The Jains criticized this opinion, claiming that if God created the world with no purpose, then he is himself without purpose, and if the world was created in a kind of sport, it was the sport of an immature and irresponsible being. Shankara responds to such criticisms by pointing out that God is in the position of a very powerful and superior individual whose needs are all taken care of, and who spends his time in occupations whose only purpose is to entertain him. In that case the motive if any out of which he acts is sport, and it would interfere with his status as the amateur par excellence if there were other considerations that influenced the nature and style of such creation.

Further reading: Deutsch 1968, Deutsch and Van Buitenen 1971.

logic   Logic in Indian philosophy developed in interesting and important ways. What is known as logic has a wider sense than logic in the Anglo-American tradition, for example, since it involves as well as the rules of reasoning in deductive thought the criteria of **knowledge** and the nature of **perception**. Although the **materialist** Lokayata tradition seems to have disapproved of logical reasoning in so far as it sought to extend knowledge from the immediate objects of experience, the other schools were interested in showing how legitimate or otherwise such extensions could be. One of the topics that came in for much analysis is the nature of negative sentences. The **Purva Mimamsakas** argue that negative sentences are arrived at through an independent means of knowledge. The Buddhists hold such sentences to be an important aspect of knowing anything to be true about the phenomenal world, but do not think that one needs to appeal to an entirely new faculty to make them possible. The main difference between the various schools lies in the appropriate analysis of generality (*vyapti*), the sort of sentence that makes a general point from a particular example. The favourite example is that wherever there is smoke, there is fire, and there are many different positions on how far, if at all, such generalizations are acceptable. The fact that this sort of topic is raised as a logical problem brings out the very broad definition of logic in Indian philosophy. The types of argument form that constitute **inference** do depend in interesting ways on the general metaphysics of the different schools, as one would expect.

An area of logic that was well developed also was the nature of the fallacy. Fallacies are judgements that appear to be good reasons for coming to a particular conclusion, but are not good reasons at all. Many of the criteria of fallacy were based on the irrelevance of a premise, on the existence of incompatible predicates, or on a premise that is too broad to fit into the syllogism.

The Buddhist Dignaga did a great deal to tidy up the structure of logic up to his time, and he considerably simplified the understanding of the structure of the syllogism. On the other hand, there is another tradition in Buddhist thought to oppose its analytical nature and replace it with more synthetic reasoning processes, thus seeking to incorporate apparent dichotomies in acceptable judgements. After all, one of the novel aspects of Buddhism is the attempt to present a doctrine that lies between the extremes of other doctrines, and in this way it transcends the contradictions the other doctrines hold out as being unbridgeable. There are interesting links between the Buddha himself and the appropriate attitude to the law of contradiction, which asserts that a statement and its contradictory cannot both be true. When he was asked whether the Buddha continues to exist after death, he compared the query to the direction in which a flame goes when it is extinguished. It is not correct to say it goes north, or that it does not go north, and one could say that it neither goes north nor does it not go north. But this is not a critique of the law of contradiction, rather it suggests that the question is so misplaced that it seems to go against that law. The fact that it seems to contradict such a law is in itself evidence of how poorly constructed the question itself is. It is this sort of question that the Mahayana school uses to suggest that all firm positions on the nature of reality are contradictory, from which it does not follow that the law of contradiction itself is tentative, since it is the basis of all argument.

Confucius had a project for the **rectification of names**, which meant that we ought to be clear on the meaning of the main terms we use, since otherwise our thought will be loose and fail to engage with current issues and problems. This point was developed by Xunzi who argued that the logic of names is designed to clarify the nature of similarities and dissimilarities. The point of having different names is to be able to use them to refer to different things that exist. He distinguished between different forms of generality, some of which deal with classes while others are of more restricted forms of generality. Chinese logic went a long way to explore the logical nature of language. For example, Huishi sought to use antinomies to throw light on the logic of the terms that are apparently thrown into conflict with each other. He was interested in statements like 'The heavens are as low as the earth, and the mountains are on the same level as the marshes.' While an ordinary person believes that the heavens are above the earth, we can when we look into the distance see that they meet. Also, some marshes are just as high as the low parts of mountains. He uses these and similar examples to show that place is relative. From a logical point of view, every place shares the category of being a place with every other place, and it is only as individuals that they can be said to be distinct from each other. This technique was followed famously by Gongsun Long who argued that 'a white horse is not a horse'. His argument was that the term 'horse' refers to a shape, while 'white' refers to a colour. 'Horse' refers to any horse, while 'white' refers to anything that is capable of having a colour. A horse may have any colour, and is a **universal** in which, as a universal, there is no colour. The point he is making is that a horse is not the same as a white horse. This and similar apparent paradoxes were used as parts of the rectification of names project, which insisted on the importance of being clear on the links between names and the objects they describe in the world.

One of the main features of Chinese logic is the firm defence of the Law of Non-Contradiction and the Law of Excluded Middle. By contrast, the Japanese thinker D.T. Suzuki argued in his defence of zen that we need to transcend these principles if we are to appreciate the logic of zen. It is important to put it in this way, and not that the logic of zen opposes dualistic logic, since there is nothing wrong with dualistic logic. The problem with it is that it is limited to one form of reasoning, and not open to the significance of intuition. There is a tendency in some thinkers to distinguish between Western and Eastern logic, where the latter is holistic and synthetic, in opposition to the analysis and piecemeal nature of the former.

Islamic philosophers were largely interested in forms of logic derived from Aristotle and the Stoics, and a great deal of work went into the development of systems of logic and reasoning. Even thinkers like al-Ghazali who were critical of the use of Greek philosophy were supporters of logic, although some thinkers were opposed both to philosophy and logic, arguing that the latter was more than a technical set of rules but involved a metaphysics. The notion of logic accepted by its supporters was as a system of rules that directs the intellect towards the truth and away from error, and logic was often seen as a tool of philosophy, rather than as a part of philosophy. Al-Farabi is the best of the earliest logicians, and his work was broadened by ibn Sina, who explained the value of logic as being capable of deriving the unknown from the known via the syllogistic method. Both thinkers wished to distinguish logic from **language**, since the latter can only provide us with rules that govern the correct use of terms within a particular language, whereas logic provides rules that are universal and cover all terms in all languages. Grammar may come to be the object of logic, but it can never be more than an object since it totally lacks the theoretical and general power of logic.

An important distinction was made between conceptualization (*tasawwur*) and assent (*tasdiq*). The former is the act of the **mind** which results in the grasp of a particular essence, while the latter is the act of the intellect which results in a judgement with a truth-value being created. Assent is only possible if conceptualization has already happened, but the reverse is not the case. We may hold ideas in our mind without wondering whether they are true or not. Conceptualization represents the definition or first premise which is then expanded through another premise via the syllogism to produce something both new and true, that is, assent. The purpose of logic is to show how knowledge may be achieved, and the best sort of knowledge is that which is certain and necessary, and so based on demonstrative reasoning. Such syllogisms are made up of premises that have to be assented to, and so their conclusions are just as certain as their premises. Dialectical reasoning, by contrast, starts off with premises that are generally accepted, but nothing logically stronger, while rhetorical syllogisms are based on less reliable premises. Sophistical reasoning is based on premises that bear some superficial resemblance to an entirely different form of premise, while poetic premises affect the **imagination** to produce a feeling. Even the lowest form of reasoning, poetry, is still to a certain extent reasoning, and this was a theme pursued generally by Islamic philosophy, that although the rational content of different forms of expression may decline quite sharply, they still have some rational content within them. The different forms of reasoning are seen as different forms of expression suitable for different people, with philosophers using demonstrative reasoning, theologians and lawyers using dialectical and worse, politicians and religious leaders using the rest, but all these different forms of reasoning may be used to put over the same proposition, albeit in varying ways.

See: **orientalism**

Further reading: Cabezon 1994, Capra 1976, Carr and Mahalingam 1997, Chan 1972, Chatterjee 1965, Chi 1969, Dainian and Cohen 1996, Dasgupta 1975, Dravida 1972, Dreyfus 1997, Fung 1970, Graham 1978, 1989, Hansen 1983, Matilal 1968, 1971, Nasr and Leaman 1996, Randle 1930, Stcherbatsky 1962, Smart 1964, Tyler 1977.

Lokayata, school of materialists – *see* **consciousness, materialism**

Lotus Sutra – *see* **Chinese** and **Japanese philosophy, faith, harmony, skilful means**

love   An important concept in Mohism is universal love (*jianai*), which is really equivalent to the virtue of being human (*ren*). This involves no distinction between people at different social and economic levels, but is to be a general benevolence. Discriminating between people is for Mozi the very opposite of love, since it leads to disharmony and separation. Loving others will result in their loving you. This notion of love stems from Mozi's cosmology, according to which the universe is a whole (*jian*) just as society is a whole, and steps should be taken to keep the parts together instead of letting them pull apart. What this idea developed into was a general policy of utilitarianism, and Mozi advocated simplicity of life and altruism in order to preserve the sort of state in which everyone could benefit both himself and others.

Buddhism defends the idea of what might be linked with love in the sense of **compassion**, while for many Buddhist thinkers physical love would be seen as an aspect of craving which gets in the way of **enlightenment**. Some **tantric** views would defend the role of physical love as a spiritual route, while within Hindu philosophy the more effective path to enlightenment which involves love would be identified with ***bhakti yoga***, love of God expressed in worship.

In Islamic philosophy the thinkers who used the concept of love seriously in their work were the **Sufis,** this being the appropriate attitude we should have to God, and the attitude he has for us. The most systematic thinker on this topic, but from a different perspective, is ibn Sina in his *Treatise on Love.* Here he analyses physical and intellectual love, and he argues that we can ennoble even our baser instincts and practices by bringing them within the control of reason as opposed to the physical part of us. Although the lower pleasures have their proper role, they can interfere with the development of the higher pleasures, since the desire to unite with the beautiful can be experienced at both a physical and an intellectual level, and the former can get in the way of the latter. There is nothing wrong with becoming involved in physical love, provided that it is within an appropriate legal and religious context.

Further reading: Aronson 1980, Goodman 1992, Graham 1978, Watson 1967.

Madhyamaka/Madhyamika One of the most important divisions of Buddhist philosophy, a part of the Mahayana tradition, founded quite possibly by Nagarjuna and his followers in order to explain that the route to liberation is through the realization of emptiness. Madhyamaka is the school of the Middle Way. It takes very seriously the idea expressed by the Buddha that everything exists only contingently. It starts from the proposition that everything is interdependent, which means that they are dependent on each other, and so have no nature of their own. They must be without any nature and so **empty** (*shunya*). If things existed in themselves then they would never change, and so there would be no change. If a thing existed in itself it would not be able to be related to other things, since those other things could not affect it. Nagarjuna criticizes the theories of those who claim that something must exist behind the world on which the world depends, yet that thing cannot itself depend on anything. He is thinking here of the **Nyaya-Vaisheshikas** and the **Mimamsakas**, who argue that we can distinguish between things that do not depend on anything else (**atoms**, or selves), while other things like qualities do depend on something else, such as substances. The **Sankhyans** think that matter is the source of the world, while the **Advaitins** appeal to *brahman* or reality as an underlying **cause**, a cause that nothing in turn has caused. Even some Buddhists go wrong here, he suggests, such as the **Yogachara** school, which claims that everything is dependent on **consciousness**, while consciousness is not dependent on anything else. According to the theory of Madhyamaka, everything is really empty of **existence** since they are dependent for their existence on something prior to them. Such a view fits in closely with the idea of no-self (*anatman*), which argues that the soul is empty in itself. A form of **meditation** (*vipassana*) is followed by this school, and other Buddhist schools, a technique based on the idea of letting go of the objects in the world, since these objects have no inherent existence. The doctrine is not that nothing exists, nor even that objects do not exist, but rather that whatever exists only exists because something else has caused it to exist. Thus this school makes extensive use of the concept of **dependent origination**. Things are a collection of *dharma*s which follow each other in an unbroken succession, as indeed we ourselves are, but these *dharma*s are only **momentary** and temporary, and they come about solely because something outside them has caused them to exist. Does this not suggest that at least the causes are real, as indeed are the effects? After all, we call them real because we see how they lead to the existence of other things, and can we not say that at least the causes of these things, however momentary they might be in themselves, are real? The answer is that the causes are no more real than their effects, in the sense that anything can lead to something taking place, even something that does not really exist. Our ideas about causation may go awry anyway, and all that it is important to grasp is that in the phenomenal world everything that takes place is brought into existence by something else. Madhyamaka sees itself as being in the middle (hence its name) between the doctrines that existents are necessary and that they do not exist at all. It sets itself self-consciously against the Yogachara school of Mahayana Buddhism, which is a form of idealism arguing that we are all capable of **enlightenment**, but for this to happen we must see beneath our ordinary experiences and thoughts to the real world behind all these phenomena. The leading concepts of Buddhism have a clear meaning, on this view, and serve to describe what is objective about reality.

The early Madhyamaka stressed the emptiness of everything, especially the key concepts of philosophy, even including the Buddha and *nirvana*. Perhaps initially the school saw itself as in opposition to the **Abhidharma** movement, with its confidence in the status of the leading categories of Buddhism. The approach followed tends to be a rigorous deconstruction of the leading categories, an attempt to show that they rest on some other concept which itself has rather dubious foundations. For example, if there is such a thing as *nirvana*, then Buddhism is wrong in thinking that nothing is permanent and an entity. On the other hand, if it does not exist, then it throws doubt on the aims of Buddhist enlightenment. It could not exist since everything that exists is part of the process of cause and effect, and this would imply that *nirvana* was contingent and temporary. It could not not exist, though, since something that does not exist has gone out of existence, and if there really was nothing really in existence, then there would be no *nirvana* either. Nagarjuna actually says quite explicitly that there is no difference between **samsara** and *nirvana*! This is less paradoxical than it seems when we consider it from the appropriate point of view, since the claim is that they are identical in the sense that they share an identical nature, the absence of inherent existence. The danger to avoid is to regard this world as empty but to see *nirvana* as an alternative world that exists somewhere else. Rather, *nirvana* is available in our world, albeit we shall have to look at that world in the right sort of way to make this possible. It is not the appropriate conclusion that one should believe in nothing, though, since Nagarjuna and other Madhyamaka thinkers stress the two ways in which reality may be approached. From the point of view of ultimate reality, nothing exists, but from the point of view of our ordinary experience, many concepts have a use and there are rules as to their appropriate application to the phenomenal world. Of course, it is just because, from the real point of view, these concepts are empty that they can be applied to a changing and contingent world. If everything had an essence and a self, it would be incapable of change, and we ourselves could not seek to develop spiritually and pass from one state to another. We could not do anything in a world that was real and perfect. So the doctrine of Madhyamaka really is in the middle, in that if it denied the conventional value of ordinary experience it could be accused of reifying the concept of emptiness itself, which would be self-contradictory. The arguments of the later Madhyamaka tended to be less rigorous in their defence of emptiness, and central concepts that the earlier view criticized are treated with more respect. Later views put far more reliance on the conclusions that are attainable through the application of reason than was the case with the earlier approach.

One of the interesting aspects of the Madhyamaka philosophical technique is its refusal to take a position. It seems to be entirely dialectical, ready to refute the arguments of others but not to defend a set of principles of its own. It was argued that Nagarjuna must accept that something exists, since surely at least his own words and arguments really exist. He is supposed to have replied that they do not really exist, but this does not reduce their capacity to respond to the arguments of others, since they work in just the same way that one dream may serve to replace or refute another. This response has a point to it, since it is enough to refute a statement that one brings against it an argument that makes it impossible to continue asserting that statement. This does not imply that one must accept the contrary or the contradiction of that statement, merely that the original statement is false.

It is important to grasp how emptiness functions in the system as the basis of our ways of looking at the ordinary world. Nothing can avoid **analysis**, if we wish to analyse it, and from this it follows that nothing really exists. Anything that can be analysed, that is, separated into its parts or taken in itself, does not possess inherent existence since it can always be redescribed in some other way, or have its existence challenged. What really exists is then emptiness, but this emptiness is not itself an inherent existing thing. It is not as though

195

there are two kinds of things, real things (which are in fact empty) and the things that we ordinarily think exist, since this would be to make something essential about emptiness. There is a distinction to be made between the existence of a table and its emptiness of inherent existence. The latter is not another way to see the table, but is rather the claim that what we generally take to be true about the table is actually based on nothing, nothing more than a way of talking.

Madhyamaka Buddhism dominated Tibet, and the thought of Tsongkhapa was influential. He argued that we need to combine realism with scepticism, acknowledging the real existence of external objects while at the same time claiming that we are systematically wrong about the real nature of those objects. Most people confuse the apparent existence of the object with its real existence, and this confusion leads to *karma* and the prolongation of our lives in the cycle of birth and rebirth. Through the use of reason and meditation we can come to experience the emptiness of existence, and achieve salvation.

In China Jizang produced Madhyamaka arguments against the idea of the existence of an entity such as the **buddha nature**, which he identified with a state of mind that transcends both ideas of self and no-self. There was a tendency for Chinese Madhyamaka thinkers to identify emptiness with an actual being, in the sense that it could serve as the source of being, something that Jizang strenuously attacked. He defended a strictly middle position between the contrasting principles outlined by Buddhism, rejecting the idea that one could be more basic or the source of the other. This is difficult to do, of course, since there is a tendency to believe that a higher level of discourse represents the truth, and Jizang argued that one must always resist prioritizing any particular point of view or theoretical language. Is not Buddhism, though, worth accepting? It is, but in just the same way that a raft is useful in getting over a river. Once one arrives at the other side, one can abandon it. There seems little doubt but that his dialectical approach contributed to the creation of the **zen** methodology, which itself consists in the ceaseless raising of questions that try to make the speaker think seriously about the confidence with which he rests his arguments on particular principles.

In Japan Buddhist thinkers have tended to see Madhyamaka and Yogachara as two aspects that can be regarded as complementary. The latter tries to explain how things are, given that they are not as they appear to be, while the former rejects all the main categories of analysis, thus throwing doubt on the whole process of doubt. A particularly important text in Japan is the *Lotus Sutra*, which explains that the Buddha has set out various paths to enlightenment for different people based on their varying interests and skills.

The unusual position of the Madhyamaka is that it has no position, in that it does not try to explain the world. All it does is criticize other explanations, although it does not stray from explanation when ethical issues arise. It insists on the 'three jewels', respect for the Buddha, the law and the monastic order. Nagarjuna is thoroughly sceptical of the ability of human reason to understand the universe, and the Madhyamaka reject attachment to any principle or methodology.

Further reading: Carr and Mahalingam 1997, Eckel 1992, Garfield 1995, Gyatso 1992, Huntington 1989, Inada 1970, Kalupahana 1975, Murti 1960, Nagao 1991, Williams 1989.

mahamudra, doctrine of the great soul – *see* **Tibetan philosophy**

Mahayana One of the two great schools of Buddhism which argued that the **buddha nature** is immanent in all beings, so that what is important is not personal salvation but **liberation** of all sentient creatures from suffering. The term means 'the greater vehicle' and is contrasted with **hinayana** ('the lesser vehicle') which is directed towards an end to the suffering of the individual, rather than to the whole of creation. There exist an infinite number of Buddhas who are intent on helping us, and even the Buddha himself did not disappear on his apparent death, but remains out of **compassion** in infinite **time** and space to help us. This form of Buddhism became very significant in Tibet, China, Japan and east Asia generally, and split up into a number of different schools. The doctrine of **emptiness** is crucial for Mahayana, since it is the foundation of the idea that there is essential equality among all sentient beings both morally and potentially. It is sensible then to have as the aim of Buddhism the **enlightenment** of the whole of the world, since the whole of the world is capable of achieving enlightenment. There is nothing inherently in the world that can stand in the way of such enlightenment, since the essences of the beings in the world are empty. They come to have those essences through something else affecting them, and why should not this eventually be the Buddha?

See: *bodhisattva*, **Madhyamaka**
Further reading: Gombrich 1988, Williams 1989.

manas – *see* **mind**

mappo, period of degeneracy – *see* **time**

materialism In Indian thought this is generally identified with the Charvaka school or the Lokayatas, those thinkers for whom the world is itself the basis of reality. Little of their work has survived, and it is generally known through refutations of them by their opponents. They adhere to perception as the sole means of acquiring **knowledge**, rejecting **inference** due to its illegitimate trust in the truth of a major premise. Such a premise is in itself unreliable since it is a **universal** proposition, and there is no perception that can justify such a judgement. Even the principle of **causality** is dubious, since it implies belief in a universal principle, so we should accept that every event in the world comes about through chance. All the main metaphysical concepts such as the self, the deity, the afterworld and so on are ruled out since they cannot be perceived. The **Vedas** are also not to be trusted, they urge belief in the hidden and often contradict themselves. Of course, it is not difficult to see how this central principle came itself to be attacked as running against the principles of materialists themselves, since the assertion that only perception may be trusted is a general claim itself, as is the claim that ultimate reality is no more than physical reality.

They categorized reality in terms of four elements, earth, water, fire and air, rejecting ether since it is not visible. These come together in a particular way to constitute the human self, and the latter is equivalent to the physical body. The difference between a live and a dead person is not due to the existence of an imperceptible *atman* or self, but rather to a particular arrangement of the parts of the body, which results in **consciousness**. Since consciousness is formed by a particular physical combination of elements, once that combination changes, consciousness disappears. There is no **afterlife** or survival of the self from one life to another, and no point in adhering to transcendent principles such as God. The only aim worth pursuing is the enjoyment of life, which is often brought about by material wealth. Even their enemies seem to accept that they did not follow a policy of licentious behaviour, but were generally self-controlled. They seem to have pursued a policy of non-harm or *ahimsa*, rejecting **violence** and meat eating.

Further reading: Basham 1971, Carr and Mahalingam 1997.

maya In the **Advaita Vedanta** *maya* represents the illusory existence of a world of variety hiding the simplicity of reality (**brahman**) through the power of ignorance (**avidya**). There is a difference between *maya* and ignorance, since the former is actually more about getting something wrong than not knowing something, because what it gets wrong is that a reality that is in fact one appears to be complex. This omnipresence of *maya* is rejected by another **Vedanta** thinker, Ramanuja, who argues that there is no point in following

Shankara's proposal to treat all our judgements as illusory. This means that we fail to acknowledge the distinction between reality and illusion on which the notion of illusion rests. Even a mistake involves an accurate grasp of something, something that looks like something real. In any case, our mistakes are embedded in the reality of God, and so there is much about them that is accurate.

Further reading: Bhatt 1975, Deutsch 1968, Smart 1964.

meditation Often connected with yoga, this is regarded as a vital route to salvation in most Indian philosophy. Before it can be tried, the body must be in a suitable position, since unless one can control the body one is unlikely to be able to control the **mind**. In just the same way that there are precise ways in which the body can by controlled, so there are different stages in controlling the mind. According to the **Sankhya Yoga** school, controlling the mind involves fixing the mind on an object, contemplating it and then entering into a trance. There are two types of trance. The weaker kind is where the thinker is absorbed in the object of thought, but is still aware that it is an object of thought. The stronger kind is where the immersion is so total that it is no longer regarded as just an object of thought, but as something identical with the thinker. The idea that meditation is an important route to salvation is always going to be important in theories that identify being dispassionate with **enlightenment**. Through meditation the individual can detach herself from her ordinary thinking and feeling, and can merge mentally with an idea that even dissolves her notion of self, itself a powerful source of error and suffering. This is a particularly important consideration for Buddhists, and through meditation one can not only appreciate the absence of a fixed self, but also experience what it is like to operate without such a self. In ordinary life, of course, we cannot operate at all without the idea of the self as something real and important. On one version of Buddhism, what the meditator is doing is uniting with **emptiness**, which brings out the basic nature of emptiness as the only viable definition of reality. But the chief function of meditation is to bring about a calming and concentrating (*samatha*) effect, to weaken the power of desire, while the sort of awareness produced through forms of meditation (*vipassana*) designed to produce a strong sense of one's mind can reduce both craving and **ignorance**.

There was also an argument in Buddhism that the higher states of **consciousness** attained in meditation could lead to rebirth in a more spiritual and less corporeal state of existence. According to Dogen, the zen thinker, **zazen** or seated meditation involves transcending the body/mind dichotomy. We all have the **buddha nature**, and we can realize it through meditation. One way of making progress on the path to enlightenment is through riddles (**koan**) or paradoxical sayings which stimulate the mind to work out what the real position is. Several Chinese approaches to meditation insist on the possibility of sudden enlightenment, reinterpreting the tendency in Indian philosophy to stress a more gradual approach. This reinterpretation often took the form of understanding the notion of stages of meditation as being really states of mind that are to a degree always present. It was combined with a view of meditation that stressed the absence of attachment, allowing the mind to flow freely without being slowed down by the introduction of value judgements, judgements about whether the objects of the thoughts are true or not. This is not the absence of thought, though, but rather it is a process that restores the original clarity of the mind, and allows the agent to use the concepts in his mind without attachment. This view of meditation has the advantage that it is resolutely non-dualistic, in that it does not see enlightenment as the goal and meditation as the means.

In the chan tradition the key Indian principles of *samadhi* (concentration) and **prajna** (wisdom) were altered to make them fit better with the Chinese orientation to sudden enlightenment. This is possible if these stages are seen as states of mind as compared with types of practice, and they were often combined in one single experience in which the whole Buddhist path could be collapsed. The chan emphasis on direct insight replaces the development of *samadhi* and *prajna*, and these came to be regarded as only useful to the less sophisticated meditators. What replaced this more gradual approach is what came to be known as the no-mind (*wu xin*) or no-thought (*wu nian*) practice. The problem with thought is the erroneous belief that the concept of a thing is the thing itself, and using concepts is a way of projecting one's own view of the world on the world itself, assuming that point of view is an accurate picture of reality. Concepts are acceptable as sorting ideas to deal with experience, but they should be used without drawing any implications of their real grasp of the nature of the world. The mind should flow freely, not being concerned about issues like validity or anything that interferes with spontaneity.

According to the **Madhyamaka** notion of meditation, the preparation starts with **analysis** into the notion of inherent **existence**. This analysis considers the arguments in favour of such existence, rejects them and then looks at the contrast between the notion of inherent existence and the notion of the everyday existence of objects in the world of experience. After this stage the meditator has to be careful to get the balance right between these different aspects of what might be seen as reality, and she has to appreciate that the concept that she considers is neither really existent nor non-existent. She will have in her mind the absence of real essence of the concept, and this is equivalent to the cognition of emptiness, since she realizes that the concept refers to emptiness. But this is not a direct awareness of emptiness, only a grasp of the concept of emptiness as being implied by the emptiness of the concept. Such direct awareness is a bit further along the process, and is equivalent to total meditative absorption. What the meditator needs to do here is place her mind without distraction and also without effort on the object. Of course, this is not easy, since the calmness that is part of the appropriate attitude may have been disrupted by the analysis that has gone into the construction of the concept of emptiness. Once the calmness is established, the meditator tries to alternate between analysis and calmness, until the analysis itself brings about the calmness. This level is known as that of insight, and if it has emptiness as its object it is called the path of preparation. Then there are four successive paths to follow, which result in the stage-by-stage removal of the conceptual elements due to this concentration on emptiness. When a direct and non-conceptual insight is achieved one has a direct cognition of the ultimate. When this is combined with the unselfish **compassion** of the *bodhisattva*, the meditator is at the first of the ten *bodhisattva* stages. One might think that this is the end of the journey, but in fact it is just the beginning. Progress has been made, in that the meditator can now after her meditation appreciate that what looks like inherent existence is just an illusion, but she still has to purify her understanding of any fragments of such essences in her moral and conceptual life. The goal is to attain Buddhahood, and this means that the essences are replaced by emptiness in the perceptual act itself.

In **Yogachara** meditation we start off by analysing the stream of consciousness as the only real factor in our experience, and then we proceed to dispense with the notion of the subject and concentrate on the notion of non-duality. This involves not the negation of the stream of experiences themselves, but rather of the mind as something distinct from those experiences. The experiences must be grasped in a non-dual manner, without distinction between knower and known, which is why consciousness is often identified with suchness or thatness. In so far as we see the experiences as the basis to real things we remain in the world of *samsara*, but if we manage to transcend that notion we can reach *nirvana*, since we have left duality behind.

See: **afterlife**, *tathagata*
Further reading: Abe 1992, Eckel 1992, Eliade 1958, Fontana 1992, Gregory 1987, Griffiths 1986, Jackson 1993, Nasr 1993, Tominaga 1990, Zaehner 1997.

Mimamsa Literally 'investigation', generally used to refer to the ways of interpreting the **Vedic** scriptures, and which became differentiated into two broad schools, **Purva** Mimamsa ('Earlier Investigation') and later **Vedanta**. Hinduism shares with many other systems texts that apparently refer to historical events and particular individuals, and these require interpretation if they are to be made generally relevant. For Mimamsa truth is to be determined in terms of the Vedic text, and **knowledge** was identified with the realistic representation of objects. Their account of the nature of *dharma* in the sense of ethical force is quite distinct. For them it is the subject of Vedic imperative statements. Since the Vedas are the source of knowledge of the supreme good, which we could not grasp except through the Vedas, we must rely on them totally to work out how to act. In fact, if we do not get the result we should, or if what we are told to believe does not seem to come out as accurate, we can be confident that in the fullness of **time**, possibly in another life, the Vedic claim will be justified. By contrast with our ordinary conventional **language**, the Vedic words are **eternal** and determinate. The doctrine of **liberation** has been added to the interpretation of the Vedas, and involves our acquiring understanding of how to stop being attracted and repulsed by events in the phenomenal world. This brings *karma* to an end, and stops the cycle of birth and rebirth for the successful individual.

The view of liberation is very different from that of the other orthodox schools, since the Mimamsa emphasis is on the Vedas and the rituals connected with them. The mantras and the Vedas have power in themselves, and they consist largely of injunctions which need to be followed. *Brahman* or reality subsists in the words themselves, so the Sanskrit language itself is far from just a conventional representation of the truth. It embodies the truth in itself, and is to be performed through recital, sacrifices and rituals. Salvation is identified with the rewards for those who organize the appropriate sacrificial rituals.

The key concept for the Mimamsakas is *dharma*. This is the principle that holds the universe together, and given the plurality of reality according to this school there is a need for such a principle. *Dharma* is often identified with virtue and vice which exists within the self or **atman** of each individual and controls their behaviour, both now and through transmigration. It shapes the world into its various forms, since it leads us to act in particular ways. We are free in that our past actions do affect our present character, but not in such a way as to determine it. We can use virtuous behaviour to counteract the negative influence of previous bad *karma*.

See: **samsara**

Further reading: Beidler 1975, Dasgupta 1975, Nakamura 1983, Potter 1972, Radhakrishnan 1966.

mind The **Nyaya-Vaisheshika** school distinguishes sharply between mind (*manas*) and soul. The mind is infinitesimal, **eternal** and unique for each particular self, and is the part of the body that makes experience possible. Since it is so small, it cannot experience many things at the same time, for this the self is necessary, and similarly the mind cannot take in composite objects. The self is at the basis of all such experiences, and is distinct from our sensory apparatus. Each self has its own mind, at least until it achieves **liberation**. While in the state of *samsara* the mind works in tandem with the self, and leads to knowledge along with the emotions, faculties and feelings of **love**, pain, hate, pleasure and will. This sort of account of the distinction between the mind and the self is also followed by the **Vishishtadvaita**, who identify the self with the 'I' that frames all our experiences. In fact, it is the constant use of such an 'I' that leads them to criticize the Buddhists for denying the existence of a constant self. Given the fact that our experiences are changeable and consciousness can lapse, it would be a mystery how we can link our experiences through a continuing 'I' unless it corresponded to some constant and unchanging subject that persisted over **time** and space. But they are rare among Hindu thinkers in having a notion of the mind that makes it rather like the soul of Western thought. We should note that the mind in the sense of *manas* is generally identified with the organ of mental apprehension, a sense that is directed at ideas or concepts which are abstracted from the other senses.

Sometimes the mind is represented by the term *chitta* which really refers to the internal constitution of an individual, perhaps better translated as '**personality**'. This term is often used in early Buddhism to suggest belief in the existence of a mental transmigrating being which is far from simple nor immune from change, but which explains the continuity of the individual from life to life, while at the same time explaining why we do not require the notion of a permanent and simple self continuing through all the changes.

A **Neoconfucian** theory called mind-monism identified ideas with the mind, and ideas (*li*) with the essence of the world. With Buddhism also there came to be an identification of mind and reality. The Nirvana school placed the **buddha nature** in the mind, but the **Madhyamaka** followers rejected this as not a genuinely middle position. When the **Yogachara** school arrived in China it was used to suggest that the mind is equivalent to suchness (*tathata*) or the ultimate reality of everything. This led to the belief that we must all be in principle **enlightened**, and this is something that can suddenly come about, doing away with the necessity for lengthy preparatory steps. Once we realize that the mind is equivalent to suchness, or facticity, the mind itself is equivalent to **emptiness**, and this knowledge can be used to free us from bondage. The illusion of suffering depends on the failure to appreciate the identity between mind and reality. This approach was criticized by Fazang who distinguishes between two kinds of mind. There is a lower kind of **consciousness** which is indeed equivalent to reality, where this means the reality of the objects in our everyday world. Then there is the mind which is equivalent to the deeper reality, the reality that lies behind this world and reflects the emptiness of being.

Islamic philosophy was very interested in the nature of the mind which it treated as linked to the soul. Ibn Sina argues that the soul is the principle that organizes the body, since the body does not itself have a part of itself which is capable of doing this. The soul has an understanding and an awareness of itself that is entirely different from its understanding of the body. However, the term *nafs* is used in a variety of senses, sometimes meaning the physical part of a human being, sometimes the rational part, and sometimes the combination of both the rational and non-rational parts. There is an intimate connection between the body and the soul, the latter being the form or perfection of the body. This means that the body is an essential aspect of the soul, and so there are difficulties in talking about the rational soul continuing to exist after the body has decayed. There are aspects of the soul such as common sense, **imagination** and memory that most of the philosophers accept are important descriptions of ways in which we operate as agents. Common sense is the faculty that combines the objects of the external senses into a concept, so that when we no longer actually experience the object we can still think about it and its qualities. Imagination combines images of external things in a way that is not determined by our experiences of those things. Memory allows us to keep hold of these concepts and images, and provides material to the other faculties.

The rational soul is either practical or theoretical. As practical it acquires knowledge in order to further the welfare of the individual, his or her family, and the state. It is assumed that there are principles that need to be grasped for this to be possible. The theoretical intellect concentrates on the universal bases of knowledge. There is a hierarchy of intellects, starting with the material intellect, that possess the potentiality to grasp the **universals**. The potential intellect can grasp the universals, but does not always do so, unlike the actual intellect, which both acquires the universals and uses them. Finally, the acquired intellect is the stage at which our theoretical intellect comes into contact with the **active intellect**, the principle behind the universals (and often represented as the intelligence of the lowest heavenly being, the moon), and this is the highest state that humanity can reach. The basis of this reasoning is the principle that the knower, the known and the act of knowledge are all the same, so that the acquired intellect is one with its objects. The best form of happiness is achieved during the state of the acquired intellect, since we here identify ourselves with the universals, which are eternal, and so enjoy eternal happiness.

See: **anatman, atman**

Further reading: Beidler 1975, Carr and Mahalingam 1997, Chatterjee 1965, Creel 1953, Garfield 1995, Griffiths 1986, Hoffman 1987, Leaman 1985.

ming jiao, teaching of names – *see* **Neodaoism, rectification of names**

Mohism The creator of Mohism is Mozi, and he opposed the central Confucian emphasis on kinship and hierarchy with the notion of the universal **love** of humanity (*jianai*), and the role of heavenly will (*tianzi*). However, like Confucius he advocated moral **education** and a political philosophy in terms of humanity (*ren*) and morality (*yi*). The point of this was to reconstruct China along more self-sufficient and **harmonious** lines, but Mohism also led to considerable development of **logic**. This is outlined in the *Mo jing* and consists of detailed discussion of various examples of dialectic. This has the role of clarifying the distinction between right and wrong, good and inefficient government, similarity and dissimilarity, names and what they denote, and how to decide on which **actions** are to be pursued. When it comes to assessing what is **knowledge**, three criteria are involved. We need to examine the source of the claim and its structure, and assess its practical implications. Later developments of the theory produced a very sophisticated theory of knowledge, in accordance with the name, fact, correspondence and action involved in a knowledge claim. The criterion of whether a name actually refers to an object lies in the pragmatic value of this belief, that is, from what follows from an action in accordance with the belief.

For Mozi *ren* or humanity is equivalent to benevolence, *jianai*. What this means is that people are naturally benevolent, and they owe a duty of love to everyone else regardless of their rank in society. If a policy of benevolence becomes universal, then this will succeed in pulling society together, while its opposite policy, that of dissension and aggression, will help it disintegrate. This moral principle actually copies a cosmological idea of the harmony of the heaven and the earth, the large and the small, the individual and the group, and so on. Whereas Confucius emphasized *li* in the sense of respect for the claims of others, Mozi sought to replace this with *yi* or a general form of utilitarianism in ethics, so that we should seek to help others whatever their social role and/or relationship to us. The ideal society Mozi had in mind was obviously one in which modest individuals grouped together to live simple but fulfilled lives helping each other, and being confident that they themselves would receive help in due course. The virtuous individual seeks to benefit the whole world and prevent misfortunes from occurring, and this can be brought about through the acceptance of universal love as the principle of action. As with Confucius, the criterion of value is not that based on the individual, but rather what is owing to society as a whole, and the welfare of the individual will be preserved if everyone follows such unselfish and right policies. Of course, it might prove difficult to persuade everyone that it is their personal interest to seek to help everyone else, even though it is and will result in reciprocal help when required. Mozi suggests that religion needs to be used to strengthen this ideal in people, since they are more likely to accept it if they think that it represents the will of Heaven. If God and lesser deities are thought to reward those who act virtuously, and punish those who do not, then this will make it much easier to motivate people to act correctly. It is worth pointing out that the actual existence of gods is not logically connected with the rationale for Mozi's ethics, just with their easy acceptability by the population as a whole.

The effective ruler has to have absolute power to punish and reward, since otherwise he will be unable to rule without opposition. Such a political organization is preferable to anarchy, and the state rests on both the will of the people and of God. Without a strong state, everyone acts in accordance with their own wishes and ideals, and chaos results, but the imposition of the state introduces only one concept of right and wrong, hopefully identical to the principle of universal love. There is no way for a community to reach this principle and turn it into practice without its incorporation in the structure of a political entity which insists on its application.

The main objections Mohism makes to Confucianism relate to the latter's lack of belief in God, the Confucian stress on the significance of funerals and music and the consequent time and expense involved, as well as the **fatalism** in the Confucian idea that everything is predetermined, which leads to passivity. The last objection is hardly accurate, but the others are, and reflect the social differences between the Confucians and the Mohists, the latter being more orientated towards less elevated classes than the well-educated and sophisticated Confucians. Hence the arguments by Mohists in favour of austerity, and in criticism of the elaborate rituals the Confucians often favoured. The Confucian response, provided in a lively way by Mengzi (Mencius) was to counter that the practices the Confucians favour all strengthen the personal links between individuals, and it is on such links that the strengthening of society depends. The idea of a general love that can serve as social cement is far-fetched, and if there is any possibility of establishing such a general benevolence it will only be via an extrapolation of love from the duties of love owed to fathers, families and the ruler.

The Mohist theory of knowledge is realist, and our knowledge is based on ideas of external objects which we receive through our experiences. A complex theory of logic was developed, which was used to analyse the idea of welfare which is the basis of their system. This theory came into play to deal with two objections to the theory, one being that the infinite number of people in the world meant that it is surely untenable to set out to love them all. The response is that there may be an infinite number of people, but the space they fill is finite, and so in setting out to love everyone one is hoping to love everyone who inhabits a finite space, which is feasible. The other objection is that if one has to love everyone, then one has to love the **evil** person who is properly punished through death. The answer to this problem is that in hating the criminal, one is hating that aspect of a human being that is criminal, not the individual himself or herself. To love the individual is not to love the criminal, even though the individual might be a criminal. So punishing criminals is not inconsistent with the principle of general benevolence.

See: **human nature**, **humanism**, **language**
Further reading: Chan 1972, Creel 1953, Fung 1970, Graham 1978, Watson 1967.

moksha   Literally 'setting free' or liberation, the aim of the spiritual life in Indian thought. It is equivalent to release from *samsara*, the cycle of death and rebirth. *Moksha* as release is often identified as being equivalent to becoming *brahman*, or realizing one's true nature. This is a state of perfection in which we transcend the normal distinctions between self and non-self, good and **evil** and so on. Some argue that it is possible to achieve release in this life, while others insist that it can only be attained in the next life.

According to the **Vedantin** Ramanuja, when the self is liberated it is no longer subject to the conditions of the ordinary world, in particular the world with selves and individuals. Yet, unlike the view of the **Advaita**, the individual self survives. What sort of survival is this? One might think that it is just a rather blank and empty formal notion of self-**consciousness**, but it seems that more than this is required. We have to remember that when liberated there is no distinction between the knowledge of the individual and the knowledge of God. In just the same way that God knows what goes on in the ordinary world, we must do the same, and the important difference here is that we shall after liberation be able to perceive that world with ironic detachment, no longer permitting its pains and pleasures to affect us. So

211

the liberated self is certainly connected to the unliberated self, they are continuous, and the liberated self will have no difficulty in recognizing herself in what had been her life of *samsara*. Liberation consists in coming close to God, and since God is the principle behind the world, in a sense when we are liberated this is carried out by God. The problem with the view of liberation that identifies it entirely with unity with *brahman* is that it is a rather inferior form of liberation, since it involves no sense of one's complete dependence on God. That is why it is important for the self to persist after liberation, since only then can it reflect on the contrast between its present and past conditions, and only if a self survives can it enjoy its new and final state of perfection.

See also: *nirvana*, **Vishistadvaita**
Further reading: Bhatt 1975, Carr and Mahalingam 1997, Hiriyanna 1985, Lipner 1986, Sharma 1964.

momentariness There is an influential Buddhist account of ontology, the nature of **being**, that does without the concept of **dependent origination**, and operates instead with the idea that reality is only momentary in nature. For Dharmakirti things exist insofar as they can realize some function, and that function is to bring about a particular result. This is only possible if the thing is always changing, since if it were to be unchanging it could have no effect on anything else, nor could anything else act on it. It follows from the fact that something exists that it is momentary. What this implies is that there are no real general concepts or **universals**, he argues, only real things. After all, universals themselves have no **causal** power, and so in reality do not exist. This is presented as a critique of **Nyaya** ontology, which does regard universals as real.

See: **atomism, time**
Further reading: Dravida 1972, Dreyfus 1997.

mu – *see* **emptiness**

Mu'tazila – *see* **Ash'ariyya and Mu'tazila**

N

nafs, soul – *see* **mind**

nahda –*see* **enlightenment**

Naiyayikas – *see* **Nyaya-Vaisheshika**

nana – *see* **knowledge**, *jnana yoga*

nembutsu   The utterance of the Amida Buddha's name (*namu-amida-butsu = nembutsu*) is supposed to result in birth in Amida's **Pure Land** at death. Japanese Buddhism has been attracted to the idea of a Pure Land, a perfect realm into which one could be reborn, and the reciting of the *nembutsu* ('All praise to Amida Buddha') reflects a constant mindfulness of Amida Buddha which is taken to be especially effective in this regard. There was an extended debate in Japan as to the relative effectiveness of different techniques for achieving **enlightenment**, and around 1175 Honen came to the view that only *nembutsu* is worth pursuing as compared with other devotional and meditative practices. This apparently easy path was opposed by the forces of orthodoxy, but came to be popular among the lay public. Honen argued that this rather drastic reinterpretation of Buddhism was appropriate since time had moved on irreversibly from the original period of Buddhism, and traditional forms of behaviour were no longer likely to be effective in achieving enlightenment. He took the drastic line that only the *nembutsu* chant now mattered, the other practices having been right in the past, where they were provided by the Buddha out of **compassion** for the limited and varying capacities of believers at that time. This theory was taken even further by Shinran who founded the True Pure Land movement, which denied the necessity of human effort even in the form of uttering the *nembutsu* to achieve enlightenment, since Amida's original promise of rebirth is the only power that can bring about such an end. These views were challenged by Myoe who interpreted the Pure Land as a mental creation brought about through **meditation**. The recitation of Amida's vow is by itself useless unless it is accompanied by the mind concentrating on the Buddha and used as an aid to meditation.

Further reading: LaFleur 1983, Maruyama 1974, Tanabe 1992, Tsunoda *et al.* 1964, Tyler 1977.

Neoconfucianism This term is often used to translate *Dao zue*, which refers to the study of the dao, or truth. Later developments of Confucianism moved away from exclusive reliance on political and ethical thought, and linked the original ideas of Confucius to wider philosophical issues. There was also the necessity to seek to refute the arguments of Buddhism and Daoism. Zhangzai argued that the ontological basis of reality is gas, and all objects are constituted of gas, and eventually return to gas. The materialization of gas in the human body leads to **human nature**, of which there are two kinds. One is the nature of heaven and earth, which is equivalent to reason and which is good, and the other is the nature of temperament which is impure and **evil**, or at least capable of evil. The individual should seek to restrain the nature of temperament and concentrate on the nature of heaven and earth through self-cultivation. This sounds rather like Buddhism, but the argument is not that the basis of reality is nothingness or **emptiness**. On the contrary, the basic building bricks of the world are made of gas, and there is no such thing as complete emptiness. What looks like total emptiness is in fact gas that has been dispersed. Feudal society represents a family that contains great variety, but the essence of everything, however diverse in appearance, is the same, so we are all parts of one thing. It follows then that we should respect not only our parents and relations, but everyone in the universe. This principle is based upon a **cosmology** that sees reality as consisting of gas, out of which everything is formed, and into which in the end everything is reconstituted. The contrast with Buddhism lies in the claim that it is impossible to seek to transcend this process. All that one can do is understand it. This view differs from the Daoist thinkers also in not valuing particularly the extension of human life. The recommendation is that one should put no especial value on longevity, nor seek to delay **death**, which is after all just a natural process. People should live ordinary lives in society and seek to do their duty, not try to transcend their social obligations nor concentrate on personal physical and spiritual preservation. Other Neoconfucians took a different attitude to the nature of reality, favouring forms of idealism, where ideas are the basic constitution of the world, but the general thesis is that feudal moral categories are to be identified with absolute and metaphysical significance. Forms of Neoconfucian thought continued to be significant right up to the twentieth century, when it came under renewed attack by the modernists in the Republican movement and then the Communists. On the other hand, even in the People's Republic of China there has been something of a rediscovery of the value of Confucius, in particular the social desirability of attitudes of respect for authority and **harmony**. Throughout the Chinese cultural world Confucius' ideas have had a very powerful effect on the ways in which people actually live.

There are some interesting similarities between the aims of Chinese Buddhism and Neoconfucianism. For the former, the aim is to teach people how to achieve Buddhahood, while for the latter it is how to become a sage. The contrast is particularly dramatic when we consider the different routes to the truth involved, since for the Buddhist the path is likely to imply a rejection of society, while for the Neoconfucian it is through participation in society. Zhou Dunyi seemed to identify the paths when he suggested that the route to becoming a sage is through having no desires (*wu yu*), which he also links to the principle of non-**action**. Having no desires leads to emptiness when the thinker is at rest, and to simple activity when one is acting. **Enlightenment** gained through such attitudes leads to **knowledge**, and **actions** based on simplicity to impartiality. Impartiality leads to universality, so that one develops the total and unbiased view of the sage. One of the points this approach stresses is the necessity to allow one's thoughts and actions to reflect one's natural goodness, whereas if we spend a lot of time reflecting on what we are going to do, all sorts of improper motives and feelings may creep in. The more we ponder action, the more selfish our thoughts become, and the less we think about what we do, the more natural our responses to situations, the more our inherent goodness can direct our activity. The complete vanquishing of selfish desires converts the **mind** to a shining mirror that is capable of reflecting the truth clearly. Enlightenment results in the construction of a brilliant mirror, capable of appreciating what each situation objectively demands without making discriminations based on personal likes and dislikes. Both Zhou and his successors made much use of the *Book of Changes* in their thought, which stresses the cyclical nature of reality and its ability to display an inherent structure which represents the principles of its operation as nature.

The *Li xue* school (literally, the school of principles) was established by two brothers Cheng Yi and Cheng Hao. The latter argued that unity with everything is the basic principle of *ren* (benevolence). If one can keep this in one's mind, and make it the foundation of action, one will become even more securely part of everything, but this is not something that is difficult or requires great effort. It should be developed in the personality as a disposition that can then be effortlessly brought into action. There is a tendency for human beings to base their actions on selfishness, which interferes in the basic unity that links all nature. The thought of that unity is an effective idea in the battle between selfishness and benevolence, and allows us to strengthen our natural desire to identify with everyone else and practise virtue. Of course, even the noblest of us may experience pleasure and pain, but this does not trouble the status of the sage. His mind is characterized by impartiality, universality and objectivity, so he observes these feelings as though they were unconnected to his self. If he really is a sage, then when these feelings arise, they arise at the right sort of time and in line with the objective description of the world. All he does is reflect reality, which means that when the cause of the emotion – the object – goes, the emotion goes with it. So the sage has emotions but is not put into bondage through them. There is a reference in *The Analects* (6: 3) to Yan Hui, a favourite pupil of Confucius, not venting his anger on those who do not deserve it, and not repeating an error, and this is a passage made much of by the Neoconfucians. Like a mirror, Yan Hui was affected by the objects in front of him, but once they went, he was not so tied in with those objects that he could not release them and the emotions that went with them. Once they go, the reflection and everything connected with them goes as well, so the mirror like the sage is in charge of what is represented, in the sense that these representations will consist entirely of objective images of the truth. Yan Hui's anger was not connected to his self, so once what stimulated the anger went, the anger went also. Thinking that emotions are important and should persist is an aspect of error, and of small-mindedness.

It is this ability to distinguish between the self and the emotions that enables the sage to be ' happy. He is happy because he takes pleasure in simple things, and ultimately in himself, since he is a simple thing. Both as an agent and when not acting he lives in accordance with the sort of person he is, and since he has a self that is not occluded by the changing events of the world of experience he blends into the nature of heaven and earth. In particular, the sage does not respect the opinions of others, the ordinary conception that happiness consists in wealth and social position.

Zhuxi brought the *Li xue* school to its culmination, arguing that *li* is the basis to reality. Everything possesses its own nature, and this makes it the sort of thing it is. This potentiality exists eternally, and when particular things are eventually constructed, this presupposes the existence of the *li*. What makes things possible is the combination of *li* and *qi* (matter or energy), whereby the latter is shaped by the former into the objects of our world. One might think that on this view the matter is passive, but this is not the case. Rather, it embodies the ability to be transformed, and what transforms it, the *li*, is not itself anything different from the principle of form. It does not have any intentions or ideas about how the matter should be shaped, these are inherent in the matter itself. That is, the matter already has a certain orientation, which is given the push to instantiation by the presence of *li*. To take a popular example of the time, before a father can have a son, which is a material relationship, there must exist the idea of such a relationship, and that idea must exist before it is brought into physical existence. Although *li* and *qi* have to operate together, there is a certain priority of the former, but this is only an ontological priority. The *qi* in the universe is identified with **yin** (when it rests) and the **yang** (when it moves), while *li* remains unchanged behind these processes of change and rest.

For a human being to exist, he must be the result of a particular kind of matter, which is what distinguishes him from other people. The *li* or principle of humanity is the same for everyone. The latter is inherently good, so the **evil** in the universe must arise due to the matter, which provides us with a specific physical and mental nature. But the **mind** is also affected by *li*, since like everything else in existence it is a blend of *li* and *qi*. We are capable of acting nobly due to the presence of *li*, but this presence is mediated by matter, and so we as agents differ in our capacity to

follow these abstract principles of **justice**. The political implications of this view are interesting, since they imply that there
must be a *li* of politics which will enable the state to be pros-
perous and harmonious. Zhuxi argues that much of the
government in China has followed the path of the interests
of the rulers, rather than being based on knowledge of how
the state really ought to be run, its *li*. Sometimes they managed
to come close to the *li*, but this is haphazard unless they have
a firm intellectual grasp of the *li*. Their political successes,
such as they are, come about through chance and are unstable.
One might think that this charge is rather harsh, since *li* is
abstract and in itself empty, so how might one come to know
it? The *li* is accessible through knowledge of the material,
which results in an understanding of the principles that exist
in the phenomenal world and within ourselves. Once we
come to the end of such a process of learning, the pure and
universal basis to the world will become evident.

A different approach to the nature of reality was taken
by Wang Shuren, who rejected dualism for a theory that the
world is an entirely spiritual entity. The mind is itself *li*, so
if there were no mind, there would be principles waiting to
be instantiated. This mind is shared by everyone and all we
need to do to behave well is to follow our natural instincts.
It follows that anyone can be a sage, and everyone is potentially a sage. All that has to be done is to follow one's original
nature and understand how to bring into action the basic
knowledge of good and evil. This knowledge is the inner
light of our mind, which represents and is at the same time
part of the fundamental unity of reality.

Further reading: Chan 1972, Creel 1953, Fung 1952, Gardner 1986,
Graham 1989, Tu Wei-Ming 1985.

Neodaoism The developments of Daoist views often merged
with other philosophical principles. For example, there was
little difficulty in linking Daoist principles with some
aspects of Buddhism, in particular the **emptiness** thesis. The
Neodaoists themselves made great use of the notion of *wu*

(**nothingness**). The Neoconfucians supported the pursuit of *ming jiao* or the teaching of names, which struck many as taking a rather superficial view of the nature of reality. The Neodaoists, by contrast, advocated *xuan xue* or the 'dark learning' as the way to approach the nature of reality, often arriving at the idea of non-being or nothingness as being the source of all **existence**. They were particularly critical of the idea that one really understands the nature of a concept where one could be mistaken, or where the link between the concept and the reality it describes is impermanent. This refers, they argued, to the emptiness that lies at the source of **being**. Confucius himself had referred to Yan Hui, his favourite disciple, as being often empty (*Analects* 11: 18). The dao, then, came to be identified with nothingness, where this means more than that it is not a thing and so unnameable. The implication of this is that there is nothing at the source of reality, that all that exists are the beings of which we have experience. This means that everything comes into existence out of itself, and although the relations between things are necessary and define those things, the things themselves come into existence originally without any prior **cause**. Both the original things and those that come later have to exist, the latter because they are necessitated by causes, and the former because the universe itself is a necessary condition for their existence.

Both the universe and society are in a constant state of flux. One cannot expect institutions to remain relevant regardless of the contemporary situation; it is easy for an institution that is initially natural swiftly to become artificial. This even applies to following the words of the sages, since the conditions under which they produced their statements may have radically changed and lost their meaning. Imitation of someone else is usually futile, since one is trying to change one's nature to bring it into line with someone else's nature, in itself a highly artificial and inefficient activity. Even the effort of imitation is dangerous, since one will not only not manage to copy the sage, but could easily lose one's own self. Neodaoism involves a less robust attitude to social bodies than existed in original Daoism, which distrusted all such institutions, but it retains the Daoist commitment to change, so if institutions are to have value they must fit in with the processes of change and be flexible. The principle of non-**action** finds interesting employment here, since it is used to describe the way in which an institution or practice changes to fit in with new circumstances, as compared with when people try to shape it in accordance with their wishes, which often results in artificial and inefficient results. The idea here is that it is far better to work with the natural tendency of an institution or a person than to oppose it and try to shape it into something radically different.

There is another strand in Neodaoism that puts a less rational interpretation on the idea of living naturally. Neodaoists acted spontaneously, often in rather strange and unconventional ways, to emphasize their attitude to the world as a place in which one should feel relaxed and at home. One of the unusual aspects of their behaviour is that it reveals an attitude of comradeship with even animals, and certainly with all other human beings. It might be thought that reacting emotionally to the events around them goes against the notion of the sage as someone who controls his emotions by not associating them with his self. To a certain extent it is true that they seem to value emotions more than earlier Daoists, but it is not emotions about personal and private events that they describe and recommend, but feelings about life and the world as a whole. Although there was an emphasis upon the acceptability of the emotions as a natural reaction to the world, this was disconnected from sensuality as far as possible, so that the emotions involved are often rather etiolated and abstract. One of the useful observations of this tendency, which is illustrated in the literature by often picaresque descriptions of disreputable behaviour, is that it points out how loose the notion of being natural is. It is certainly true that this form of being a philosopher appears to be more attractive than many of the alternatives!

See: **language**
Further reading: Chan 1972, Kaltenmark 1969, Leaman 1996, Wu 1963.

nibbana   A Pali term (*nirvana* in Sanskrit) for the highest possible
level of happiness. For the Buddhists this is a state in which
the individual no longer craves anything and sees beneath the
layers of illusion and **ignorance**. This results in a feeling of
total peace and inner freedom, where the mind experiences
purity and stability. The point of thinking of things as impermanent, suffering and non-self is to put oneself on the track
to experience *nibbana*. It represents the opposite of these
imperfections, and so is what is not conditioned by something else, what cannot change, what is not **empty** and what
is not contingent. It cannot decay, and is a whole that cannot
be broken up into its parts. It consists of a permanent, happy
and self-subsistent essential unity. But it is not the opposite
of non-self, in the sense of being a self, since *nibbana* is in
itself entirely empty, so it is completely empty of self.

According to the Theravada school, the only people who
can enjoy *nibbana* are those who become *arahat*s, who achieve
liberation through detaching themselves from the ordinary
attachments of the world, including the notion of the self
and the importance of one's cravings. Both *nibbana* and *arahatta*
(the state of being an *arahat*) are the highest **dhamma**, which
leads to two interesting questions. One is whether this state
can really be the result of earlier states, since this seems to
go against the idea that *nibbana* is perfect and unconditioned.
The other is whether the *arahat* who continues to live manages
to detach himself entirely from suffering, which is certainly
the case of *nibbana* itself. The *arahat* manages to avoid the
suffering that arises due to change in something to which he
is attached, but not the fact that sensations are often unpleasant
nor that things are imperfect due to being brought about by
something else. There is no way in which someone who
lived within this phenomenal world could avoid such aspects
of that world. The *arahat* can enter *nibbana* completely on
death, when the body ceases to affect the individual, but in
this life he cannot constantly experience such perfection.
None the less, he is very different from most people in that
he has removed from his character the capacity for attachment, with all the emotions and illusions connected with it.

His mind is pure of such ignorance, but it is still subject to physical conditions and these have an impact on his character, in so far as that character is physically determined by outside forces. This is inevitable, but is to a degree mitigated by the ways in which the *arahat* regards these conditions as conditions, with concentration and **compassion**. It is sometimes argued that the *arahat* could escape the effects of such **dependent origination** since his sense faculties would stop operating during his life, so that he would no longer be interested in knowing anything about the phenomenal world. This leads to the possibility of the temporary cessation of the **personality**, as the *arahat* dips in and out of *nibbana*.

It is not only the *arahat* who can perceive *nibbana*, but it is only he who can enter it. Lesser saints can grasp it, but not enter it. This is not a different form of perfection, and *nibbana* is complete and undifferentiated in form, whether experienced in this life, at death or just seen from afar. The latter case describes the position of the individual who observes the dependence of phenomena on **causes** and their ephemeral state, and who at the same time glimpses the uncaused and permanent reality behind them. So although there is only one *nibbana*, human beings have considerable flexibility with respect to their approach to it.

Further reading: Gombrich 1971, 1988, Kalupahana 1976, Williams 1989.

Nichiren Buddhism – *see* **faith**

nirguna brahman, absolute *braham* – *see* **lila**

nirvana, ultimate liberation – *see* ***nibbana***

niyati, fate – *see,* **fatalism**

noesis – *see* **knowledge**, *prajna*

non-violence – *see* ***ahimsa***

nothingness – *see* **emptiness**

nous poetikos – *see* **active intellect**

Nyaya-Vaisheshika   Although there were in fact two schools, the Nyaya and the Vaisheshika, their agreement on so many key issues has led to them being generally put together under a joint name. *Nyaya* means a theory of **inference**, and *Vaisheshika* a study of ultimate things. This has been an extraordinarily long-lived school, starting in the fourth century BCE and continuing up to today. This school believes that the being of the external world is not dependent on **consciousness**, and so is realist. There are four sorts of **knowledge**, and these are **perception**, inference, analogy and verbal evidence. They analysed general statements, statements like 'where there is smoke, there is fire' as based on a regular association of ideas, ideas for which counter-examples are not known. They tended to argue that the truth of such a statement is based on a particular kind of perception of its truth, which abstracts the general features of what is perceived and so allows us to understand the truth of the general statement as a whole. Knowledge is a relation to objects, and it is on that relation that its character rests; there is no scope for any knowledge that makes itself self-evident just through some quality it has. A distinction should be made between the mode of knowing and the knowledge itself, since what leads to our having knowledge (the cause of the knowledge) not only brings about the knowledge but also provides evidence for its truth. The truth of knowledge is determined by the ways in which it is grounded in sufficient and appropriate evidence.

Perception is the most basic form of knowledge, and involves matching up thoughts with objects in the external world. What we see consists of parts, but we actually see the whole thing, and we are entitled to claim that it is one thing. The Buddhists are wrong in arguing that things only seem to be things, and they also err in their thesis that what we take to be continuing existence of the same things is illusory. Their central thesis that all we really perceive are sense data, not the objects themselves, is attacked roundly by the Nyaya. This school argues that it is possible to establish the rational basis of our knowledge of the world. Inference is a more complex form of knowledge, and the problem with it is that it is knowledge based on prior knowledge. Since there is no possibility of actually observing that which the inference seeks to describe, one has to accept particular rules of valid inference to have any confidence in the reliability of this method. As we have seen with 'where there is smoke, there is fire', this involves what is sometimes called inductive **logic**, and the rules for which such claims are valid are very complicated indeed according to the Nyaya-Vaisheshikas. The idea is that someone notices smoke on a hill, and she is familiar with the fact that when there is smoke in the kitchen, it is caused by fire. So it seems that since this is certainly not the only experience of the links between smoke and fire we can assert with some confidence that there is a fire on the hill, if there is smoke. The Nyaya-Vaisheshikas are very interested in using the notion of a relationship in explanations of how the different parts of reality and our knowledge function. The criterion of knowledge known as verbal evidence is a good indication of this, since this refers to linking a term with the object that it means, in other words, the identification of a relation. The relationship between a term and what it refers to is not so natural that it does not require **analysis** in this way, they would argue. Even if we all know the meanings of the words and the sentences we use, we need to form some idea through inference of the relationship which the speaker thinks obtains between what he says and reality in order to know what is meant.

Their account of meaning made it dependent on God according to earlier versions of the theory, and then on convention. Sentences need to be grammatically well-formed, semantically appropriate and relevant if they are to have meaning, with the later addition of the requirement that they have an intention that can be understood. Otherwise the sentence will be **ambiguous** and will fail to express a clear meaning.

According to this school, the highest good for human beings is the ending of suffering and **liberation**. Although the ultimate goal is turning away from this life and its delusions, the route to this end is through gaining knowledge of the nature of reality. What is this reality? To a certain extent it is the main categories that define reality, and these are substance, quality, **action**, generality, particularity, inseparability and non-**existence**. Reality itself cannot be simple, and to describe it we need to talk about a substrate, its properties and relations. The attributes of the substrate will be some mixture of the categories. There are in turn nine kinds of substrate – earth, water, fire, air, space, direction, **time**, **mind** and self. The self is different both from the mind and the body. The self is the 'I' that accompanies all personal experience, and cannot be the same as the body since the latter does not in itself have experience (as evidenced by what happens when a body loses organs, but still remembers how they operated). Nor can the self be the same as the mind, since the mind is **atomic**, and so cannot by itself grasp a multiplicity of objects all at once. What happens when we experience something is to bring together a variety of our senses in producing a judgement, which we could not do unless the mind came into contact with all the senses at the same time. It can do this since it is so small, and since it is infinitesimal it takes no time to travel around all the senses and bring them all to the self which perceives them as its object. Not only does this theory explain how we can bring together a variety of senses in one judgement, it also refutes the **Sankhya** and **Advaita** view that the mind is infinite. If it were infinite, it would be everywhere and we should know everything. Since we do not, it cannot be infinite. Given the existence of transmigration, each individual must have a constant self which goes through existences from birth to birth. The self must be both eternal and immutable, since otherwise we should lose our identity as we moved into different bodies.

Action or **karma** is the same as movement, and is a property of substance. It links substances with each other, but cannot be inherent in matter since it leads to continual alteration. The principle of generality gives many' things their common character, and in spite of its existence in many substances, it is in itself one. An important distinction was drawn between different kinds of generality, some of which really pick out essential differences between things, while others just describe inessential distinctions. The essential qualities involve **eternity**, commonness and inseparability. The point of these criteria is to distinguish between essential and merely accidental properties, and a great deal of intellectual effort was put into the precise definition of which properties are essential, and how essential properties relate both to each other and to their substrates.

The world is a combination of heterogeneous entities which each have ontological reality and so the relations of conjunction, inseparability and **causation** are all external. A cause is an invariable event that regularly precedes its effect. An effect is something that comes into existence, and so negates its prior non-existence. Some aspects of the cause are essential, and others are not. An essential cause is of the same sort of material as the effect, like the thread in a piece of cloth. Some aspects of the cause are not essential, as for example it is not essential that the threads have a certain colour, nor is it essential for a particular person to have woven the cloth. The effect is a genuinely new creation, since it has negated an antecedent non-existence, and although it had to happen once the earlier causal conditions were all in place, both causes and effects are real. We should recall that for the Nyaya-Vaisheshikas, non-existence is a category, so the earlier non-existence of the effect is just as real as the eventual effect itself when it is instantiated.

The goal of life is liberation and the ending of life in **samsara**. Some have argued that the idea of transcending both

227

the pleasures and pains of this life is not a particularly appetizing one, since we shall then no longer experience any desires, intentions or thoughts. This might be the state that awaits some people after **death**, but there is another, more appealing notion of *moksha*, and this involves only the elimination of the unwelcome qualities of life, not everything. Such an individual will continue to enjoy all the desirable qualities, and can still participate in the world, albeit only in a positive way. Yet is it not the case that the mind, being immortal, will continue to operate as it did pre-liberation, and so invalidate any attempt at such perfection? This does not constitute a serious problem since the idea is that although the mind does continue, it does not affect the self, which has managed to disengage itself from the negative aspects of mind, and, of course, the body. Evil is equivalent to the identification of the self with the mind and the body, and once we stop such identification, we are able to transcend both and replace our ignorance with knowledge.

Further reading: Chatterjee 1965, Matilal 1968, 1971, 1986, Randle 1930.

nyorizo – *see* *tathagatagarbha*

Ohrmazd – *see* **evil**

orientalism In the decades following Indian independence it became popular to associate the West with materialism and the East with spirituality. But this is merely part of a much older movement by which the West romanticized the East, treated it as 'the Other', and as a result failed to undertake an objective study of its culture. Sometimes the attitude was one of exaggerated respect, and sometimes of extreme hostility, and this is characteristic of placing the East in a special category. The term became pejorative after the publication in 1978 of Edward Said's book *Orientalism* in which he examined and criticized the ways in which Western scholars had approached the Middle East. He claims that the concept of the orient is in fact largely a European invention. In philosophy orientalism might be defined as the notion that the ways of thinking of people in the East are essentially very different from those of the West, so that the kinds of philosophy that were produced there have to be understood using alternative hermeneutical techniques as compared with Western philosophy. Sometimes what is taken to be a very basic difference between Western and Eastern forms of philosophy is regarded positively, in the sense that the orient has managed to maintain a grasp of spirituality lost in the West.

Sometimes this is regarded more negatively, and Eastern philosophy is taken to be unable to achieve the levels of **analysis** that have been attained in Western thought.

Further reading: Clarke 1997, Nasr and Leaman 1996, Said 1985, Sen 1997.

P

panna, wisdom – *see prajna*

paradox – *see koan*, logic

perception – *see* inference, knowledge, *prajna*

personality   According to Buddhism the personality consists
of five factors:

1• The body.
2 The feelings associated with experience.
3 The ability to organize experience into knowledge.
4 The will and the ability to pay attention.
5 The ability to be conscious.

These aspects of personality are strongly linked to the
phenomenon of dependent origination, which argues to
the causal linking of everything within the imperfect world.
Through ignorance we tend to misidentify the real, and this
sets off a sequence of beliefs and actions that mire us even
more firmly within the world of birth and rebirth, *samsara*.
What we should notice, but are prevented from noticing due
to ignorance, is that our dispositions and feelings are characterized by impermanence and suffering, and are not part of
a real self.

Of course, the notion of the personality plays an important role in the subsequent Buddhist controversies over the nature of the self. There was a group of thinkers called the Personalists (Pudgalavadins, from *pudgala* or person) who argued that the person is neither equivalent to nor different from the five factors of human personality. It cannot be different from them since if it were, the self would be **eternal**. It cannot be identical to them since if it were then the self would be the same as the body, which hardly fits in with Buddhism. They argued that the self is a type of collective notion that is more than the sum of its parts. The person is a collective name for the *skandhas* or various groups of events that make up the individual.

Their opponents, the Theravadins and the **Sarvastivadins**, argued by contrast that the personality factors can be known but that is the limit of our knowledge of the person. In other words, they would analyse the notion of person in terms of its parts, the aspects of the personality available to us. The Personalists, by contrast, would analyse those parts as constituting a new entity, something over and above the parts themselves. After all, they said, if there can be morality then there must be a moral person, and if there can be knowledge a knowing subject. What is the point of speaking about **compassion** if there is no person for whom compassion is appropriate? As they argue, if the *arahat* manages to escape from the phenomenon of craving, he would disappear as an individual unless his personality was something over and above the personality factors. Yet we speak of the same person continuing as an *arahat*, not someone entirely new coming into existence. Although they used the notion of a person, they avoided the concept of *atman*, the concept of the permanent self, arguing that their concept of the self avoided the objections the Buddha had made to the notion of a real self.

Given the problems with the notion of the self, a number of intriguing difficulties arise. For example, since people are affected from life to life due to their previous **karma**, how acceptable is that given that rebirth brings about what looks like a different person? How far is there continuation of character from life to life? Now, it might be thought that this is only a problem if one denies that there is some linkage between personality traits, and all that Buddhism does is deny the existence of a real permanent self, and this in fact is the way to resolve the issue. In fact, it is even reasonable to suggest that *karma* from a prior life which has not yet brought about its results can pursue what is regarded as the original person into the next life, with the consequences of those results affecting her rebirth. This seems reasonable, since unless *karma* affected the original agent, there would be no personal continuity. On the other hand, there are difficulties in holding on to a notion of personality proceeding through rebirths since there is no particular start of the cycle of birth and rebirth, and there is no particular pattern to the shape the future takes, except that it is shaped by past actions or *karma*. Although most accounts have it that one maintains the same gender through all rebirths, this is certainly not necessary, and there are many references to particular decisions in one life affecting the gender one has in a succeeding life. On the other hand, given that there is no memory, or only vague memory, of past lives, what is involved in claiming that the 'same person' is born again is difficult to grasp, but this serves again to emphasize the incoherence of the notion of the real self.

Personality comes out on the Theravidin account as a stream of conditioned mental and physical processes, with a degree of persistence existing over **time** and rebirths. Then responsibility for one part of the process is passed on to another part of the process across time. What gives the personality its dynamism is the prolongation of desires, or even possibly the attempt to transcend them through **enlightenment**, and the ordinary notion of the self persists in so far as the individual seeks to benefit himself, herself or itself in satisfying the variety of desires that are thought to be important. If the individual succeeds in achieving the state of *arahat*, then this process comes to an end, since the personality merges with reality itself and its individuality disintegrates.

233

Although there are references to personality in the sense of *atman* and **purusha** (soul) in Hindu thought, this is far from the soul with which Western philosophy is familiar. Even the **Sankhya** school with its account of the existence of many *purusha*s is not advocating the existence of souls that go from one existence to another, since what makes these souls different from each other is their **material** aspect. The transmigrating personality we find in the **Upanishads** and most orthodox Hindu schools is a complex entity which keeps on changing as it runs through successive existences, and there is generally taken to be an element of material identity that makes it possible to link the individual through the variety of lives.

See: **anatman**
Further reading: Beidler 1975, Collins 1982, Raju 1985.

prajna A Sanskrit term meaning 'wisdom' (Pali, *panna*) which is used in Buddhism to refer to the sort of thinking that is linked with insight into the true nature of reality. It is one of the three parts of the Buddhist path (along with *shila* and *samadhi*). It is the most significant of the perfections, six in total, along the path to becoming a Buddha. In Buddhist accounts *prajna* is often regarded as coming about after conceptual **analysis** into the nature of reality, which is preliminary to a more direct way of finding out, a form of non-conceptual intuition that enables the thinker to achieve the ultimate truth.

Different schools have interpreted this notion in various ways. In **Abhidhamma** it is related to the accurate understanding of the flow of mental events and their objects. The **Madhyamaka** and **Prajnaparamita** emphasize the significance of **emptiness**, so for them wisdom is not in itself a perfection unless it is directed to the discernment of the emptiness of everything. Wisdom is a state of **consciousness** that is direct intuitive consciousness of emptiness itself. In **Yogachara** wisdom is the flow of non-conceptual consciousness, which is itself the ultimate reality. *Prajna* is throughout identified with direct experiential understanding, by contrast with dualistic thinking, but its precise nature is linked in each school with its particular notion of the nature of the ultimate truth. Nagarjuna, the Madhyamaka thinker, argues that there are three stages to the pursuit of wisdom, the first two being knowledge, which can be acquired through study, and independent reflection, which culminate in the personal development of the individual to the stage where he or she appreciates the emptiness of everything.

Further reading: Kalupahana 1975, Nagao 1991, Puligandla 1975.

Prajnaparamita A Buddhist term for the 'perfection of wisdom', generally applied to some of the Mahahayana sutras. These stress two features, the **emptiness** of everything and the supremacy of the *bodhisattva*, especially in connection with his or her **compassion**. This is total, and is not just directed at the individual who has managed to achieve **enlightenment**, but is directed at all sentient beings. Wisdom is crucial to such a process, since it is the perfection that is capable of leading the others. But we should be careful about identifying *prajna* with wisdom, since the former is more of a mental state, a form of **consciousness** that excludes doubt. This represents a way of thinking that results from **analysis**. The central teaching of these writings is that there is no self, no essence and nothing exists essentially, and so there can be no reference to some level of reality that ultimately exists, such as the *dharma*s, for instance. It is difficult to over-emphasize the difficulty of this as a doctrine to be followed, since it requires the individual to let go completely of every attachment to anything he or she might regard as reality. Another problem with a form of wisdom based on analysis is that there is an insistence throughout the literature on the *bodhisattva*'s refusal to use analytical thought. One might have expected that *prajna* would have involved an analysis of the nature of emptiness, but instead this is replaced by what sometimes appears to be a sort of mental blackness. It is difficult to appreciate the role this can have for salvation. More positively, though, the goal is really an end to conceptualizing tendencies and the attainment of a pure consciousness.

The *bodhisattva* is concerned not only with her salvation, but with **liberation** and the attainment of complete Buddhahood, and also with the liberation of all creatures. She generates infinite compassion and her acts are entirely directed towards helping others. What is important here is the way in which these unselfish **actions** take place; they must be entirely unselfish and so they are since they are motivated by no expectation of anything essential that is actually helped. Being totally unselfish will even involve turning over one's merit for the welfare of others, and applying **skilful means** to express the truth in ways acceptable to listeners.

Further reading: Inada 1970, Keown 1992, Williams 1989.

prakriti   A cause of other things, the original source of the world of experience and matter, closely related to the concept of nature. In **Sankhya** thought the effect is logically linked with the cause, and so the nature of **causality** and particular causes is an inherent feature of the material world. The causal nature of the world is not necessarily an aspect of delusion, although the variety of ways in which causality manifests itself can mislead us into thinking that the variety of the world is a true reflection of a real variety and complexity. This variety is brought about through *prakriti* in order to allow humanity to enjoy the application of the senses and to use them to free itself through **knowledge**. The **Nyaya-Vaisheshika** argue that the world has its origins in a variety of ultimate real beings which are simple and atomic. The **Sankhya Yoga**, by contrast, look to its origins in a single substance that pervades the world, and this is *prakriti*. We cannot actually experience this matter, but we can infer its existence from the nature of the existence of that which we can experience. How does something as basic as *prakriti* manage at the same time to be one thing and yet complex enough to lead to the diversity of the phenomenal world? The answer is that a thing can be both one thing and yet also consist of elements that stand in opposition to each other, in the sense that the parts of something often look as though they are so different that they could hardly be parts of one thing, yet they manage to operate as such parts. The important point is that the aspects of nature are just aspects of one thing, and so when a cause brings about an effect, the cause continues in the effect, although of course the·cause and the effect are different. For example, the potter is the efficient cause of the pot, and although he is very different from the pot itself, the pot could not have come about except through his efforts, and so the notion of the pot is not entirely distinct from the notion of the potter. Nor is the potter separate from the pot, since all that he did was bring the pot from potentiality into actuality. This is even more obvious in the case of the material cause of the pot, the clay.

The natural basis of all these changes is itself unchanged by them, since it incorporates all the potentialities for diversity within a constant equilibrium. The notion of change and evolution as a kind of cycle fits in nicely with this view of nature, since the idea here is of a process that follows a particular pattern and then returns to the state from which it started. Some of the more basic aspects of *prakriti* involve the development of the most important categories of the phenomenal world, leading to the ability of human beings to receive experience and deal with it appropriately. These physical accompaniments of *purusha*, spirit, are of two kinds, one that is subtle enough to continue with the individual through his births and rebirths, while the gross body is cast off at **death**. This subtle body is only abandoned on the **liberation** and exit from *samsara*, the cycle of birth and rebirth.

According to the **Vishishtadvaita**, *prakriti* is not actually independent of spirit, nor is it independent of God. The **Dvaita** view is that the effect is neither existent nor non-existent before it is instantiated, and these descriptions are treated as aspects of the point of view that we can have of different stages of causation, not aspects of the nature of matter itself.

Prakriti is itself made up of three *guna*s, three qualities of the first matter, and these are *sattva* (**harmony**), *rajas* (motion) and *tamas* (inertia). These represent the specific way in which matter is organized within a particular individual, so that someone who is rather greedy would be dominated by *rajas*, while someone who was fairly lazy and dull is controlled by *tamas*. Both matter and spirit are without beginning and **eternal**, and the aspects of matter cannot affect the spirit. Matter is affected by different permutations of its qualities, and ends up as an object that can be perceived, whereas spirit remains throughout the perceiving subject. They need to be combined in order for anything to be accomplished in the ordinary world, since matter by itself could not bring anything about, lacking direction as it does, and spirit could not do anything in that world since without matter it would have no channel with which to operate.

Further reading: Dasgupta 1975, Radhakrishnan 1966, Smart 1964.

prama, result of knowing – *see* **knowledge**

pramana, faculty of knowing – *see* **knowledge**

pratityasamutpada, dependent origination – *see* **dependent origination, fatalism**

pudgala – *see* **personality**

Pure Land This is a form of Buddhism based on the idea that there is a pure land or land of happiness which may be attained by calling on the appropriate Buddha. Although this school originated in both India and China, it became very popular in Japan. Its most important figure is Honen who was a part of the **Tendai** school until he broke off to argue that **enlightenment** could be achieved through the invocation of the name of Amida, the Buddha Amitabha. He distinguishes between two routes to salvation, one being very difficult and dependent upon one's own efforts, while the other is easier and is brought about by the Buddha whom one addresses. It is clear that this comes close to theism, since Amida is identified with ultimate reality and the cause of the phenomenal world. It is not difficult to see why this view blended happily with **Shingon** and Tendai approaches, since they all employed the notion of the objectification of the principles of worship and grace, and emphasized the significance of visualization.

There was a particularly influential development of the school by Shinran, who argued that the influence of Amida could rapidly bring to an end the process of *karma*. Amida had acquired so much merit during his existence that it serves as a form of credit which can suddenly save his followers. Even the individual who is not especially virtuous may be saved if he prays to Amida and is rewarded accordingly. On the other hand, there is no point in practising devotion in order to be saved, since this will not result in salvation. Prayer itself has to be seen as a spontaneous reflection of the nobility and perfection of Amida, and if seen in that view may lead to an appropriate response. This is sometimes called the True Pure Land or Jodo Shinshu school, and was quite worldly in its orientation, since it allowed ordinary lifestyles to achieve salvation.

See: **nembutsu**
Further reading: LaFleur 1992, Tsunoda *et al.* 1964, Yamasaki 1988.

purusha This refers to the spiritual aspect of **being**, although it originally occurs in the *Rig Veda* where it is described as a sort of cosmic person, whose sacrifice led to the creation of so many different things and beings. The **material** aspect of being, *prakriti*, cannot encapsulate the phenomenon of **consciousness**, our ability to be aware. According to **Sankhya Yoga**, both *purusha* and *prakriti* are equal and independent in their roles as the two basically explanatory concepts. We can infer the existence of the former through the same process that was engaged in for the latter, by working back from the purposive nature of things. There are many things in nature that provide evidence of teleological structure, and so we can infer that there is some *purusha*, some instinct or design that directs the way in which things are arranged. The contrast with *prakriti* is that we work back from the phenomena of nature to their material cause, whereas with *purusha* we work towards the aim or direction of nature, its final cause. Unless there existed a realm of *purusha*, there would be no scope for emancipation from the realm of physical nature. *Purusha* is unchanging and requires the participation of *prakriti* in order to know anything or be involved in the doing of anything. Of course, the difficulty is going to be explaining how such different concepts can be linked together, as they must be in ordinary human behaviour. *Purusha* without *prakriti* is inactive, while *prakriti* without *purusha* is undirected. They have to work together for us to be able to operate in the world, and neither could be the source of the other. By contrast with *prakriti*, *purusha* is manifold, since after all we know from our experience that people are different from each other, and if there were only one **consciousness** then after the **liberation** of one individual everyone would be limited, which we know is not the case. Matter takes on a particular form because of the needs of consciousness, some of which relate to our lives in the phenomenal world, while others are directed towards our eventual escape from that world altogether. These alternatives are not genuine alternatives, since the route to liberation is through our lives in this world. While the individual regards herself as a consciousness that has to work with matter in order to exist, she will remain within the realm of the cycle of birth and rebirth. But once the individual appreciates the difference between *purusha* and *prakriti*, and realizes that she is herself nothing but the former, **eternal**, free and uncontaminated with the material aspects of the world, then she is liberated from the world.

According to the Sankhya, there are a mass of *purusha*s in existence, and one might think these are individual souls and selves that persist through change. This is not the case, though. The *purusha* is pure spirit, abstract consciousness, and it has no marks of the phenomenal world, the latter being entirely a result of matter. This leads to explaining the different selves that come into existence through the cycle of birth and rebirth as being constituted largely from matter, although the soul is assumed to control the configuration of the elements of the matter to a certain extent. One wonders how to differentiate between *purusha*s that are entirely free of matter, although it would probably be argued that they are distinct as a result of the different ways in which their individual beings illuminate themselves.

See: **samsara**

Further reading: Carr and Mahalingam 1997, Larson 1969, Radhakrishnan 1966, Raju 1985.

Purva Mimamsa – *see* **Mimamsa**

qi The best way to understand this Chinese term is as equivalent to energy, as a kind of fluid medium that is activated in the balance between complementary and opposing forces. For example, *qi* is brought into existence in the relationships between *yin* and *yang*, since once those forces have come into a particular position they create a field of energy. The concept was used by Mencius in an ethical way to argue that human beings could bring about most virtue by reflecting in themselves the diverse forces in the universe.

See also: **being, cosmology, Korean philosophy, Neoconfucianism**

rajas, passion – *see* **Dvaita**, *prakriti*, **yoga**

rectification of names The main concern of Confucius'
theory of meaning was the relationship between **language**
and behaviour, and it is vitally important for language to
work successfully so that it gets a grip on the rituals that
constitute the right way to live and act. Ritual (*li*) establishes
the paradigms for the use of language, and the basis of ritual
is *ren* or humanity. The main point of getting names
right is to establish the correct kind of state, since if the
names are wrong, the way people speak will go awry, resulting
in chaos and disharmony. No one will know how they are
to act or what forms of behaviour are acceptable or otherwise. In later Chinese philosophy the precise links between
a name and what it describes was analysed in a wide variety
of different ways. This theory was extended beyond its pragmatic aspects by Xunzi to explain the logical links between
names and objects in the natural world, and he argued
that it is very important to be clear on the precise meanings
of names and the process through which they act as names
if we are to be able to use language without sinking into
confusion.

See also: **ambiguity**
Further reading: Graham 1978, Hansen 1983.

243

ren   A Chinese term often translated as 'benevolence', but also meaning '**humanity**'. This linking of concepts brings out nicely the Confucian idea of identity between a harmonious society and a moral universe.

See also: **harmony, Mohism, Neoconfucianism**

ru lai zang – *see* **tathagatagarbha**

S

saguna brahman, the absolute as the creator – *see lila*

samadhi, concentration – *see* **meditation**, *prajna*

samatha – *see* **meditation**

samsara   The notion of 'wandering' is important in philosophies inspired by Indian forms of thought, and is used to
represent the continual process of birth, **death** and **afterlife
and rebirth**. During this wandering one may spend time in
non-human form, either enjoyably or not, as a result of one's
previous behaviour (*karma*). Even though there are pleasant
aspects of physical existence, it is generally identified as
suffering and is regarded as a state from which the **enlightened** individual manages to escape.

Further reading: Carr and Mahalingam 1997.

samsari, someone undergoing the cycle of birth and rebirth –
see **Jain philosophy**

Sankhya   A school of Hindu philosophy, based on a
cosmology in which **mind** and matter emanate from an

245

original source as a result of the imperfections in the three basic modalities, or types of **being**. Human **consciousness** tends to fall into error by identifying with the effects of *prakriti* or the **causal** principle, in that the material and mental effects produced in the world seem to be important and interesting. What it should do is sharply distinguish between itself and the causal processes in the world, emphasizing the distinctiveness of human spirituality against the mental and material aspects of the world.

Further reading: Larson 1969, Radhakrishnan and Moore 1957.

sarupya, agreement of knowledge with its object – *see* **knowledge**

Sarvastivada A Buddhist school of thought that pre-dates Mahayana and was the dominant trend in Northern India during the early centuries of Mahayana. Literally meaning 'all exists', it relates to a particular theoretical problem. The theory of *karma* suggests that particular **causes** in the past will have particular effects in the future, and yet the theory of the impermanence of the world (*anicca*) implies that such long-standing and powerful links across **time** are questionable. How can a present event be linked with something that happened a long time in the past? The solution put forward by the Sarvastivada school is that the time at which something takes place is actually a part of the nature of the thing, the way in which it takes place or exists, and so an event in the past that apparently no longer exists does in fact exist, albeit in past time. Then there is no general problem in understanding how the past can affect the present and future.

This school identifies the phenomenal world with **atoms**, so that everything in it is **momentary**. The basis of the ordinary world is change, which affects both the **mind** and matter. This is a useful thesis given the difficulties in Buddhism of accepting the dichotomy between **being** and non-being, a dichotomy that is to be replaced with the notion of becoming. The Sarvastivada theory manages to justify the use of the notion of time, which was often heavily criticized in Theravada Buddhism, and combines a belief in atomism with disbelief in the soul. Atoms that make up compound objects really exist, as do the past and the future.

Further reading: Kalupahana 1976, Lopez 1988.

sattva, real, existing – *see* **Dvaita**, *prakriti*, **yoga**

shari`a – *see* **law**

shaykh, spiritual leader – *see* *guru*, **Sufism**

sheng, development – *see* **causation**

shi, reality, actuality, power – *see* **Legalism**

Shi`a, Shi`ism Literally 'the party' of God (*shi`at Allah*), representing a particular attachment to `Ali, the Prophet's cousin, and to the family of the Prophet. Among that family is generally included the line of Imams who are taken to be the rightful leaders of the Islamic community. They operate as spiritual guides to the community, and are taken to be in communication with higher levels of reality. In philosophy the Shi`a tended to adopt enthusiastically the principles of Neoplatonism, and some Shi`a communities such as the Isma`ilis were very open to the use of philosophy as a route to understanding the nature of reality and the place of human beings in it. As with Sunni thought, which the Shi`a set themselves against, the forms of philosophy that have been produced are various, but there is often an orientation towards mysticism.

See: **Sufism, sunni**
Further reading: Nasr and Leaman 1996.

*shi`at Allah*, party of God – *see* **Shi`ism**

shila, ethics – *see **prajna***

Shingon Buddhism Like most philosophical movements in Japan, this arrived from China, and is a specifically Japanese version of **tantra**. This fits in with Buddhism in that the tantric ideas can be represented as an esoteric version of the more standard concepts and teachings of the religion. What is unusual about this approach is that it seeks to revive the **buddha nature** which is inherent in everyone through concentration upon a particular Buddha, and as a result to integrate oneself with reality. That reality, if it is ultimate reality, manifests itself in two different ways, both as enlightened **consciousness** behind the things of the world of experience, and as those things themselves. So to grasp this notion of reality one has to practise both **meditation** to align oneself with the enlightened consciousness, and ritual to understand the phenomena. Meditation leads to the attainment of non-duality, so that we mentally blend with reality and stop distinguishing between the self and the other. The human body can serve as a site for Buddhahood since in a sense it embodies the whole universe. The external actions needed are those that make possible the uniting of the body and the **mind**, and these involve special postures and mantras. The Shingon school was founded by Kukai and defended the notion of attainment of buddha nature while still within a particular physical frame. He discussed the variety of philosophies that then existed as aspects of different ways of looking at the world which lead to different kinds of experience. He criticized each in turn on account of their incompleteness, something that could only be resolved by his own doctrine of esoteric Buddhism.

See: **enlightenment**
Further reading: Kukai 1972, Yamasaki 1988.

shu, method, technique – *see* **Legalism**

shunya – *see* **emptiness, Madhyamaka**

shunyata – *see* **emptiness**

Shunyatavada, philosophy of emptiness – *see* **emptiness, Madhyamaka, Mahayana**

shura, consultation – *see* **democracy**

skandhas, group – *see* **personality**

skilful means There is a detailed discussion in Buddhism about the availability of *nirvana*, spiritual **liberation**, to everyone. Many in the Mahayana tradition would claim that since we can achieve this state through accepting the **emptiness** of the world, then anyone can in principle achieve this state. After all, we only require an acknowledgement of the illusory state of *samsara*, the cycle of birth and rebirth, to put ourselves well on the road to ending our suffering and reaching **enlightenment**. So anyone can reach enlightenment, there is no reason why it should be restricted to only a few. On the other hand, the ways of bringing them to this position vary. People need to be addressed in ways that make sense to them, and skilful means (*upaya* in Sanskrit; *hoben* in Japanese) need to be employed to help everyone attain the path to liberation most surely. Buddhas and *bodhisattvas* are particularly skilled in their understanding of which means are likely to be most effective. The use of skilful means may even involve expressing heretical views or breaking moral laws. There is a charming example in the *Lotus Sutra* in which a father (the Buddha) deceives his sons by telling them that he has toys for them, when he has not, in order to get them out of a burning house (*samsara*). There is also a story of how the Buddha, in a previous life, killed a man who intended to kill five hundred others, which would have resulted in the murderer spending a very long time indeed in the lowest hell. The act of killing was motivated entirely by **compassion** both for the potential murderer and for those who would otherwise have been killed. There are many similar stories in the literature of Buddhism.

One thing these stories have in common is the acceptability of adapting the teaching of the truth to the particular circumstances of the audience. It does not follow, however, that the moral laws that are flouted become unimportant, but the necessity to use these morally questionable techniques has an effect upon the character of the actor himself or herself despite the virtuous motives that inspire them. The notion of skilful means also played a part in opening up Buddhism to non-Buddhist ideas, since such incorporation could be regarded as a compassionate use of existing materials to get over an important point to those who would otherwise not appreciate it.

Yet the notion of skilful means plays an important part in the controversy over whether enlightenment can be sudden or must be gradual. There came to be a division of the Buddha's teachings between the gradual ones, which relied on expedients to accommodate his enlightened insight to the understanding of unenlightened people, and sudden teachings which are appropriate for those who have achieved a higher level of enlightenment. For the *bodhisattva*s there is no necessity to use skilful means, since their capacity to understand is highly developed. The more gradual approach helps to prepare people slowly for the final message, which he delivered just before he died. Indeed, the whole approach of the Buddha brings out the policy of skilful means in producing statements that seem quite perplexing. For example, sometimes he implies that the *tathagatagarbha* (the **buddha nature** that we all possess) is equivalent to the self. Yet we know that it is also a key principle of his that there is no self, and he was worried that some might regard this principle as nihilistic. This would lead them to reject it. So he talked about a self where there is no self, and he talked about a non-self where there is a self, to get his point over to those who would otherwise be unable to accept it. The buddha nature is really non-self, but to a certain extent it is a self. It is a self in the sense that each sentient being can become a Buddha, and to that degree only we can talk about the existence of a self.

The basis of skilful means is the defence of openness and flexibility to others, the ability to question the security with which some feel themselves to be on the path to the highest end. The lower aims of becoming an *arahat*, for instance, are perfectly acceptable as stages on the route to Buddhahood, and some people will find that this is as far as they can really go, since they are presented with this as their route to salvation. But once they have achieved this, they should appreciate that this is only a resting place on the path to the eventual end, Buddhahood, and they thought that this limited stage might be the end (for them) through the skilful teaching of the Buddha. They thought that there were a variety of routes to salvation (a variety of vehicles – *yana*) and they were encouraged in this thought by the compassion of the Buddha who realized that this was the way to convey the truth to them. But in fact there is only one vehicle to salvation, and that is in becoming Buddhas ourselves. To give an example, again from the *Lotus Sutra*, the Buddha's teaching is like the rain that falls equally on all plants, but those plants absorb it in line with their particular natures.

*See: **anatman***
Further reading: Pye 1978.

song, sincerity – *see* **human nature**

suchness – *see **tathagata***

suf, wool – *see* **Sufism**

Sufism A specifically Islamic form of mysticism designed to help its followers understand the nature of divine unity (*tawhid*). It is based upon the following of a mystical path, under the guidance of a teacher (*shaykh*), and the end of the path is a direct experience of divine reality, although the precise nature of this is described in different ways by different schools of Sufis. The term itself comes from the Arabic for wool (*suf*) which refers to the simple clothes of its original practitioners, and by contrast with many believers the Sufis led solitary and simple lives in order to bring them nearer to God and immerse the individual human soul within the unity of God. A term for their approach to God is *dhawq* or taste, representing the desire for a personal experience of God as opposed to an intellectual or legal understanding of divinity. They sometimes call their approach to prayer *dhikr*, which means remembering, in the sense that prayer reminds us of our real role in the universe as part of the unity of God, and helps us cast off the superficial ways of thinking that arise from our customary and mistaken view of the world as consisting of many separate and independent things.

There are many schools of Sufism, and there is also a wide variety of explanations of the central doctrines. As one might expect, given the centrality of mystical experience to much, but not all, Sufism there is extensive discussion of how to distinguish between genuine and fallacious mystical experience.

See: **guru**, **meditation**
Further reading: Nasr 1989, 1993, Nasr and Leaman 1996.

Sunna, **Sunni Islam**   Literally, custom or law, a reference in Islam to the life of the Prophet. Along with the Traditions (*hadith*) and the Qur´an, this is often taken to be the basis of authority in Islam, in particular in Sunni Islam, by far the largest group of adherents to Islam by contrast with the **Shi`a**.

Further reading: Nasr and Leaman 1996.

susupti, dreamless sleep – *see* **atman**

svadharma, duty linked to caste – *see* **dharma**

T

tamas, darkness – *see* **Dvaita**, *prakriti*, **yoga**

tanha, craving – *see* **Four Noble Truths**

tantra Literally 'weaving' or 'thread', *tantra* refers to a number of Hindu and Buddhist texts with esoteric meaning. It represents a loose collection of ideas for achieving **liberation** via working with the body, **mind** and spirit and their imperfections as opposed to rejecting them, and this is possible because we as microcosm mirror the universe as macrocosm.

In Hindu *tantra* philosophy the universe has emanated from the supreme and hidden reality in progressively cruder ways, ranging from mind and space until we get to air, fire, water and· earth. All these levels are also present in every human being, with energies concentrated on different parts of the body. These levels are often linked with parts of human physiology, but most significance is given to the **meditative** meanings of the levels, which can be altered and directed in positive ways through appropriate techniques. Tantric· practices. are different from **Vedic** ones in that they are more universal, being applicable even to those·groups of people such as women who are generally excluded from the Vedic techniques. Tantra involves the acquisition of a spirit force through the teaching of a *guru*, which involves a variety of ritual practices along with the transmission to the pupil of a mantra which he or she has to repeat regularly to overcome difficulties that may occur. More elaborate procedures are involved for the individual who wishes to attain perfection, since this person has to develop spiritual excellence through mastering the mental disciplines, and in the end can produce miracles and put aside all mortal concerns. As one might imagine, the processes involved here are very complex. One generally has to work with an image, and it is necessary to pray to it, bring it to life in one's mind and for this to be possible one has to genuflect before it with what are called the eight limbs (the legs, hands, chest, mind, head, speech or look), completely submitting oneself to the image. The point is to impress upon oneself in a total sense the presence of the deity. Often this process will start with an elaborate worship of the *guru*, and end similarly.

There are a wide variety of versions of Tantric practice, some of which only relate to purification of the upper half of the body, while others make the effort to imagine a tree of **knowledge** growing in one's lotus heart. This is like a tree with *dharma* as its root and knowledge as its trunk, whose eight petals are the virtues and vices. What is common to these practices is the differentiation of worship between the animal, human and divine. The animal is ordinary worship, worship that is carried out routinely and does not succeed in increasing spirituality. Human worship fixes the mind on the deity, but stops at that point. Finally, divine worship succeeds in imparting the idea that the individual is only a differing form of the deity, and this is the highest level.

There is a close connection between *tantra* and the disciplines of **yoga**, the latter being based on a form of mysticism linking humanity and the divine. Through acting and thinking in appropriate ways one is able to achieve union with ultimate reality. A variety of practices can be followed to this end, some emphasizing worship while others stress breath control and special postures. The practice of *tantra* has undergone some exotic variations which bring in what are commonly regarded as forbidden practices, often given an esoteric meaning by their adherents, and this has brought the whole tradition under something of a cloud. In Buddhist thought *tantra* refers originally to a series of texts designed to promote **enlightenment** through meditation. It is important to have a spiritual guide, a *guru* or lama, who links the present disciple with a previous master. The teacher shows the pupil how to meditate on a deity, how to acquire the power of a particular text, and finally how to go about applying a text. This is an important aspect of Mahayana Buddhism, in particular its notion of the inseparability of *nirvana* and *samsara*. Since everything is essentially **empty**, there is no point in distinguishing sharply between these two apparently very different aspects of human development initially. Everything after all comes from the same cause. Understanding this leads to the basis of the tantric processes in accordance with which what might look like defiling actions can be transformed through wisdom (*prajna*) into perfections. Tantrism has had a particularly important impact on Tibetan Buddhism.

See: **Shingon**

Further reading: Eliade 1958, 1969, Karmay 1988, Radhakrishnan and Moore 1957, Saran 1997.

Taoism – *see* **Daoism**

Tao Te Ching – *see* **Dao De Jing**

tasawwur, conceptualization – *see* **knowledge**, **logic**

tasdiq, judgement, assent – *see* **logic**

tat tvam asi, 'That art thou'. – *see* **Vedanta**

tathagata This is an expression the Buddha uses of himself, as appropriate for a description of **liberated** beings. It literally means 'thus gone' or 'thus arrived' and describes someone who has attained the height of **enlightenment**.

See: **enlightenment**, *tathagatagarbha*

tathagatagarbha A school of Mahayana Buddhism that became popular in China (*ru lai zang*; *nyorizo* in Japanese) and means the embryo or womb of Buddhahood, the idea that the **buddha nature** reposes in creatures like a seed, waiting for propitious conditions to help it to grow, *tathata* being equivalent to suchness or thusness, the real way things are. This doctrine regards all sentient creatures as already Buddhas, and so in themselves enlightened. It follows that **enlightenment** cannot be a state of transcending this world, but rather the recognition of the connections between the individual and everything in the world. Then there is no need for a lengthy apprenticeship for the attainment of enlightenment, the latter can be suddenly acquired. Critically, this means that enlightenment is not the preserve of monks, ascetics or scholars, but can be enjoyed by ordinary people leading ordinary lives. This is very different from the position of Theravada Buddhism, for instance, which is prevalent today in South and South East Asia, and which denies enlightenment as a likely goal of the lay population. But the main problem of *tathagatagarbha* is that it provides little account of the nature of **ignorance**. If ignorance comes from the **mind** itself, how can the nature of that mind be regarded as essentially pure? On the other hand, if ignorance comes from somewhere else, how can the mind be regarded as the source of both *nirvana* and *samsara*?

This problem is solved in the **Yogachara** school by the argument that ignorance arises out of the *alayavijnana*, the storehouse consciousness that is the source of all impure *dharma*s. How then do we ever acquire pure *dharma*s? The answer is that these must come about from outside the mind, and on many Indian views which regard *avidya* as having no objective basis, this is not a problem. Knowledge replaces ignorance, and ignorance just disappears. Chinese solutions tended to take a different approach, stressing the dual way in which reality may be viewed. That is, through ignorance one may take that which would otherwise have been seen as *nirvana* as *samsara*. To a certain extent this reflects what might seem to be a central paradox surrounding this notion, that sentient beings are already enlightened, yet they become enlightened in the future. The solution seems to be that every such being has within itself the potentiality to become a Buddha, and this potentiality is itself pure and uncontaminated. But it is occluded by ignorance, and although it remains there throughout, it does not develop in the ways in which it otherwise might. Sometimes it looks as though this potentiality is equivalent to the self, and it is in the sense that it represents a potentiality in every sentient creature, but it is not in the sense that the self might be regarded as a real essence. But like the ordinary conception of the self there is something permanent and real in sentient beings, and this is the buddha nature. The point about this is to counter the idea that Buddhism is nihilistic, and spends all its time discovering suffering and denying reality. It is important to be able to make positive claims about those aspects of the structure of being that are in themselves positive, and the buddha nature is just such a thing. So we can admit that it shares some at least of the characteristics of the self while at the same time denying that it is equivalent to the real self. But it is certainly real.

Many controversies arose within Buddhist philosophy about the exact status of *tathagatagarbha*, and especially about its precise relationship with the notion of the self. There was a particularly interesting such controversy in Tibetan philosophy. Does the doctrine really teach that there is something permanent and real in existence, the potentiality to become a Buddha, or is this merely a way of cloaking the genuine position, which is that this is equivalent to **emptiness**? That is, if the thesis was clearly that this potentiality was the same as emptiness, then the apparent nihilism of it would deter a lot of putative followers, so the Buddha in his **compassion** phrased it differently, but the real teaching is the one that identifies this potentiality with emptiness. The dispute ranges

257

over whether the assertion is that something, the ultimate reality inherent in all sentient beings, exists, or whether there is no such thing as an ultimately real entity.

The Soto Zen thesis of Dogen denies that all sentient creatures have the buddha nature, since this is too dualistic. It is better to say that everything is the buddha nature, and not only sentient creatures. The buddha nature does not lie behind the appearances, the phenomena, but is literally part and parcel of those appearances. This means that there is no need to engage on long and difficult paths to enlightenment, since we are already enlightened. But to realize that we are enlightened is not quite as simple as this, it involves an attitude of complete unity with the particular object of thought, an openness to its character and perfection as reflecting complete reality.

Further reading: Abe 1992, Chan 1972, Creel 1953, Dreyfus 1997, Fung 1952, Griffiths 1994, Jackson 1993, King 1991, LaFleur 1985, Williams 1989.

tathata, suchness – *see tathagatagarbha*

tawhid, divine unity – *see* **Sufism**

Tendai   The Tendai movement is a Japanese version of the Chinese Buddhist *tian tai* school set up by Saicho on his return from China. He argued for the sudden view of **enlightenment**, and the school discusses in detail the concept of enlightenment or *hongaku*. This is a kind of non-dual **consciousness** that exists behind the flow of things and experiences. It stands in between **ignorance** and complete enlightenment, denying the existence of absolute truth but also not accepting the point of view of ignorance. Enlightenment is present at all times, even during ignorance, but we need to know how to discover it. This form of Buddhist philosophy in its original Chinese form emphasized the significance of the *Lotus Sutra*, and in particular the idea that all the vehicles of Buddhism are basically just one vehicle. The school went on to develop in a number of different directions, including a more esoteric Shintoist direction, and a **zen** direction.

Further reading: Swanson 1989.

Theravada Buddhism   A Pali term for 'doctrine of the elders' that represents the form of Buddhism popular in ancient Ceylon (Sri Lanka) and South East Asia. Theravada is rudely characterized as 'hinayana' by the Mahayana school, since the former accepts as a valid aim the 'lesser' goal of the *arahat*, or the personal **enlightenment** of the individual as compared with the enlightenment of everyone.

Further reading: Gombrich 1988.

tian   A Chinese term for heaven, taken by Confucius to have an effect on human beings. According to Mozi, the ruler should identify his will with that of heaven in order to align the state with the natural flow of things. He criticizes Confucius for doubting that heaven intervenes directly in human affairs, arguing by contrast that retribution is a fact and that natural disasters are an expression of heaven's dislike of improper conduct by the ruler.

Although *tian* is not to be identified with a transcendent deity, since *tian* is not so much the creator of the world but the world itself, it does operate on humanity. Heaven plays a part in the activities of human beings, and in particular the most noble human beings, and can indirectly communicate with humanity.

See: **human nature**
Further reading: Hall and Ames 1997.

tianli, laws of heaven – *see* **human nature**

tian tai, Tendai school – *see* **Chinese philosophy, emptiness, Korean philosophy, Tendai** *tianzi*, will of heaven – *see* **Mohism**

Tibetan philosophy   Tibetan philosophy is Buddhist, and consists of a specifically Tibetan orientation in Buddhist thought. Buddhism came to Tibet initially in the seventh century, from a variety of sources: China, Central Asia and, most importantly, India. The first wave of Buddhism was related to **tantrism** and **Madhyamaka** Buddhism, while there was also an important strain of *chan* (zen) philosophy coming from China. This led to an early controversy in Tibet, between the Indian form of philosophy which argued that **enlightenment** can only be achieved by slow and gradual procedures, and the Chinese form which emphasized the sudden route to enlightenment. The argument was won by the Indian faction, and the Madhyamaka position become the orthodox one in the country. Perhaps the greatest contribution of Tibetan philosophy to Buddhist thought as a whole is the energetic translation of texts for many centuries, especially those tantric texts that were produced in such large numbers in India. There were also many translations of the commentaries on the sutras, which are important since they are often of texts no longer extant in Sanskrit, and which survive only in Tibetan.

The most productive period of Tibetan thought came between the thirteenth and fifteenth centuries. An influential idea at the time was that the highest Buddhist teaching is of the great completeness, which represents the **mind** as the basis of reality. In itself it is perfect, eternal, pure, makes no distinction between subject and object, completely one and infinite. The **ignorant** finite mind thinks that what it sees is real, but this is entirely wrong, and it forgets the connection that exists between the finite mind and its infinite source, its original nature. What the mind should not do is set out to rediscover its pure and **liberated** condition, since it is not as though there is a reality behind the appearance. The reality is there already in the workings of the finite mind, and what we need to do is appreciate this fact. What is required to attain this state of purity is to engage in a series of practices designed to reduce and eliminate the influences of *karma*, which then results in the mind removing all thoughts and experiences, and finding its true nature again.

An important intellectual concern of the Ga-gyu is the doctrine of the great seal or symbol (*dzogchen* = *mahamudra*). This is a state of enlightenment that unifies appearances with the reality. It is always present, and can be reached through **meditation** which frees the mind of discursive and so dualist thought. The most enlightened mind is the ordinary mind, which is in itself lucid and simple. The ordinary mind is like a clear mirror in that it reflects reality without adding anything to it, while the more sophisticated mind is like a clouded mirror which misrepresents reality as divisible in terms of subjects and objects. What we need to do is not reject the ordinary mind, even though it may include all kinds of errors, but we should work from those errors to illuminate the truth that lies within them. Once we can recognize the links that exist between the worldly mind and the ordinary mind, we are aware of how alongside our delusions a natural truth persists through all existence.

The Sa-gya movement produced a wide variety of different forms of philosophy, including tantrism, Madhyamaka Buddhism, **logic** and epistemology. The Ge-luk produced a very impressive thinker, Tsongkhapa, who concentrated on arguing that even apparently contradictory philosophical schools are in fact consistent, so that the logical methods and the contemplative methods are in fact doing the same sort of thing. One of their most interesting ideas is that there is no inconsistency in using concepts that strictly speaking are in themselves empty. He also suggested that the only route to enlightenment is through the logical analysis of the parts of experience. The Ge-luk thinkers also adhered to a form of realism, arguing for the reality of everyday objects.

One of the intriguing distinctions between Tibetan and Indian Buddhist philosophy is the extreme systematization of the former. They argued that there is a hierarchy of philosophical schools, each of which is an improvement on its predecessor, and the philosophical curriculum should involve working one's way up through the different schools until one ends up with the highest, generally the Prasangika/ Madhyamaka school of Candrakirti. Of course, we should remember that Tibet came across these schools of thought relatively late, and so was able to take a more global view of them than was perhaps available to thinkers further east, or even to Indian philosophers themselves. Let us take as an example the way in which epistemology was discussed. The most elementary theory was taken to be that of naive realism, the idea that what makes a thing appear as a thing is the fact that it is as it is. This notion came to be criticized since it ignores the role images play in our knowledge of objects, and on the better view what we have experience of is not directly of objects but of the sense data linked to the objects. This, of course, leads to the problem that we might have a set of sense experiences that lead us to think that they have a particular cause in a certain object, but we may be wrong, since a variety of objects can give rise to sense experiences that can mislead us. We can use this sort of argument to arrive at a form of idealism, and assert that all that exists is really ideas, experiences that are dependent on the mind. What is taken by Tsongkhapa as being the best view is a combination of realism and idealism. We should be realist in the sense that we should accept that external things exist distinctly from the mind, but we should also be idealist in that we should break the link between sense experiences and the objects that are supposed to be the sources of those experiences. Objects exist, but the experiences we have do not give us a good idea of what they are like. Of course, where we go wrong is in thinking that the sorts of objects that we seem to experience really exist, since nothing really exists except **emptiness** (in the sense that it is a state lacking an inherent nature) and we use this false confidence in the reality of the world to embed our commitment to the world and to the cravings and desires that go with it. This cements us in the production of **karma** which fixes us in the cycle of birth and rebirth. What we should do is use reasoning to work to the conclusion that objects do not have intrinsic existence, and thus prevent the accumulation of yet more *karma*, so entering the path to salvation. It is clear from examining this form of **inference** that epistemology in Tibetan thought reached very high levels of development indeed, as did logic. The arguments about the precise nature of key Buddhist concepts, like emptiness for example, were pursued in a rigorous manner, and continue to be today. The analysis of the different philosophical interpretations available to the Tibetan thinker are part of an educational model that sees merit in working through theories to learn from them even if they ultimately come out to seem unsatisfactory. In this way one appreciates that the truth or lack of it is not to be found in the thought of a particular individual, but these different approaches reflect the fact that reality has no essence. Theories that deny this are useful in so far as they can eventually be seen to be unsatisfactory, which adds to the plausibility of the Buddhist notion of **being**.

See: **samsara**
Further reading: Dreyfus 1997, Gyatso 1992, Karmay 1988.

time   In Chinese philosophy the **Mohists** provided a scientific account of time (*jiu*), regarding it as the sum of all the various units that represent the continuity of the workings of matter. They linked time with movement, and this is not dissimilar from Confucius' identification of time with a flowing river. Zhuangzi refers to time as the active force that brings about the creation of heaven and earth, and the notion of time seems to be the notion of something infinite. Daoist accounts of time tend to downplay its significance, since past, present and future are merely parts of a pattern that never really alters. In any case, the universe will eventually become entirely still, so time will at some point lack any significance at all.

On the zen account of **being**, Dogen emphasizes the role of change and motion. He has an unusual concept of time which runs against the ordinary idea of it as a measure of flow. Being is identical with impermanence and change, and so time must be more than just change, since this would mean that we could think of the future as something that is going to come into existence, while the past is what has gone out of existence. There is no such thing as the continuity of time, all that exists is the reality of individual times, of each individual moment. This means that we cannot think in terms of sequences connected to each other in accordance with laws. An advantage of this view is that it avoids the dualism of seeing time as a framework within which we work towards certain ends. For example, we should not view the **buddha nature** as something we wish to attain in the future after practice in the past, unless we realize at the same time that the buddha nature is not only the aim of our practice but also its starting point. This fits in nicely with Theravadin arguments that neither the past nor the future exis.

In Tibetan Buddhism the ambition of the practitioner is to become **enlightened** in his lifetime, and this means transcending **death** during this life. This involves overcoming what might be thought of as the ordinary notion of linear time, since death is a part of the definition of time, given that time runs out for the person who dies at the point of death. What we need to do is to replace linear with cyclical time, the idea being that in this way we can control time, as against the usual notion of time controlling us. It is difficult to know how to describe this alternative notion of time, since we really only understand it if we have managed to achieve it. Our ordinary conceptual scheme is too infected with the ordinary notion of linear time for this deeper concept to make sense, until we manage to overturn our **language** and experiences to allow in this other notion.

The account of time provided in Japanese Buddhism plays an important part in the rather dramatic developments of Amida Buddhism and the arguments for **violence** provided by Nichiren. The **Tendai** movement prioritized the *Lotus Sutra* above everything else, and in particular a view of historical time. It was taken that the world would pass through three different periods of time in which the Buddhist teachings would figure. First there was a period of authenticity during which the real teaching could be adopted, then there was a time when it could be followed but not really understood. Finally, and this was the period Nichiren and others identified with the thirteenth century and difficult contemporary conditions in Japan, is the period of *mappo,* the degenerate time, during which it is necessary to consider radical reformulations of Buddhism to fit the times. The use of time to explain the necessity to reinterpret Buddhism is a frequent theme within the Japanese tradition.

In Islamic philosophy time plays an important role in the controversy over the **creation** of the world. Many thinkers argued on Aristotelian lines that time is a reflection of change, so that there was no change before the world was created, which means that if there always is time then the world must always have been in existence. God could not have created the world at a particular time, since that would have been to create not only the world but also time itself, and we could not call the start of time a time. Al-Ghazali challenges this view by arguing that we can think of a time before time, as it were, so that we can think of God being by himself before creating the world, and then bringing the world, and time itself, into existence. Other philosophers tried to explain away the problem by arguing that the world is continually emanating from God, and so is re-created at particular times, and yet the whole process is itself **eternal**, so in a sense the world is eternal. Iqbal reproduced in his work a familiar **illuminationist** notion of two different concepts of time, *dahr,* which represents the unchanging view of time as a perspicuous grasp of reality, as compared with *zaman,* the ordinary linear concept. The former is the view held by God, and can be experienced by us to a certain degree during mystical experience.

See: **momentariness**

Further reading: Abe 1992, Allinson 1989a, Chung 1992, Nasr and Leaman 1996, Rodd 1980, Yampolsky 1990.

triaratna, three jewels of right behaviour – *see* **ethics**

trishna, grasping – *see* **Four Noble Truths**

U

umma, community – *see* **violence**

universals The problem of universals is to explain the concept of universal concepts which apply to a variety of different objects. Realists argue that such different objects share a common feature, which exists independently of human awareness. Anti-realists deny this, arguing that universals belong to the human **mind** and its interaction with **material** things. The **Nyaya** suggest that universals have meaning because they refer to real general qualities. Such principles are very important for our ability to know the nature of the world, since they permit us to apply categories to that world. On the whole, the Hindu view is a variety of realism, which is hardly surprising, since realism fits in with the notion of *dharma*, the system of the universe. The latter provides a way of working out what to do in every situation, while the universals provide similar guidance for our linguistic and intellectual projects. The **Sankhya** view is that there is really only one universal, out of which every other apparent universal stems as a manifestation of nature or *prakriti*. The Naiyayikas by contrast produce a vast number of different universals, and they play an essential role in both thought and **language**. General terms refer to universals that are associated with them, and when we say that many different things share a quality, we mean that they all refer to the same universal. Were we unable to use such universals, we could not understand the world, and when we bring concepts to the world, we are not bringing to the world just our ideas, but our ideas in so far as these reflect reality.

The Buddhist response to this form of realism was to deny the reality of universals. For example, Dharmakirti argued that the Nyaya account of universals is incoherent since universals are taken to exist apart from their particulars. It follows, he argues, that they cannot be related to those particulars. There are only two ways in which things can be related. Either they share the same nature, or they are distinct but related **causally**. Since the universals and the particulars are supposed to exist separately, they cannot share the same nature. Nor can they be causally related, since they are supposed to exist together at the same time. It follows that universals and individuals must be unrelated, which is completely the contrary of the conclusion that the Naiyayikas try to draw. The Nyaya response was to counter that it follows from this that there is no such thing as general concepts at all, which is clearly wrong. Many Buddhists did not wish to reject all such concepts, but they did want to deny that universals are just like things that are in existence and waiting to be discovered. Rather, universals are ideas that we produce as a result of our experience of individuals, and in themselves they do not share anything in common. Universals neither exist nor do not exist, in the sense that they do not have the same form of existence as individual things, and they do have a valid use.

See: **logic**
Further reading: Dravida 1972, Dreyfus 1997, Matilal 1968, 1971.

Upanishads   A compilation of Sanskrit writings, some of great antiquity, that represent varying approaches to the meaning of reality. These texts tend to break with the **Vedic** tradition of representing worship as the route to **knowledge** and salvation, arguing by contrast that the seeker after the truth needs to discover the meaning of his soul. We need to turn away from the appearance of reality which is our ordinary world and grasp the nature of the self and its ability to flourish once it is denied the ordinary attachments of life. Most of the key concepts of Indian philosophy such as *atman*, *brahman*, *yoga*, *maya*, *dharma* and the principles of **asceticism** appear in the Upanishads, which finds their epitome in the *Bhagavad Gita*. This work raises many of the general issues of the Upanishads in highly concrete form and explores the problems of trying to understand how to live a good and authentic life. The Upanishads continue to be a source of philosophical **meditation** within Indian thought, and many of the major Indian thinkers, in particular Shankara, base their general theories on the principles and ideas of the Upanishads.

Further reading: Radhakrishnan 1953, *Upanishads* 1996.

upaya – *see* **skilful means**

Vaisheshika One of the *darshanas* of Hindu philosophy, founded by Kanada around the second century BCE. The central thesis is that spiritual development and **liberation** can be achieved by completely understanding how the world of experience is made up of six basic categories – substance, quality, activity, commonness, particularity and inherence. Vaisheshika is a realist school, with an **atomistic** basis, and distinguishes **mind** from spirit. The former is minute, while the latter is infinite, and both are eternal.

Further reading: Carr and Mahalingam 1997, Hiriyanna 1932, 1985.

Veda Literally meaning '**knowledge**', this is a collection of Hindu verses from very early on, starting perhaps around 1000 BCE. Although the doctrines and rituals the Vedas describe are now often very distant from current Hinduism, they are full of philosophical interest in their accounts of the nature of human beings and destiny. The object of human life in the Vedas is not the attainment of **liberation**, but the observance of *dharma*. It is through **action** that we can come as close as possible to reaching wealth, happiness and in the end heaven. When we speak we should try to use the proper **language** which has been established in religion, and if we are no longer sure what the precise meaning is, we need to become clear on what the practical force of

269

the words is, since if we at least follow that we shall not go far wrong.

Further reading: Radhakrishnan and Moore 1957.

Vedanta One of the six *darshana*s of Hinduism, literally the 'culmination of the Vedas'. It has tended to dominate the other *darshana*s, and concentrates on **knowledge** of the divine power. It is often used to describe the thought of the later **Mimamsa**, and given the emphasis in the school of concentrating on religious texts, it analyses the arguments of the **Upanishads**. An important philosopher in this tradition was Badarayana, who argued that *brahman* is the source, sustaining force and end of the world. It works through individual souls, which are in themselves **atomic**, but is not affected by the contingency of the souls, which merely reflect the power of *brahman*. Moral behaviour leads to knowledge of *brahman*, and needs to be combined with worship and turning our backs on the pleasures and pains of the phenomenal world. **Liberation** means acquiring knowledge of *brahman*, and it is inhibited by **ignorance**, but our futures are very much a matter of our **action**s through *karma*. Although the world has come about through God and his *lila* or play, God has no control over our futures which are entirely regulated in accordance with *karma*.

The Vedanta thinkers produced a range of detailed and important arguments, in particular those like Shankara who argued for a strict monism or non-dualism (**Advaita**). This was opposed by Ramanuja, who argued that the self could not be equivalent to the divine, since this would vitiate the point of worship. God is linked to the world in the sense that it is his body that helps make sense of the famous Upanishadic saying 'That are thou' or *tat tvam asi*. The human soul is also to a certain extent part of God's body, and although we do not, of course, understand all aspects of this relationship, we are justified in having confidence that we have some correct judgements about reality. By contrast with Shankara, Ramanuja insists on the survival of the soul after liberation, since the latter expects the soul to **meditate** on the contrast between its liberated state and its earlier form of life, and how could this be done unless there were just one soul?

Whereas Shankara was a committed monist in his commitment to the Vedanta, and Ramanuja weakened this slightly with his distinction even after liberation between God and the individual, Madhva was a dualist. He stressed the compound nature of the world, in which there exist many souls, plenty of matter and, of course, a distinction between God and other souls. Whereas Ramanuja had suggested that *karma* came under the control of God, so he could relieve us of it should he wish, Madhva adhered to a kind of determinism here. God is the source of the things in the world, and they continue to behave in accordance with their very varying natures. These natures are generally characterized by the different ignorant points of view of the things themselves, and the entire group of these things act out their natures in a sort of **harmony** under the general, but not particular, direction of God in the sense that they all originate in him. Once they are in operation, though, there is no possibility of his intervention in the world to either help or hinder.

See: **Dvaita**, **Vishishadvaita**
Further reading: Beidler 1975, Carr and Mahalingam 1997, Deutsch 1968, Deutsch and Van Buitenen 1971, Nakamura 1983.

vikalpa – *see* **imagination**

violence Some varieties of Buddhist philosophy justify killing if it furthers the interests of the *dharma*. The Japanese thinker Nichiren is perhaps the most famous defender of such a view. He was writing at a time of great disruption in Japan, and he accounts for this as the result of the **evil**ness of humanity and the consequent departure of those deities who protect the country. He also was disgusted by the wide variety of doctrines that prevailed in Buddhism at the time. This public dissension is responsible for the sad state of the country and the solution is to intervene and prevent these dubious doctrines from being broadcast. There are examples in the literature, after all, of the Buddha in a previous life killing Brahmins to prevent them from slandering Buddhism, which also saves them from the punishment that they would otherwise have suffered. This sort of argument formed part of the justification for the abandonment of pacifism as an essentially Buddhist doctrine.

In Islam the use of violence is acceptable provided that it accords with strict rules of defending the Islamic community (*umma*). On the other hand, there is often a distinction between the greater and the lesser *jihad* or struggle, where the former is the struggle to overcome our baser instincts for the sake of our nobler spiritual aspirations. The lesser *jihad* is physical struggle or war, and should also be carried out ultimately for religious motives, but it must be recognized that once physical combat is initiated, it is very difficult to maintain the purity of motive which is desirable from a spiritual point of view.

See: **ahimsa**
Further reading: Bondurant 1965, Rodd 1980.

vipassana, form of meditation – *see* **Madhyamaka, meditation**

Vishishtadvaita   This refers to the non–duality of qualified or differentiated beings. Ramanuja treats the chief problem of the **Upanishads** in reconciling *brahman* with the individual self and also with the universe in an interesting way. He argues that we do identify things that are really distinct, but only some such identifications are possible. That is, we can identify a colour with a subject by saying that the subject is the colour, although we know that really the subject and the colour are entirely different entities. Other identifications do not work, though, and we have to say that one thing has another thing, rather than is the same as it. This is because there are different strengths in the relationship between different entities, so that some merely link qualities to each other through conjunction, while others form an intimate relation that is inseparable, in the sense that one thing cannot exist unless the other exists, and vice versa, and one thing cannot be known unless the other is known also. This is very much the relation between *brahman* and the world or the soul. God is inseparable from the soul and the world, and neither can exist or be known without him. They are all different, but none the less closely linked in this logical manner. Ramanuja's interpretation of the Upanishads is ingenious, since it deals very plausibly with the language of the text. When it talks about the self, the world and *brahman* as though they are separate, it reflects how we experience our world. When all these are related to each other, they are meant to be inseparable but not identical.

A crucial category for Ramanuja is substance (*dravya*), and among its modes are matter, soul and **God**. Matter (***prakriti***) is not independent of spirit or God, since it is the body of God. This means that the entire phenomenal world develops under the guidance of God. The self (*jiva*) is not independent of God either, nor is it identical with him. Souls are many, and although there is reference in the text to them being all the same, this refers to their characteristics, not to a denial of their variety. There are three kinds of soul. Some were never in bondage and have always been free, others have become free after passing through many tribulations and having achieved self-discipline, while some are still in the system of transmigration. God, the souls and matter form an organic whole, just like the individual person with its unity of soul and body. God is both the efficient and the material cause of the universe, since nothing else could have brought it into being, there being nothing else in existence that could have done it. We should be clear, though, that he is completely unrelated to the **evil** that is consequent on the changing nature of the world, since this is a characteristic of the souls and the matter of that world. Ramanuja is highly critical of the notion of an indeterminate *brahman*, a notion that the **Advaita** seem to use. The notion of something without any qualities is incoherent, and it is an error to think that denying that reality has some qualities implies that it has absolutely no qualities.

There are two routes to perfect freedom and happiness, one available to everyone and the other restricted to members of the higher **castes**. The former is complete self-surrender, and involves understanding **knowledge** of the status of the world and its-links with reality. The latter is a process of *bhakti* or worship that involves a curriculum including *karma yoga*, *jnana yoga* and *bhakti yoga*. The first is carrying out one's duty in the right spirit, which cannot be a selfish one. The second is to help one realize the real nature of oneself in relation to God, and of matter in relation to God. This involves meditating on the self and its nature, and on its relationship to God. It is this **meditation** on our dependence on God that establishes another distinction between this view and that of the Advaita. *Bhakti yoga* is constant meditation on the nature of God, mixed with **love**. We can only fully achieve this goal once the physical part of us has disappeared. Even then, though, we can contemplate the ordinary world, but we shall no longer be affected by its pains and pleasures. On the contrary, the world is seen as a reflection of reality by the liberated soul, and the latter experiences bliss at the sight of what causes suffering when he is immersed in it.

See: **purusha**, **samsara**
Further reading: Bhatt 1975, Lipner 1986, Potter 1972.

vyapti, generalization – *see* **logic**

wei, intangible – *see* **Daoism**

wei wu-wei, action through non-action – *see* **Daoism**

wu, nothingness – *see* **Neodaoism**, **zen**

wu nian, no-thought – *see* **meditation**

wu xin, no-mind – *see* **meditation**

wu yu, absence of desires – *see* **Neoconfucianism**

X

xi, inaudible – *see* **Daoism**

xuan xue, the dark learning – *see* **Neodaoism**

xue, learning – *see* **enlightenment**

Y

yana, vehicle (of enlightenment) – *see* **skilful means**

yi, invisible – *see* **Daoism, Mohism**

Yi jing – *see* **Book of Changes**

Yin–Yang school   The classic text is the *Yi jing*, the **Book of Changes**, and this formed the basis to the Chinese occult sciences. Often obscure, it provides great scope for interpretation and prediction, based as it is upon a metaphysics of change and underlying order. The idea that reality consists of relationships between opposite and opposing principles has proved to be very suggestive, and came to play a huge role in the development of Chinese **cosmological** thinking. Often, though, the notions of *yin* and *yang* should not really be understood in an ontological sense to be the constituents of reality, but rather different ways of looking at a world that may be experienced in a variety of different ways. *Yin*, or 'the shady side' is contrasted with 'the sunny side' *yang*, and the idea is that everything has at least two aspects to it. Relationships between people and natural objects can best be understood by exploring these sorts of relationships that exist between them.

Further reading: Graham 1989, Hall and Ames 1995.

yoga Probably means 'work' in the sense of spiritual activity, but also union with the divine. It is often used to refer to some of the different approaches of the Indian religions, in particular those that depend on physical activity. The term is identified by Ramanuja with an unmediated and intuitive grasp of reality, to be attained by the harmonious interplay of actions and wisdom which makes it possible for us to come into contact with God. We can approach God through solitary devotion alone, but this is not likely to be a successful path, especially when we consider how we find it easier to act than to renounce action, and given the obligations we acquire through life in a community. We should work in such a way as to diminish our selfish concerns, out of a motive of pure **love** for God and to establish moral and social **harmony** in the world.

As a philosophical system yoga combines the dualistic realism of **Sankhya** with a commitment to theism. Its main doctrines are found in the *Yogasutras* of Patanjali of perhaps the second century BCE. It is based on the Sankhya idea of **prakriti** being composed of three aspects – *sattva* (brightness or illumination), *rajas* (emotion or motion) and *tamas* (dullness or inertia). They are always found together, but the precise proportion may vary. If the *sattva* predominates, then we can attain an experience that is like a direct perception of reality with no emotional or physical distortion. The term *yoga* is often identified with concentration, which is an aspect of the route to achieving **liberation**. The self is in bondage as long as it identifies itself with the body and the **mind**, and this error leads to a hiding of the truth that the self is pure and **eternal**, in itself distinct from the world of matter, the mind and our reasoning faculties. To achieve the opposite of error, **knowledge**, we need to restrain our physical and mental faculties and use our pure consciousness alone. In this way the reality of that consciousness will manifest itself, by contrast with the sort of self that exists when we are subject to the pains and pleasures of the body and mind. Through such concentration one can liberate oneself from the world of suffering, and escape the cycle of **death** and rebirth. The complete purification of the intellect, the *buddhi*, results in its shining like a mirror in which the soul is at last visible. The point of yoga is to bring to an end the workings of our ordinary mental functions and physical attachments. There are generally agreed to be eight steps to liberation, each of which is equivalent to a particular state of mind:

1 Self-control involves stopping harming anything living, adhering to the truth in thought and action, not stealing, not accepting superfluous gifts from others, and practising prudence.
2 Then one cultivates oneself, in the sense of acquiring good dispositions to allow for purification. This amounts to purification of the body through washing and eating pure food, and also purifying the mind by developing virtuous habits and attitudes, studying the scriptures and constantly thinking about God.
3 There needs to be the application of appropriate postures for meditation. To be able to do this one would need to follow the teaching of an authority, and through it one can preserve both physical health and mental concentration. The underlying aim is to bring about control of the body and also the mind.
4 Breathing needs to be controlled in order to assist the steadiness of the body and mind. Breath control can increase the process of concentration.
5 The senses have to be redirected away from the phenomenal world to the self itself. Once one can do this it is possible to transcend the ordinary distractions of life and as a result concentrate on what it is important to contemplate, the level of reality.
6 Steady attention on an object is important since it involves practice in fixing the mind.
7 Then comes **meditation** on the object, which if properly carried out enables the thinker to understand the real nature of the object behind its appearance.
8 The final stage is complete concentration of the mind on the object of thought whereby the mind is so immersed

in the object that it loses itself and identifies itself with the object. Consciousness turns in on itself and becomes its one illuminated nature. All that is left is the pure consciousness of the self (*purusha*).

This path should not be thought of as being easy to follow, since it in fact represents a complex and arduous process of training. It does not result in unconsciousness, but rather a state where we transcend the distinction between acts of consciousness and the objects they perceive. The end is intuition from which distorting subjective emotions have been eradicated.

Further reading: Carr and Mahalingam 1997, Eliade 1958, 1969, Pereira 1976.

Yogachara One of the Mahayana forms of Buddhism that stressed the significance of calmness and insight **meditation** as the route to **enlightenment**. The theory developed into a very complex system, basically positing itself in between the realist **Sarvastivada** and the nihilist Shunyatavada. Matter does not really exist, but some things do exist, in particular ultimate truth and **consciousness** in itself. Sometimes called Chittamatra, or thought only, because of the doctrine that the Buddha is produced by thought, although as with Mahayana doctrine in general, such a producing **mind** is itself not essentially real. Sometimes reference is made to the *alayavijnana*, a sort of universal mind out of which the things we experience in the world emanate. The implication is that what we take to be real is just a reflection of something created by mind. This school of philosophy has had an immense effect on Hindu and Buddhist **logic** and epistemology.

It is based on the principle that there are three kinds of **knowledge** – illusory, relative and absolute. What we think of as the real world and the selves within it are only aspects of the universal consciousness. To attain Buddhahood we have to pass through ten stages of becoming a *bodhisattva*, and the goal is to unite, through *bodhi*, with the Buddha. If we succeed, the subject/object dichotomy is transcended and replaced by unity with pure consciousness. Once we achieve this higher level of consciousness we shall appreciate that the distinction between *nirvana* and *samsara* is itself illusory, the latter being a feature of diversity and the former of sameness. Reality from the point of view of *samsara* is a matter of constant flux, while from the point of view of *nirvana* it is blissful stability. The confidence with which this school of Buddhism used orthodox concepts was attacked by the **Madhyamaka** school, which sought to criticize those concepts as falsely encouraging us in an attitude of confidence in their reality.

According to this school, there are three aspects to what can be known. The first is the conceptualized aspect, and describes the falsifying effect of **language**. Words imply that things have a real existence when they do not. The use of concepts to stand for things suggests that concepts are things, but all they are are concepts. Of course, a feature of conceptualization is the fact that there is a knower and an object of knowledge, both of which, as they are ordinarily understood, very suspect ideas from a Buddhist perspective. The second aspect is the dependent aspect, and brings in the **dependent origination** of *dharma*s, the fact of **causality**. What this does is connect our experiences to suggest that the basis of those experiences are real things, but this is merely an illusory effect of causality, and only serves to deepen our suffering and **ignorance**. The point of criticizing this aspect is to argue that the way in which we decide what causes what effect is quite arbitrary, and yet we treat it as more than just a particular way of slicing up experiences. We treat it erroneously as an indication of the nature of how things really are. It does not follow, though, that there is no reality behind our experiences, because there is. There has to be, since unless there were something real, there could not be judgements that go awry, since they must be awry in relation to something that is real. Something real must exist, but it is in itself indescribable. Once our concepts approach an experience, the real basis to it remains hidden and inexpressible. One of this school's leading thinkers, Dharmakirti, argued that the difference between a correct perception of a thing and an illusory perception of it is rather like the difference between the real thing and a counterfeit thing. What leads to our distinguishing between them is the fact that we can link the real thing to reality in specific sorts of ways which we cannot do with the illusory thing. So there are criteria of objectivity with respect to our experience.

The final aspect, and the route to the escape from illusion, is that of the perfected aspect. This is the suchness or thus-ness (*tathata*), what might be called the facticity of things, that is attained in meditation. We might think that we could not say anything about this level of reality, since to say anything at all about it we need words and concepts, which in themselves are entirely unsatisfactory ways of approaching the truth. But the situation is not quite so difficult, since the perfected aspect works by grasping the fact that there is a flow of experiences, which is equivalent to **emptiness**. So long as it is appreciated that this flow of experiences is not mediated by essentially existing things we are free of the conceptualized aspect, and quite right to think that the flow of experiences itself exists. An example of how the three aspects work is given in the idea of water seen in a mirage. The water as seen rather than real water is the dependent aspect. The water that is experienced by the perceiver falsely as real water is the conceptualized aspect, while the absence of real water in the water in the image is the perfected aspect. The theory has a neat way of relating the same sort of facts to both *samsara* and *nirvana*. Ordinarily we just tend to break up the flow of experiences into stable objects and real selves, and we want to benefit ourselves and satisfy our desires. But this is nothing else but *samsara*, and the more enthusiastically we partake of such descriptions of reality, the more embedded we are in the cycle of birth and rebirth. On the other hand, we can come to appreciate this in meditation, and we may come to realize that the flow of experiences is just that, a flow of experiences without even any real distinction between the self and the objects of experience, and we can then attain *nirvana*. The same facts, then, can serve either to deepen our bondage, or to help us transcend the world of illusion.

The main distinction between this school and the Madhyamaka is that the former argues that something exists, namely, emptiness. But does this not fall foul of the struggle against duality? That is, we seem to be in the position of adhering to the existence of two sorts of things, emptiness and the non-existent. The argument is that no duality is implied by the thesis that emptiness does not mean the absence of real existence, since the thought of such absence is empty, but none the less itself really exists. The Madhyamaka contrast emptiness and real existence, while the Yogachara contrast emptiness with the subject–object relation. Thinking about what does not really exist is equivalent to the consciousness, the flow of perceptions and experiences, but as an undifferentiated stream of experiences. Once we apply concepts to that stream of consciousness, we apply the concept of real existence to it, and so go awry, but that stream itself is quite real. Outside the consciousness those experiences have no material basis, but as experienced by the consciousness they are real. When we differentiate them into material objects, we bring in duality, separating the mind from the external world, and so introduce error and enter *samsara*. The Madhyamaka position understands emptiness as the lack of inherent existence, while the Yogachara takes emptiness to mean the lack of a subject and an object in our experiences, since all that there is is a flow of changing perceptions.

Further reading: Murti 1960, Nagao 1991, Puligandla 1975, Radhakrishnan and Moore 1957.

Z

zaman – *see* **time**

zazen · The Japanese Rinzai school is often contrasted with the Soto school on the grounds that the former emphasizes sudden **enlightenment**, while the latter is in favour of gradual enlightenment. The Soto school stresses the practice of 'just sitting', but the grounds for this belief are interestingly close to the notion of sudden enlightenment. The trouble with the **koan** practice, according to Soto, is that it reifies enlightenment, it places it at the end of a process and makes it something that we try to attain. Yet since our very nature is to be enlightened, to look for enlightenment can only add to the delusions that prevent us from realizing our enlightened nature in the first place. While we are 'just sitting' we avoid giving **meditation** the status of a means to an end, which is dualistic and objectionable. 'Just sitting' may find that sudden enlightenment is its approach just as much as in the case of the Rinzai.

Further reading: for references *see* **zen**.

zen   The Chinese school of Buddhism called *chan*, or *zen* in Japanese, was formed at the start of the seventh century CE, and a century later split into two competing groups. One was committed to gradualism (largely the Northern school) while the other defended subitism, where the former refers to the necessity of a gradual approach to **enlightenment**, the latter to the possibility of sudden enlightenment. A similar split occurred in Tibet, where the local Chinese subitists were locked in controversy with the Indian gradualists. This controversy was affected by Daoism also from an even earlier date, and became particularly important because it linked up with already existing Chinese ideas. After all, the Confucians and the Daoists had argued about the respective values of cultivation and intuition, and this conflict was apparently reformulated but not essentially changed in the Buddhist debate. In China there seems to have been an attraction by the iconoclastic Daoists for the sudden enlightenment Buddhists, which deepened the distrust of the Confucians.

The name of this school comes from Chinese and Japanese phonetic readings of the Sanskrit *dhyana*, or **meditation**, and the school uses this description to emphasize the differences that it recommends by comparison with previous Buddhist schools. There is a tradition, common to many mystical traditions, that the creator of the religion, in this case the Buddha, transmitted an exoteric teaching in his scriptures, and also an esoteric teaching to chosen disciples. This was said to have been handed down to Bodhidharma, who came to China between 520–6, where he founded the chan school. This split into a Northern and a Southern School. First, it contrasted the sudden approach to enlightenment to the gradualism of existing traditions, and later it devised a language designed to bring about enlightenment through terse and challenging language. One of the principles of chan is to teach only through personal contact, and many of the responses by teachers to metaphysical questions are paradoxical. For instance, a query about the basic principles of Buddhism might be answered by physical **violence**, or some statement about the weather or the price of beans! The point being made in this muscular way is that there is no point in talking about that which cannot be talked about. One must do all that one can to avoid falling into what the chan called the net of words. This might seem paradoxical, and it is intended to be paradoxical, since the attempt at expressing the inexpressible can only be paradoxical. As a result many chan teachers refused to debate, since they saw no point in entering a debate that presupposes that *wu* or nothingness is in fact something, and can be discussed. Hence silence often seemed to be the best response to questions.

The chan path to cultivation involves the practice of non-cultivation. The best way to attain enlightenment is to carry out one's ordinary tasks without making any deliberate effort. This means that one manages to live naturally and avoids setting out to attain complicated ends through one's activity. If activity manages to have no further effects, then one's accumulation of **karma** will become exhausted and **liberation** possible. Yet the question obviously arises as to the difference between living an ordinary and simple life and so achieving salvation, as compared with just living an ordinary life. Does this teaching, if it is a teaching, imply that all that we need to do to achieve salvation is live ordinary lives? This seems to make the route to salvation far too easy, and actually attained by most people. But in fact what is involved in living simply is very complicated, since it is not enough just to live ordinary lives. What is important is the motivation out of which one's actions take place, and in ordinary life one carries out such actions with ends in sight and out of attachment to one's desires and ambitions. Initially to learn to act without effort or attachment itself requires effort and attachment to a conception of oneself, in just the same way that if one is going to forget what one is doing, one has to learn to forget. Eventually one is able to act without effort, without making an effort to act in such a way, and one can forget to remember that one has to forget.

Enlightenment is a matter of seeing the dao. Such contact is identical to being one with it, since it is a state in which all distinctions disappear. In such a state there is no distinction, for example, between the knower and what is known, and it is impossible to express what this is in ordinary **language**, since ordinary language is based on the distinctions that are no longer in existence. This state is the knowledge that is not knowledge, and is certainly very different from mere **ignorance**. The nature of this form of enlightenment is not the attainment of additional knowledge, but the understanding that what had previously appeared to be a problem is no longer a problem. This does not mean that the enlightened individual lives in any different way from anyone else. He acts in the same way as the rest of the world, but what he does has a different significance for him. The ordinary actions are carried out without attachment and so do not affect his character.

A particularly interesting version of zen was produced by Dogen. According to him everything is already the **buddha nature**, thus avoiding the dualisms of the subject and object, potentiality and actuality, and means and end. If the buddha nature is not an object, then it is not something we can acquire. We cannot acquire it because we already are identical to it. It is not something to be realized in the future, but it is here now as part of the basic nature of everything. Finally, Buddhist practice is not a means to an end, and the idea that we can gradually approach enlightenment is an error.

Further reading: Abe 1985, 1992, Buswell 1983, Gregory 1987, Heine 1989, 1993, Heisig and Maraldo 1994, LaFleur 1985, McRae 1986, Tsunoda *et al.* 1964.

Zhou yi – *see* **Book of Changes**

REFERENCES AND FURTHER READING

Some of the books in this list contain reference material which is relevant to almost every concept mentioned in the book, and they are often not separately listed under Further Reading. They appear in this list with an asterisk.

Abe, M. (1985) *Zen and Western Thought*, Basingstoke, Macmillan
—— (1992) *A Study of Dogen: His Philosophy and Religion*, ed. S. Heine, Albany, State University of New York Press
Adelmann, F. (1982) *Contemporary Chinese Philosophy*, The Hague, Nijhoff
Allinson, R. (1989a) *Chuang Tzu for Spiritual Transformation*, Albany, State University of New York Press
—— (ed.) (1989b) *Understanding the Chinese Mind: The Philosophical Roots*, Oxford, Oxford University Press
Ames, R. (1994) *Self as Person in Asian Theory and Practice*, Albany, State University of New York Press
Ames, R. and Callicott, J. (1989) *Nature in Asian Traditions of Thought*, Albany, State University of New York Press
Angel, L. (1994) *Enlightenment East and West*, Albany, State University of New York Press
Aronson, H. (1980) *Love and Sympathy in Theravada Buddhism*, Delhi, Motilal Banarsidass
Basham, A. (1971) *History and Doctrines of the Ajivikas*, Delhi, Motilal Banarsidass
Beidler, W. (1975) *The Vision of Self in Early Vedanta*, Delhi, Motilal Banarsidass
Bhagavad Gita, trans. W. Johnson (1994) Oxford, Oxford University Press

Bhatt, S. (1975) *Studies in Ramanuja Vedanta*, New Delhi, Heritage Publishers

Billington, R. (1990) *East of Existentialism: The Tao of the West*, London, Unwin Hyman

—— (1997) *Understanding Eastern Philosophy*, London, Routledge

Bishop, P. (1993) *Dreams of Power: Tibetan Buddhism and the Western Imagination*, London, Athlone Press

Bondurant, J. (1965) *Conquest of Violence*, Berkeley, University of California Press

Bowker, J. (1991) *The Meanings of Death*, Cambridge, Cambridge University Press

Boyce, M. (1975) *A History of Zoroastrianism: The Early Period*, Leiden, Brill

—— (1984) *Textual Sources for the Study of Zoroastrianism*, Manchester, Manchester University Press

Brockington, J. (1996) *The Sacred Thread: Hinduism in its Continuity and Diversity*, Edinburgh, Edinburgh University Press

Burch, G. (1976) *Search for the Absolute in Neo-Vedanta*, Honolulu, University of Hawaii Press

Buswell, R. (trans. and ed.) (1983) *The Korean Approach to Zen: The Collected Works of Chinul*, Honolulu, University of Hawaii Press

Cabezon, J. (1994) *Buddhism and Language: A Study of Indo-Tibetan Scholasticism*, Albany, State University of New York Press

Capra, F. (1976) *The Tao of Physics: An Exploration of Parallels between Modern Physics and Eastern Mysticism*, London, Fontana

*Carr, B. and Mahalingam, I. (eds) (1997) *Companion Encyclopedia of Asian Philosophy*, London, Routledge

Carter, R. (1989) *The Nothingness beyond God: An Introduction to the Philosophy of Nishida Kitaro*, New York, Paragon House

Chakraborty, A. (1996) *Mind–Body Dualism*, New Delhi, D.K. Printworld

Chakravarty, A. (ed.) (1961) *A Tagore Reader*, New York, Macmillan

Chambliss, J. (ed.) (1996) *Philosophy of Education: An Encyclopedia*, New York, Garland

Chan, Wing-tsit (1972) *A Source Book in Chinese Philosophy*, Princeton, Princeton University Press

Chapple, C. (1993) *Nonviolence to Animals, Earth, and Self in Asian Traditions*, Albany, State University of New York Press

Chatterjee, M. (1983) *Gandhi's Religious Thought*, Notre Dame, Notre Dame University Press

References and Further Reading

—— (1996) *Studies in Modern Jewish and Hindu Thought*, London, Athlone Press

Chatterjee, S. (1965) *The Nyaya Theory of Knowledge*, Calcutta, Calcutta University Press

Cheng, C. (ed.) (1989) *Sun Yat-sen's Doctrine in the Modern World*, Boulder, Col., Westview Press

Chi, R. (1969) *Buddhist Formal Logic*, Delhi, Motilal Banarsidass

Chung, B. (1992) *Zhuangzi Speaks!*, Princeton, Princeton University Press

Clarke, J. (1997) *Oriental Enlightenment: The Encounter between Asian and Western Thought*, London, Routledge

Cleary, T. (1991) *The Essential Tao*, San Francisco, HarperCollins

Collins, S. (1982) *Selfless Persons*, Cambridge, Cambridge University Press

Collinson, D. and Wilkinson, R. (eds) (1994) *Thirty-Five Oriental Philosophers*, London, Routledge

Confucius, trans. R. Dawson (1993) *The Analects*, Oxford, Oxford University Press

Conze, E. (1962) *Buddhist Thought in India*, London, Allen & Unwin

Cook, F. (1977) *Hua-yen Buddhism: The Jewel Net of Indra*, University Park, Pennsylvania State University Press

Cooper, D. (1996) *World Philosophers: An Historical Introduction*, Oxford, Blackwell

*Craig, W. (ed.) (1998) *The Encyclopedia of Philosophy*, London, Routledge

Creel, H. (1953) *Chinese Thought: From Confucius to Mao Tse-Tung*, Chicago, University of Chicago Press

Dainian, F. and Cohen, S. (ed.) (1996) *History and Philosophy of Science and Technology*, Dordrecht, Kluwer

Daizhen (1990) *Tai Chen on Mencius: Explorations in Words and Meaning*, trans. A. Chin and M. Freeman, New Haven, Yale University Press

Dasgupta, S. (1975) [1922] *A History of Indian Philosophy*, Cambridge, Cambridge University Press; repr. Delhi, Motilal Banarsidass 1975

Datta, D. (1972) *Six Ways of Knowing*, Calcutta, University of Calcutta Press

de Bary, W.T. (1988a) *The Message of the Mind*, New York, Columbia University Press

—— (1988b) *Sources of Indian Tradition: Introduction to Oriental Civilizations*, New York, Columbia University Press

—— (1996) *The Trouble with Confucianism*, Cambridge, Mass.; Harvard University Press

de Bary, W., Chan Wing-tsit and Watson, B. (1960) *Sources of Chinese Tradition: Introduction to Oriental Civilizations*, New York, Columbia University Press

de Bary, W., Embree, A. and Heinrich, A. (eds) (1989) *A Guide to Oriental Classics*, New York, Columbia University Press

de Bary, W. T. and Haboush, J. (eds) (1985) *The Rise of Neo-Confucianism in Korea*, New York, Columbia University Press

Deutsch, E. (1968) *Advaita Vedanta: A Philosophical Reconstruction*, Honolulu, University of Hawaii Press

—— (1975) *Comparative Aesthetics*, Honolulu, University of Hawaii Press

Deutsch, E. and Bontekoe, R. (eds) (1997) *A Companion to World Philosophies*, Oxford, Blackwell

Deutsch, E. and Van Buitenen, J. (1971) *A Source Book of Advaita Vedanta*, Honolulu, University of Hawaii Press

Dilworth, D. and Viglielmo, V. (1998) *Sourcebook for Modern Japanese Philosophy: Selected Documents*, London, Greenwood Press

Dravida, R. (1972) *The Problem of Universals in Indian Philosophy*, Delhi, Motilal Banarsidass

Dreyfus, G. (1997) *Recognizing Reality: Dharmakirti's Philosophy and its Tibetan Interpretations*, Albany, State University of New York Press

Dundas, P. (1992) *The Jains*, London, Routledge

Eckel, M. (1992) *To See the Buddha: A Philosopher's Quest for the Meaning of Emptiness*, San Francisco, HarperCollins

Eliade, M. (1958) *Yoga: Immortality and Freedom*, Princeton, Princeton University Press

—— (1969) *Patanjali and Yoga*, New York, Schocken

Fakhry, M. (1983) *A History of Islamic Philosophy*, London, Longman

—— (1997) *A Short Introduction to Islamic Philosophy, Theology and Mysticism*, Oxford, Oneworld

Faure, B. (1993) *Chan Insights and Oversights: An Epistemological Critique of the Chan Tradition*, Princeton, Princeton University Press

Filippi, G. (1996) *Mrtyu: Concept of Death in Indian Traditions*, New Delhi, D.K. Printworld

Fingarette, H. (1972) *Confucius: The Secular as Sacred*, New York, Harper & Row

Fontana, D. (1992) *The Meditator's Handbook: A Comprehensive Guide to Eastern and Western Meditation Techniques*, Shaftesbury, Element

Fung, Yu-lan (1952) *A History of Chinese Philosophy*, trans. D. Bodde, Princeton, Princeton University Press

—— (1970) *The Spirit of Chinese Philosophy*, trans. E. Hughes, Westport, Conn., Greenwood Press

Gandhi, M. (1969) *The Collected Works of Mahatma Gandhi,* Delhi, Government of India Publications

Gardner, D. (1986) *Chu Hsi and the Ta-Hsueh*, Cambridge, Mass., Harvard University Press

Garfield, J. (ed.) (1995) *The Fundamental Wisdom of the Middle Way*, New York, Oxford University Press

Gombrich, R. (1971) *Precept and Practice*, Oxford, Clarendon Press

—— (1988) *Theravada Buddhism: A Social History from Ancient Benares to Modern Colombo*, London, Routledge

—— (1997) *How Buddhism Began: The Conditioned Genesis of the Early Teachings*, London, Athlone Press

Gonda, J. (1970) *Visnuism and Sivaism*, London, Athlone Press

Goodman, L. (1992) *Avicenna*, London, Routledge

Graham, A. (1958) *Two Chinese Philosophers: Ch'eng Ming-tao and Ch'eng Yi-ch'uan*, London, Lund Humphries

—— (1978) *Later Mohist Logic, Ethics and Science*, Hong Kong, The Chinese University Press

—— (1981) *Chuang-tzu: The Inner Chapters*, London, George Allen & Unwin

—— (1989) *Disputers of the Tao: Philosophical Argument in Ancient China*, La Salle, Ill., Open Court Press

—— (1992) *Two Chinese Philosophers*, LaSalle, Ill., Open Court Press

Gregory, P. (ed.) (1987) *Sudden and Gradual*, Honolulu, University of Hawaii Press

Griffiths, P. (1986) *On Being Mindless: Buddhist Meditation and the Mind–Body Problem*, La Salle, Ill., Open Court Press

—— (1994) *On Being Buddha: The Classical Doctrine of Buddhahood*, Albany, State University of New York Press

Gross, R. (1993) *Buddhism after Patriarchy*, Albany, State University of New York Press

Gudmunsen, C. (1977) *Wittgenstein and Buddhism*, London, Macmillan

Guenther, H. (1972) *Buddhist Philosophy in Theory and Practice*, Harmondsworth, Penguin

—— (1976) *Philosophy and Psychology of the Abhidharma*, Berkeley, Calif., Shambhala

Gyatso, J. (ed.) (1992) *In the Mirror of Memory: Reflections on Mindfulness and Remembrance in Indian and Tibetan Buddhism*, Albany, State University of New York Press

Hakeda, Y. (1972) *Kukai: Major Works*, New York, Columbia University Press

Hall, D. and Ames, R. (1987) *Thinking through Confucius*, Albany, State University of New York Press

—— (1995) *Anticipating China: Thinking through the Narratives of Chinese and Western Culture*, Albany, State University of New York Press

—— (1997) *Thinking from the Han: Self, Truth, and Transcendence in Chinese and Western Culture*, Albany, State University of New York Press

Han Fei (1964) *Han Fei Tzu: Basic Writings*, trans. B. Watson, New York, Columbia University Press

Hansen, C. (1983) *Language and Logic in Ancient China*, Ann Arbor, University of Michigan Press

Harvey, P. (1990) *Introduction to Buddhism*, Cambridge, Cambridge University Press

—— (1995) *The Selfless Mind: Personality, Consciousness and Nirvana in Early Buddhism*, Richmond, Curzon

Heine, S. (1985) *Existential and Ontological Dimensions of Time: Heidegger and Dogen*, Albany, State University of New York Press

—— (1989) *A Blade of Grass: Japanese Poetry and Aesthetics in Dogen Zen*, New York, Peter Lang

—— (1993) *Dogen and the Koan Tradition: A Tale of Two Shobogenzo Texts*, Albany, State University of New York Press

Heisig, J. and Maraldo, J. (eds) (1994) *Rude Awakenings: Zen, the Kyoto School, and the Question of Nationalism*, Honolulu, University of Hawaii Press

Henderson, J. (1984) *The Development and Decline of Chinese Cosmology*, New York, Columbia University Press

Hick, J. (1997) *God and the Universe of Faiths*, Oxford, Oneworld

Hinnells, J. (1978) *Spanning East and West*, Milton Keynes. Open University Press

Hiriyanna, M. (1932) *Outlines of Indian Philosophy*, London, George Allen & Unwin

—— (1985) *Essentials of Indian Philosophy*, London, George Allen & Unwin

Hoffman, F. (1987) *Rationality and Mind in Early Buddhism*, Delhi, Motilal Banarsidass

Hoshino, K. (ed.) (1997) *Japanese and Western Bioethics*, Dordrecht, Kluwer

Hourani, G. (1985) *Reason and Tradition in Islamic Ethics*, Cambridge, Cambridge University Press

Huntington, C. (1989) *The Emptiness of Emptiness*, Honolulu, University of Hawaii Press

Inada, K. (1970) *Nagarjuna: A Translation of his* Mula-madhyamaka-karika *with an Introductory Essay*, Tokyo, Hokuseido Press

293

Inada, K. and Jacobsen, N. (eds) (1984) *Buddhism and American Thinkers*, Albany, State University of New York Press

Izutsu, T. and Izutsu, T. (1981) *The Theory of Beauty in the Classical Aesthetics of Japan*, The Hague, Nijhoff

Jackson, R. (1993) *Is Enlightenment Possible? Dharmakirti and rGyal-tshab-rje on Mind and Body, No-Self and Freedom*, Ithaca, NY, Snow Lion Publications

Jayatilleke, K. (1986) *Early Buddhist Theory of Knowledge*, Delhi, Motilal Banarsidass

Kaltenmark, M. (1969) *Lao Tzu and Taoism*, Stanford, Calif., Stanford University Press

Kalupahana, D. (1975) *Causality: The Central Philosophy of Buddhism*, Honolulu, University of Hawaii Press

—— (1976) *Buddhist Philosophy: A Historical Introduction*, Honolulu, University of Hawaii Press

—— (1986) *Nagarjuna: The Philosophy of the Middle Way*, Albany, State University of New York Press

Karmay, Ś. (1988) *The Great Perfection: A Philosophical and Meditative Teaching of Tibetan Buddhism*, Leiden, Brill

Kemal, S. (1991) *The Poetics of Alfarabi and Avicenna*, Leiden, Brill

Keown, D. (1992) *The Nature of Buddhist Ethics*, New York, Curzon

King, S. (1991) *Buddha Nature*, Albany, State University of New York Press

Kitagawa, J. (1966) *Religion in Japanese History*, New York, Columbia University Press

Kjellberg, P. and Ivanhoe, P. (1996) *Essays on Scepticism, Relativism, and Ethics in the Zhuangzi*, Albany, State University of New York Press

Kukai (1972) *Kukai: Major Works*, New York, Columbia University Press

LaFleur, W. (1983) *The Karma of Words: Buddhism and the Literary Arts in Medieval Japan*, Los Angeles, University of California Press

—— (ed.) (1985) *Dogen Studies*, Honolulu, University of Hawaii Press

—— (1992) *Liquid Life: Abortion and Buddhism in Japan*, Princeton, Princeton University Press

Lal, B. (1973) *Contemporary Indian Philosophy*, Delhi, Motilal Banarsidass

Laozi, (1989) *Lao-Tzu: Tao Te Ching*, trans. R. Henricks, New York, Ballantine

Larson, G. (1969) *Classical Samkhya: An Interpretation of its History and Meaning*, Delhi, Motilal Banarsidass

Lau, D. (1963) *Lao-Tzu: Tao Te Ching*, Harmondsworth, Penguin

—— (1970) *Mencius*, Harmondsworth, Penguin
—— (1979) *Confucius: The Analects*, Harmondsworth, Penguin
Leaman, O. (1985) *An Introduction to Medieval Islamic Philosophy*, Cambridge, Cambridge University Press
—— (ed.) (1996) *Friendship East and West: Philosophical Perspectives*, Richmond, Curzon
—— (1997) *Averroes and his Philosophy*, Richmond, Curzon
—— (ed.) (1998) *The Future of Philosophy*, London, Routledge
Lee, P. (ed.) (1993) *Sourcebook of Korean Civilization*, New York, Columbia University Press
Ling, T. (ed.) (1981) *The Buddha's Philosophy of Man*, London, Dent
—— (1997) *Buddhism and the Mythology of Evil*, Oxford, Oneworld
Lipner, J. (1986) *The Face of Truth: A Study of Meaning and Metaphysics in the Vedantic Theology of Ramanuja*, Basingstoke, Macmillan
Lopez, D. (ed.) (1988) *Buddhist Hermeneutics*, Honolulu, University of Hawaii Press
Lopez, D. and Rockefeller, S. (eds) (1987) *The Christ and the Bodhisattva*, Albany, State University of New York Press
McDermott, R. (ed.) (1987) *The Essential Aurobindo*, Great Barrington, Mass., Lindisfarne Press
McGreal, I. (ed.) (1995) *Great Thinkers of the Eastern World*, New York, HarperCollins
McRae, J. (1986) *The Northern School and the Formation of Early Ch'an Buddhism*, Honolulu, University of Hawaii Press
Mao, Tse-tung (1961–77) *Selected Works of Mao Tse-tung*, Peking, Foreign Languages Press
Martin, R. and Woodward, M. (1997) *Defenders of Reason in Islam: Mu'tazilism from Medieval School to Modern Symbol*, Oxford, Oneworld
Maruyama, M. (1974) *Studies in the Intellectual History of Tokugawa Japan*, trans. M. Hane, Princeton, Princeton University Press
Ma'sumian, F. (1997) *Life after Death: A Study of the Afterlife in World Religions*, Oxford, Oneworld
Matilal, B. (1968) *The Navya-Nyaya Doctrine of Negation*, Cambridge, Mass., Harvard University Press
—— (1971) *Epistemology, Logic and Grammar in Indian Philosophical Analysis*, The Hague, Mouton
—— (1986) *Perception: An Essay on Classical Indian Theories of Knowledge*, Oxford, Clarendon Press
May, R. (1996) *Heidegger's Hidden Sources: East-Asian Influences on his Work*, trans. G. Parkes, London, Routledge

Minor, R. (1978) *Sri Aurobindo: The Perfect and the Good*, Columbia, Mo., South Asian Books

Moore, C. (ed.) (1968) *Philosophy and Culture: East and West*, Honolulu, University of Hawaii Press

Mozi (1974) *The Ethical and Political Works of Motse*, trans. Y.-P. Mei, Taipei, Ch'eng Wen Publishing Company

Murti, T. (1960) *The Central Philosophy of Buddhism: A Study of the Madhyamika System*, London, Allen & Unwin

Murty, K. (1959) *Revelation and Reason in Advaita Vedanta*, New York, Harper & Row

Nagao, G. (1991) *Madhyamaka and Yogacara: A Study of Mahayana Philosophies*, Albany, State University of New York Press

Nakamura, H. (1983) *A History of Early Vedanta Philosophy*, Delhi, Motilal Banarsidass

Nasr, S. (1981) *Islamic Life and Thought*, Albany, State University of New York Press

—— (ed.) (1989) *Islamic Spirituality: Foundations*, London, SCM Press

—— (1993) *The Need for a Sacred Science*, Albany, State University of New York Press

—— (1996) *The Islamic Intellectual Tradition in Persia*, ed. M. Amin Razavi, Richmond, Curzon

*Nasr, S. and Leaman, O. (eds) (1996) *History of Islamic Philosophy*, London, Routledge

Needham, J. (1956) *Science and Civilization in China*, vol. II, Cambridge, Cambridge University Press

Netton, I. (1991) *Muslim Neoplatonists: An Introduction to the Thought of the Brethren of Purity (Ikhwan al-Safa')*, Edinburgh, Edinburgh University Press

Nishida, Kitaro (1990) *An Inquiry into the Good*, trans. M. Abe and C. Ives, New Haven, Conn., Yale University Press

Nishitani, Keiji (1985) *Religion and Nothingness*, trans. J. van Bragt, Berkeley, University of California Press

—— (1991) *Nishida Kitaro*, trans. Y. Seisaku and J. Heisig, Berkeley, University of California Press

O'Flaherty, W. (ed.) (1980) *Karma and Rebirth in Classical Indian Traditions*, Berkeley, University of California Press

Park Sung-bae (1983) *Buddhist Faith and Sudden Enlightenment*, Albany, State University of New York Press

Parrinder, G. (1997) *Avatar and Incarnation: The Divine in Human Form in the World's Religions*, Oxford, Oneworld

Patnaik, P. (1994) *Shabda: A Study of Bhartrihari's Philosophy of Language*, New Delhi, D.K. Printworld

—— (1997) *Rasa in Aesthetics,* New Delhi, D.K. Printworld

Peerenboom, R. (1993) *Law and Morality in Ancient China,* Albany, State University of New York Press

Pereira, J. (1976) *Hindu Theology: A Reader,* Garden City, NY, Doubleday

Piovesana, G. (1997) *Recent Japanese Philosophical Thought 1862–1996: A Survey,* Richmond, Curzon

Potter, K. (1972) *Presuppositions of India's Philosophies,* Westport, Conn., Greenwood Press

*—— (1977–) *The Encyclopaedia of Indian Philosophies,* Delhi, Motilal Banarsidass

—— (1988) *Guide to Indian Philosophy,* Boston, Mass., G.K. Hall

Pruden, L. (trans.) (1988–90) *Abhidharma Kosa Bhasyam,* Berkeley, Asian Humanities Press

Puligandla, R. (1975) *Fundamentals of Indian Philosophy,* New York, Abingdon Press; second edition (1997) New Delhi, D.K. Printworld

—— (1997) *Jnana-Yoga: The Way of Knowledge,* New Delhi, D.K. Printworld

Pye, M. (1978) *Skilful Means,* London, Duckworth

Radhakrishnan, S. (1953) *The Principal Upanishads,* New York, Harper & Brothers

—— (1966) *Indian Philosophy,* London, George Allen & Unwin

Radhakrishnan, S. and Moore, C. (eds) (1957) *A Source Book in Indian Philosophy,* Princeton, Princeton University Press

Raju, P. (1985) *Structural Depths of Indian Thought,* New Delhi, South Asian Publishers

Ramamurty, A. (1996) *Advaita: A Conceptual Analysis,* New Delhi, D.K. Printworld

Randle, H. (1930) *Indian Logic in the Early Schools: A Study of the Nyayadarsana in its Relation to the Early Logic and other Schools,* London, Oxford University Press

Reichenbach, B. (1990) *The Law of Karma: A Philosophical Study,* Honolulu, University of Hawaii Press

The Rider Encyclopedia of Eastern Philosophy and Religion (1989), London, Hutchinson

Rodd, L. (1980) *Nichiren: Selected Writings,* Honolulu, University of Hawaii Press

Rosenthal, E. (1958) *Political Thought in Medieval Islam,* Cambridge, Cambridge University Press

The Routledge Encyclopedia of Philosophy (1998), London, Routledge

Said, E. (1985) *Orientalism,* Harmondsworth, Penguin

Saran, P. (1997) *Tantra: Hedonism in Indian Culture*, New Delhi, D.K. Printworld

Scharfstein, B.-A. (ed.) (1978) *Philosophy East/Philosophy West: A Critical Comparison of Indian, Chinese, Islamic and European Philosophy*, New York, Oxford University Press

Schilpp, P. (ed.) (1952) *The Philosophy of Sarvepalli Radhakrishnan*, New York, Tudor Publishing Company

Schram, S. (1989) *The Thought of Mao Tse-tung*, New York, Cambridge University Press

Sen, A. (1997) 'Indian Traditions and the Western Imagination', *Daedalus* 126, 2, pp. 1–26

Sharma, C. (1964) *A Critical Survey of Indian Philosophy*, Delhi, Motilal Banarsidass

Smart, N. (1964) *Doctrine and Argument in Indian Philosophy*, New Jersey, Humanities Press

*—— (1999) *World Philosophies*, London, Routledge

Solomon, R. and Higgins, K. (eds) (1993) *From Africa to Zen: An Introduction to World Philosophy*, Lanham, Md., Rowman & Littlefield

Stcherbatsky, F. (1962) *Buddhist Logic*, New York, Dover

Streng, F. (1967) *Emptiness: A Study in Religious Meaning*, New York, Abingdon Press

Swanson, P. (1989) *Foundations of T'ien-t'ai Philosophy*, Berkeley, Calif., Asian Humanities Press

Tanabe, G. (1992) *Myoe the Dreamkeeper*, Cambridge, Mass., Harvard University Press

The Thirteen Principal Upanishads, trans. R. Ume and G. Haas (1995) Oxford, Oxford University Press

Thurman, R. (1984) *Tsong Khapa's Speech of Gold in the 'Essence of True Eloquence'*, Princeton, Princeton University Press

Tominaga, N. (1990) *Emerging from Meditation*, trans. M. Pye, London, Duckworth

Tsunoda, R., de Bary, W. and Keene, D. (1964) *Sources of Japanese Tradition*, New York, Columbia University Press

Tu Wei-Ming (1985) *Confucian Thought: Selfhood as Creative Transformation*, Albany, State University of New York Press

—— (1988) *Centrality and Commonality: An Essay on Confucian Religiousness*, Albany, State University of New York Press

Tuck, A. (1990) *Comparative Philosophy and the Philosophy of Scholarship: On the Western Interpretation of Nagarjuna*, New York, Oxford University Press

Tyler, R. (1977) *Selected Writings of Suzuki Shosan*, Ithaca, NY, Cornell University Press

Ueda, Y. and Hirota, D. (1989) *Shinran: An Introduction to his Thought*, Kyoto, Hongwanji International Center

Upanishads, trans. P. Olivelle (1996) Oxford, Oxford University Press

Vatsyayan, K. (ed.) (1995) *Prakriti: The Integral Vision*, 5 vols, New Delhi, D.K. Printworld

Wang, H. and Chang, L. (1986) *The Philosophical Foundations of Han Fei's Political Theory*, Honolulu, University of Hawaii Press

Ward, K. (1998) *Concepts of God*, Oxford, Oneworld

Warder, A. (1980) *Indian Buddhism*, Delhi, Motilal Banarsidass

Watson, B. (1967) *Basic Writings of Mo Tzu, Hsun Tzu, and Han Fei Tzu*, New York, Columbia University Press

Wilhelm, R. (trans.) (1967) *The I Ching or Book of Changes: The Richard Wilhelm Translation rendered into English by Cary F. Baynes*, Princeton, Princeton University Press

Williams, P. (1989) *Mahayana Buddhism: The Doctrinal Foundations*, London, Routledge

Wu, J. (1963) *Lao Tzu*, New York, St John's University Press

Wu, L. (1986) *Fundamentals of Chinese Philosophy*, Lanham, Md., University Press of America

Yamasaki, T. (1988) *Shingon: Japanese Esoteric Buddhism*, Boston, Mass., Shambhala

Yampolsky, P. (ed.) (1990) *Selected Writings of Nichiren*, New York, Columbia University Press

Zaehner, R. (1969) *The Bhagavad Gita, with Commentaries Based on Original Sources*, London, Oxford University Press

—— (1975) *The Dawn and Twilight of Zoroastrianism*, London, Weidenfeld & Nicolson

—— (1997) *Hindu and Muslim Mysticism*, Oxford, Oneworld

Zhuangzi (1968) *The Complete Works of Chuang Tzu*, trans. B. Watson, New York, Columbia University Press

INDEX OF TERMS

Abhidhamma *see* Abhidharma
Abhidharma Buddhism **1–2**; and
the doctrine of emptiness 102;
opposed· by Madhyamaka 194;
and *prajna* 234
action **2–4**; and absence of 221;
in Advaita 5, and avoidance of
contrived 84; in Chinese
philosophy 2; and communism
73; and *karma* yoga 161; and
language 173; and Mohism
208; and Nyaya 226; and
personality 231; practical
orientation of Chinese
philosophy 71–2; and
Prajnaparamita 236; principle
of in Buddhist thought 42; in
Vedanta 270; and the Vedas
270; and zen 3; *see also karma*
active intellect **4**, 167; 207; *see
also* knowledge
adhyasa 4; and *avidya* 34
Advaita **4–8**; and aesthetics 9;
on *brahman* as cause 192;
criticized by Vishishtadvaita
273–4; on difference 96; and
hierarchy of being 35; on
ignorance 136; on the
individual self when liberated
211; and *karma* 159; and

knowledge 164; and language
172; on *maya* 199; on the one
reality 49; and the self 29, 77;
and Vedanta 270; *see also*
Shankara
aesthetics **9–10**; and Advaita 9;
and imagination 140; and
Islamic philosophy 9; of
morality in Daoism 84
afterlife **10–14**; and Buddhism
10–12; in Islamic philosophy
12–14, 16; and materialism 199;
see also death, *karma, samsara*
ahimsa **14**; and Jainism 149; and
karma 159; leading principle
of ethics 111–12; and
materialism 199
Ahriman **15**; and death 88; and
evil 114
ahura 15
Ahura Mazda **14–15**
ajiva 15, 79
Ajivikas **15**; and fatalism 122;
and Jainism 149
alayavijnana 15, 79; and
tathagatagarbha 256; and
Yogachara 280
ambiguity **15–16**; and *brahman*
50; in Islamic philosophy 178;
and Nyaya 226

300

INDEX OF THINKERS

317

F/BFO4001/2444 /·10 /04.